THE MAKING OF THE ENGLISH LANDSCAPE

THE CAMBRIDGESHIRE LANDSCAPE

THE MAKING OF THE ENGLISH LANDSCAPE
Edited by W. G. Hoskins

The Cambridgeshire Landscape

Cambridgeshire and the southern fens

by

CHRISTOPHER TAYLOR

HODDER AND STOUGHTON
LONDON   SYDNEY   AUCKLAND   TORONTO

For
KATHERINE and JONATHAN

Preface

ANYONE WHO ATTEMPTS to write the history of the Cambridgeshire landscape is soon made to realise what he owes to previous workers in the county. And what workers! Maitland, Seebohm, Mary Bateson, Helen Cam, Gray, Miller, Kosminsky, Fox and Darby are but a few of the better known ones. There is also a group of magnificent local historians, geographers and archaeologists such as Palmer, Teversham, Fowler and Lethbridge, whose work, though now sometimes regarded as out of date, reveals the most careful attention to detail, which is not always found today. My only justification for daring to follow such scholars is that I have tried to write a slightly different kind of history from most of theirs. Nevertheless my debt to them is immense.

The work involved in collecting together all the ideas provided by these and many other writers and relating it to the development of the landscape has been eased by a number of people and organisations. Once more my grateful thanks go to the Royal Commission on Historical Monuments which has permitted me to use much of the material in its archives. More important, it was the Commissioners who, in their wisdom, sent me away from the soft clay vales and rolling chalk downlands of Wessex to work in the harsher landscape of East Anglia. The change was of great benefit to me and, I hope, to them.

My colleagues in the Commission's Cambridge office have my special thanks, not only for all the general help they have given but for the way they have guided me through their worlds of ecclesiastical and vernacular architecture. I have gained much from their tuition. Many other friends and colleagues have helped in various ways, some allowing me to use their unpublished work. These include Mr A. P. Baggs, Mr D. Dymond, Dr O. Rackham and Mr J. Ravensdale. The staff of the Cambridge County Record Office have also given great assistance.

However, my greatest debt is to the Board of Extra-Mural Studies in the University of Cambridge. It was they who persuaded me to act as a tutor for a class on the making of the Cambridgeshire landscape at a time when I knew little about either the county's landscape or its making. To the Board and to the small group of students who stayed with me for four years go my sincere thanks.

The editor of this series, Dr Hoskins, has with great kindness and forbearance improved this book after my wife twice typed it into a readable form. I am most grateful to both of them.

It may be that readers of this book will feel that in concentrating on the harsh technical details of the making of the Cambridgeshire landscape I have not been appreciative enough of its undoubted attractions. My excuse is perhaps best expressed in the words of a couplet directed towards my fellow scholar and townsman Dr Samuel Johnson:

> Bred up in Birmingham, in Lichfield born,
> No wonder rural beauties he should scorn.

Whittlesford,   C. C. TAYLOR
Cambridgeshire

Contents

List of plates

ACKNOWLEDGMENTS

The author wishes to thank the following for permission to use their photographs:

The Royal Commission on Historical Monuments (England): Plates 1, 4, 11, 12, 13, 14, 15, 16, 17, 20, 21, 27, 29, 31, 32, 33, 37, 38 (Crown Copyright Reserved)
The Committee for Aerial Photography, Cambridge: Plates 2, 3, 5, 8, 9, 10, 19, 23, 26, 34, 36 (photographs by J. K.

St Joseph, Cambridge University Collection: copyright
reserved)
B.K.S. Surveys Limited: Plates 6, 22
The National Monuments Record: Plates 7, 40
Aerofilms Limited: Plates 24, 25, 35 (copyright reserved)
Fairey Surveys Limited: Plate 28
Mr M. J. Petty: Plate 30
Plate 18 is taken from J. Kip's *Britannia Illustrata* (1708)
and Plate 13 is a drawing by Relhan in the Cambridge
Antiquarian Society Library

List of maps and plans

Editor's Introduction

SOME SIXTEEN YEARS ago I wrote: "Despite the multitude of books about English landscape and scenery, and the flood of topographical books in general, there is not one book which deals with the historical evolution of the landscape as we know it. At the most we may be told that the English landscape is the man-made creation of the seventeenth and eighteenth centuries, which is not even a quarter-truth, for it refers only to country houses and their parks and to the parliamentary enclosures that gave us a good deal of our modern pattern of fields, hedges and by-roads. It ignores the fact that more than a half of England never underwent this kind of enclosure, but evolved in an entirely different way, and that in some regions the landscape had been virtually completed by the eve of the Black Death. No book exists to describe the manner in which the various landscapes of this country came to assume the shape and appearance they now have, why the hedgebanks and lanes of Devon should be so totally different from those of the Midlands, why there are so many ruined churches in Norfolk or so many lost villages in Lincolnshire, or what history lies behind the winding ditches of the Somerset marsh lands, the remote granite farmsteads of Cornwall, and the lonely pastures of upland Northamptonshire.

"There are indeed some good books on the geology that lies behind the English landscape, and these represent perhaps the best kind of writing on the subject we have yet had, for they deal with facts and are not given to the sentimental and formless slush which afflicts so many books concerned only with superficial appearances. But the geologist, good though he may be, is concerned with only one aspect of the subject, and beyond a certain point he is obliged to leave the historian and geographer to continue and complete it. He explains to us the bones of the landscape, the fundamental structure that gives form and colour to the scene and produces a certain kind of topography and natural vegetation. But the flesh that covers the bones, and the details of the features, are the concern of the historical geographer, whose task it is to show how man has clothed the geological skeleton during the comparatively past—mostly within the last fifteen centuries, though in some regions much longer than this."

In 1955 I published *The Making of the English Landscape*. There I claimed that it was a pioneer study, and if only for that reason it could not supply the answer to every question. Four books, in a series published between 1954 and 1957, filled in more detail for the counties of Cornwall, Lancashire, Gloucestershire and Leicestershire.

Much has been achieved since I wrote the words I have quoted. Landscape-history is now taught in some universities, and has been studied for many parts of England and Wales in university theses. Numerous articles have been written and a few books published, such as Alan Harris's *The Rural Landscape of the East Riding 1700–1850* (1961) and more recently Dorothy Sylvester's *The Rural Landscape of the Welsh Borderland* (1969).

Special mention should perhaps be made of a number of landscape-studies in the series of Occasional Papers published by the Department of English Local History at the University of Leicester. Above all in this series one might draw attention to *Laughton: a study in the Evolution of the Wealden Landscape* (1965) as a good example of a microscopic scrutiny of a single parish, and Margaret Spufford's *A Cambridgeshire Community* (*Chippenham*) published in the same year. Another masterly study of a single parish which should be cited particularly is Harry Thorpe's monograph entitled *The Lord and the Landscape*, dealing with the Warwickshire Parish of Wormleighton, which also appeared in 1965.[1] Geographers were quicker off the mark than historians in this new field, for it lies on the frontiers of both disciplines. And now botany has been recruited into the field, with the recent development of theories about the dating of hedges from an analysis of their vegetation.

But a vast amount still remains to be discovered about the man-made landscape. Some questions are answered, but new questions continually arise which can only be answered by a microscopic examination of small areas even within a county. My own perspective has enlarged greatly since I published my first book on the subject. I now believe that some features in our landscape today owe their origin to a much more distant past than I had formerly thought possible. I think it highly likely that in some favoured parts of England farming has gone on in an unbroken continuity since the Iron Age, perhaps even since the Bronze Age; and that many of our villages were first settled at the same time. In other words, that underneath our old villages, and underneath the older parts of these villages, there may well be evidence of habitation going back for some two or three thousand years. Conquests only meant in most places a change of landlord for better or for worse, but the farming life went on unbroken, for even conquerors would have starved without its continuous activity. We have so far failed to find this continuity of habitation because sites have been built upon over and over again and have never been wholly cleared and examined by trained archaeologists.

At the other end of the time-scale the field of industrial archaeology has come into being in the last few years, though I touched upon it years ago under the heading of Industrial Landscapes. Still, a vast amount more could now be said about this kind of landscape.

Purists might say that the county is not the proper unit

[1] *Transactions of the Birmingham Archaeological Society*, Vol. 80, 1965.

for the study of landscape-history. They would say perhaps that we ought to choose individual and unified regions for such an exercise, but since all counties, however small, contain a wonderful diversity of landscape, each with its own special history, we get, I am sure, a far more appealing book than if we adopted the geographical region as our basis.

The authors of these books are concerned with the ways in which men have cleared the natural woodlands, re-claimed marshland, fen and moor, created fields out of a wilderness, made lanes, roads and footpaths, laid out towns, built villages, hamlets, farmhouses and cottages, created country houses and their parks, dug mines and made canals and railways, in short with everything that has altered the natural landscape. One cannot understand the English landscape and enjoy it to the full, apprehend all its wonderful variety from region to region (often within the space of a few miles), without going back to the history that lies behind it. A commonplace ditch may be the thou-sand-year-old boundary of a royal manor; a certain hedge-bank may be even more ancient, the boundary of a Celtic estate; a certain deep and winding lane may be the work of twelfth-century peasants, some of whose names may be made known to us if we search diligently enough. To discover these things, we have to go to the documents that are the historian's raw material, and find out what happened to produce these results and when, and precisely how they came about.

But it is not only the documents that are the historian's guide. One cannot write books like these by reading some-one else's books, or even by studying records in a muni-ment room. The English landscape itself, to those who know how to read it aright, is the richest historical record we possess. There are discoveries to be made in it for which no written documents exist, or have ever existed. To write the history of the English landscape requires a combination of documentary research and of fieldwork, of laborious scrambling on foot wherever the trail may lead. The result is a new kind of history which it is hoped will appeal to all those who like to travel intelligently, to get away from the guide-book show-pieces now and then and to know the reasons behind what they are looking at. There is no part of England, however unpromising it may appear at first sight, that is not full of questions for those who have a sense of the past. So much of England is still unknown and unexplored. Fuller enjoined us nearly three centuries ago

"Know most of the rooms of thy native country
before thou goest over the threshold thereof.
Especially seeing England present thee with
so many observables."

These books on The Making of the English Landscape are concerned with the observables of England, and the secret history that lies behind them.

Exeter, 1970   W. G. HOSKINS

1. Cambridgeshire before the Saxons

The natural landscape. The pre-Roman scene. Roman Cambridgeshire.

The natural landscape

CAMBRIDGESHIRE, OR MORE strictly the administrative county of Cambridgeshire and the Isle of Ely, can by no stretch of the imagination be considered one of the most beautiful counties of England. No one, except a few die-hard Cambridgeshire dwellers, can wax eloquent on the glories of the county's landscape. The area has never produced a major poet to sing its praises, nor a writer to describe its beauties. In spite of the fact that many of the great names in English literature passed through the University, none of them left any writing of merit on the landscape of the county. Even William Wordsworth, who was up at St John's College from 1787 to 1791 and who was by no means unappreciative of a landscape, wrote nothing on the countryside of Cambridgeshire.

Most people, including the present writer, who have come to the county from elsewhere are usually dismayed by their first impressions. The city of Cambridge itself is of course truly magnificent, but unless one is prepared to visit it on a wet Sunday morning in winter one risks being trampled underfoot by the many thousands of tourists who go there, or mown down by traffic in what must be one of the most congested places in this country. The glory of Ely Cathedral tempts the visitor across the fens but there is little else at first sight. It is the flatness of the Cambridgeshire landscape more than anything which repels the casual visitor or indeed the landscape historian. Yet while it is true that there is little relief, it is quite wrong to assume that there is nothing of interest to see. As in any part of our country the marks of man's activity from the remotest prehistoric period to the present day are indelibly stamped on the landscape, though it is perhaps more difficult to unravel the pattern here in Cambridgeshire than in some other areas. But this is a challenge in itself to any landscape historian worth his salt.

In any case the county has its charms and special places even if they are of a different order from those elsewhere. To walk across the fens on a bright frosty day in winter can be a great experience even to the non-historian. One can travel for miles along river banks and see hardly more than half a dozen other human beings. The air is sharp, the ground crisp, and there is endless interest in the vegetation, wild life and water creatures. And if one is prepared to look around more carefully and to do a little historical research beforehand, the apparently endless flat landscape comes alive with the visible remains of pre-historic water-courses, medieval drainage works, eighteenth-century wind-pumping mill sites and much else. Everything soon falls into its historical place, whether it be the long-abandoned channel of a fourteenth-century drain or the ugly brick shed housing a diesel engine, whose steady throb indicates that the work of drainage, initiated by the Romans, is still going on.

Much of Cambridgeshire is not fenland at all but gently rolling chalk and clay land which gives a remarkably varied landscape with a very different history and appearance. Here too one can find places both of beauty and of interest where most people never go. Even in the height of summer, when the main roads are jammed and the fenland rivers are crowded with pleasure boats, one can wander through the lanes of south Cambridgeshire to an isolated church situated within the long-forsaken ramparts of a mighty Norman castle. Here it is possible to walk along the street of a deserted village which originally grew up outside the castle and then shrank away to a green field again when the castle was abandoned. Elsewhere in the county one can explore the tiny villages on the heavy western claylands and decipher the complex history of the early medieval exploitation of the woodland there; or investigate the fen-edge villages and find the traces of old canals, basins and wharves to which, in the medieval period and later, barges came bringing goods from as far away as Scandinavia. All this and much more is waiting to be discovered by those who are prepared to look, ask questions and look again.

The physical landscape on which all this is based is extremely simple. The southern half of the county can be termed the 'uplands', though the maximum height is nowhere much above 400 feet and most of it is considerably lower. The rest is all fenland, virtually flat, all under twenty feet above sea level, some even below sea level, with nothing but the scattered fen 'islands', themselves rarely more than fifty to sixty feet high, to relieve the monotony. But this two-fold division hardly helps us to appreciate the problems and advantages with which man has, throughout history, been faced as he slowly tamed and shaped the landscape. We need to look deeper into this natural landscape before we can venture into its alteration by man (Fig. 1).

The uplands vary considerably in what they have had to offer generations of settlers, farmers, builders and traders. Much of the eastern, southern and south-west uplands are chalk downlands, gradually rising in gentle undulations to the south. The general character is of rounded ridges and minor escarpments with intervening hollows or dry valleys carrying but little surface water now. These dry downlands

23

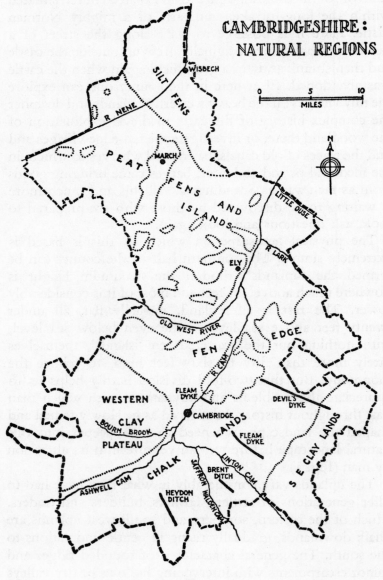

CAMBRIDGESHIRE:
NATURAL REGIONS

SILT FENS

WISBECH

R NENE

PEAT

FENS

MARCH

AND

ISLANDS

LITTLE OUSE

R LARK

ELY

OLD WEST RIVER

EDGE

FEN

R CAM

FLEAM DYKE

DEVIL'S DYKE

WESTERN

CLAY

PLATEAU

BOURN. BROOK

CAMBRIDGE

CLAY

LANDS

FLEAM DYKE

LINTON CAM

S E CLAY LANDS

ASHWELL CAM

CHALK

BRENT DITCH

HEYDON DITCH

SAFFRON WALDEN CAM

0   5   10
MILES

N

Fig. 1

are still largely empty of settlement even today and have perhaps never been occupied intensively by man. Nevertheless their light soils and former pastures provided many of the basic requirements for successive peoples who from the prehistoric period to the present day have lived alongside the three main branches of the River Cam which flow east and north-west in broad open valleys through these chalklands towards Cambridge (Plate 1). In the west the chalk is replaced by the generally flat area between 200 and 250 feet known as the Western Clay Plateau. Here the chalk and clays are covered by glacial deposits and these produced a thick forest cover which largely prevented prehistoric settlement. However, the existence of the Bourn Brook, cutting its way through the centre of the plateau on its way to join the River Cam, as well as a host of minor streams around the plateau sides, enabled the Romano-British people of the county to move into the area and exploit its potentialities. It was these first settlers who started to clear the woodland, and their Saxon successors completed the task. Even by the eleventh century it was a fully developed landscape which later people have altered but little. In contrast, in the south-east of the county, where similar glacial material overlies the chalk, the removal of the forest cover and subsequent settlement was much slower and not completed until well on into the medieval period. Even today it remains a rather remote area with few main roads and only scattered minor settlements.

The fenlands too are by no means all the same in spite of their modern appearance. Often very minor differences have controlled man's activities from prehistoric times onwards. The southern part is mainly on peat which was laid down during post-glacial times to finally produce a wild, marshy and inhospitable landscape crossed by great winding rivers later to become the modern Ouse, Cam and

Nene. Roman, medieval and more recent engineers and farmers have all, with varying degrees of success, struggled to bring the peat fens under control. The fact that it is now one of the richest agricultural areas of England is a monument to their combined efforts and all have left their mark on it. From the relatively safe fen edges and island refuges countless generations dug ditches, embanked rivers and pumped water and as a result the present landscape there has slowly emerged (Plate 31). In the far north the fenlands are based on silt deposited by rivers and various incursions of the sea. Here the landscape is more monotonous, without even islands to break the skyline (Plate 2). But the remains of the work of Roman and medieval farmers can be traced as well as the visual results of the wealth produced from cattle and sheep that grazed for centuries on the rich siltland pastures. The impact of man's hand on the making of the landscape is everywhere. Let us now move on and examine it all in detail.

The pre-Roman scene

Because the county is, and has for long been, intensively cultivated, there are few upstanding remains of the prehistoric period. The vast majority of the dwelling and burial places of the pre-Roman inhabitants have been reduced to a few scraps of pottery and flint, or are visible only from the air when conditions are right. Some Bronze Age burial mounds survive, mainly in the south of the county on the higher chalklands, but these are fast disappearing under the annual assault of the plough. A single Iron Age fortress still crowns the Gog Magog Hills just south-east of Cambridge, but even this is a shadow of its former self as a result of partial destruction to make a landscaped garden in the eighteenth century. Yet the few physical remains of prehistoric people cannot be ignored, for their builders moulded and altered the landscape around them and played their part in producing the total landscape we see today. In any case we must be careful when assessing the remains that do exist, for if we take them at their face value we shall produce a quite wrong interpretation. We must use, carefully, all the available archaeological evidence if we are to understand not only where prehistoric people lived but what effect they had on the landscape.

The old idea, still unfortunately current in some places, was that prehistoric people lived mainly on the light, easily worked chalk soils, in quite different areas from those occupied by later peoples. This concept has received much support from Cambridgeshire where the remote part of the broad chalk zone which occupies much of the southern part of the county is dotted with the remains of Bronze Age burial mounds. But the fact that these remains have survived, at least until the present century, in this area has nothing to do with the distribution of prehistoric peoples. It is entirely due to the fact that they lie in areas which, until the early nineteenth century, or even later, were open pasture land. An interesting exercise in which the remaining burial mounds are plotted on a map showing the areas of permanent pasture before parliamentary enclosure indicates that over ninety-five per cent of them lie in these areas. There is no doubt that similar prehistoric sites existed elsewhere but have been destroyed by centuries of ploughing. This has recently been proved beyond doubt in the area east of Cambridge by systematic air-photography over a number of years. The number of Bronze Age burial mounds known there has not only been doubled, but instead of the distribution being limited to the higher chalk slopes, they are now known to lie around and even within modern villages. One of the most remarkable of these air-photographs actually showed the ditch of a Bronze Age burial mound in the back garden of a medieval house in Swaffham Bulbeck.

If we take the whole of the available archaeological evidence we can see that by and large prehistoric and Roman people, far from living on the exposed and empty chalklands of the county, occupied the rich river valleys, the good fen-edge soils and the higher, drier fen islands. This is important if we are to understand the history of the Cambridgeshire landscape. It means that the Saxon settlers of our county did not pour into a largely empty countryside, picking the best sites for their new villages, but moved into a fully settled and largely tamed landscape with the best places for settlement already taken and the best land already under cultivation. So the making of the Cambridgeshire landscape is a process that has been going on for not 1500 years but for at least 10,000 years and perhaps much longer. It is not always easy to see in the present landscape exactly what our remote prehistoric forebears achieved, but the fact that they lived where we live and worked much the same land that we now cultivate must always be borne in mind. The foundations of the modern landscape were laid down in the very remote past long before the Saxon era.

So the landscape historian must move into the often mysterious world of the archaeologist, whose methods, terminology and 'proof', often based on inspired guesses, appal the true historian. The path through this world is dangerous and lined with pitfalls for the unwary, but it must be trodden if the beginnings of the history of the landscape are to be understood.

The landscape of the county throughout the prehistoric period was of course very different from the one we see today. When man first came into Cambridgeshire, some 10,000 to 12,000 years ago, after the last great Ice Age, the fens as we know them did not exist. The northern part of the county was a flat, but relatively dry, area, across which rivers flowed to the sea, at that time far out in the middle of the present North Sea. During the early part of the prehistoric period the basin now occupied by the fenlands sank slowly and almost imperceptibly in relation to the sea level. As a result the vast areas of peat which cover most of the southern fens were deposited. This was not a sudden or indeed a constant process. It not only took many centuries but there were many minor pauses in the deposition, the details of which are more of geological than historical interest. In the north of the county the deposits were largely of silt rather than peat, laid down by recurring advances of the sea. Towards the end of the prehistoric period thick deposits of silt were laid down around the southern margins of the Wash and extended into the northern part of Cambridgeshire. Across this vast fenland basin great and small rivers wound their way slowly towards the sea. Again they were very different from today's rivers. The Ouse meandered to the north of March via Wisbech to the sea, while the Cam flowed north-west of Ely to join the Ouse south of Wisbech. The present Ouse flowing to the sea by King's Lynn did not exist except as a minor stream beyond the boundaries of our county. The old and long-abandoned courses of these rivers and their many tributary streams can still be seen in the modern landscape, for, as a result of the shrinkage of the peat fen through drainage, the silt beds of the rivers are now actually raised as low, light-coloured banks winding across the fens (Plate 28). The recognition of these 'roddons', as the old river beds are called, is not merely of geological interest, but vital for the landscape historian. Subsequent settlement in the fens from prehistoric times to the nineteenth century has often been conditioned by the existence of these roddons. The relatively high, dry and stable silt banks have always attracted dwellings of all periods in contrast to the low, wet and unstable peat.

This digression into the history of the physical landscape is highly relevant to the study of the man-made landscape in Cambridgeshire for the changes in the natural landscape of the county have played a more important part in man's activities than in many other areas of England.

The people who first started the alteration of the landscape of Cambridgeshire were the so-called Mesolithic peoples. They wandered across the county in small numbers between 8000 and 5000 B.C. Their impact on the landscape was relatively small: they were ill-equipped for altering their environment on anything but a minor scale. As yet the known places where they lived are few but this is largely due to the difficulty of finding such places rather than actual proof of a tiny population. The evidence, slim as it is, suggests that the Mesolithic people in Cambridgeshire lived along the fen edges, on sandy hillocks in the peat fens and perhaps on the larger fen islands. This is what one would expect from a hunting and fishing people. On the other hand no one has ever looked for, let alone found, the remains of these peoples along the river valleys in the south of the county and therefore the absence of any Mesolithic occupation in these areas is probably more apparent than real. One must always remember with archaeological material that its distribution very often reflects only the distribution of archaeologists and may have no significance as regards the actual areas occupied by prehistoric people.

Some time before 5000 B.C. these hunters were succeeded by a larger and technically more advanced group known as the Neolithic peoples. These were potentially much more capable of altering the landscape, for their way of life was based on a mixed farming economy, with arable fields or plots, and cattle, sheep and goats. It is likely that the grazing animals of these people produced the grass-covered chalk downlands of the south of the county which remained largely intact until the eighteenth century. There is evidence, even within the fens, that some limited clearance of the then ubiquitous trees and shrubs had taken place by about 4000 B.C., presumably by small groups of these Neolithic people living on the higher islands and sandy hillocks within the fens. While the limited number of finds of these people precludes any real certainty in the matter, the general picture seems to be that Neolithic farmers occupied the lower ground along the fen edges, the drier areas within the fens and perhaps some of the larger river valleys in the south of the county. There is no proof that these people actually lived on the sites of the present villages and there probably never will be, but the important feature is that they seem to have lived in the same *areas* as medieval and later peoples. This, as we shall see, is a recurrent feature throughout the prehistoric and Roman period in Cambridgeshire.

Around 2500 B.C. the Beaker peoples, so-called from the distinctive type of pottery they used, moved into the county from abroad, probably via the Wash and the fenland rivers. Their economy was very similar to that of their Neolithic predecessors, though they did use bronze tools to a limited extent. They appear to have intermarried with the earlier peoples and the result, in archaeological terms, is a mixed material culture. There is no doubt from the distribution of finds relating to these people that their primary areas of settlement were the same as those of their predecessors. After 2000 B.C. when we move into the true Bronze Age the same pattern of settlement is found, though with the greatly increased number of finds and sites of this period, the details are clearer. Though some, but not all, of the burial mounds of the Bronze Age people were sited on the relatively high land of the chalk in the south of the county, no definite settlement sites are known there. The great bulk of the archaeological material again indicates that these people were living on the fen islands, along the fen edges and within the valleys of the River Cam. Those burial mounds which were placed on the higher lands are not without significance here. The vast majority are deliberately sited on spurs and false crests where they could clearly be seen from the adjacent valleys or fen edges where their occupants' descendants lived.

After 800 B.C. we are in what is archaeologically the Iron Age. This does not necessarily mean a radical change of people, but merely an advance in technology. Therefore one need not expect, nor indeed do we find, a change in land-use or occupation sites. There is evidence of Iron Age occupation in and around Cambridge, along the fen edges at places such as Horningsea and Reach and within the river valleys of the south of the county at places such as Trumpington, Haslingfield, Barrington, Foxton, Abington Pigotts, Hauxton, Linton and Bartlow. Air-photographic evidence suggests many additional sites in these same areas. In view of the later medieval form of settlement in these valleys it is not without significance that the Iron Age settlements here appear to have been commonly placed in pairs either side of a ford, e.g. as at Grantchester and Trumpington, Barrington and Foxton, exactly the same pattern that recurs in both the Roman and medieval periods in the same area. Within the fens evidence of Iron Age occupation is slight though finds indicating settlement have come from Little Downham, near Ely; while at Stonea, near Wimblington, there are the still-extant remains of a small embanked settlement almost certainly of Iron Age date. Both these sites are of course on fen islands. The lack of Iron Age occupation in the fens compared with the plentiful evidence of Bronze Age settlement there is probably due to the renewed subsidence of the fenlands and the deposition of a considerable thickness of peat at this time.

This produced a very marshy environment which was to become the basic landscape of the southern fens until relatively recently.

Outside these areas of primary settlement we have little evidence of Iron Age occupation. In the higher chalkland and forested areas there is little indication of settlement except for a few fortified or semi-fortified sites which of necessity had to be in good defensive positions. Wandle-bury hill fort on the Gog Magog Hills just south-east of Cambridge is the largest of these and the only one to survive the vicissitudes of later ages in a visible form. Isolated Iron Age burials, often in earlier Bronze Age burial mounds, are known, but these probably have no significance in terms of settlement. In the few places in the south of the county where Iron Age settlements are known to exist away from the major river valleys it is interesting that they occur in or close to existing villages where local topography has always provided a good habitation site. One such was discovered at Thriplow, south of Cambridge, well inside the chalklands but near permanent springs whose water provided both the Iron Age people and their successors with the basic necessity of life.

The sum of the archaeological evidence for prehistoric Cambridgeshire, in terms of the history of the county's landscape, is this: that throughout the long centuries before the coming of the Romans, Cambridgeshire was continuously occupied by peoples living in and cultivating the areas along the major rivers, on the fen edges and on the fen islands. These areas, which we can term those of primary settlement, are where the majority of the larger settlements still lie today. There is no evidence whatsoever that prehistoric people lived anywhere else than in those places which, it is alleged, only the Saxons found so inviting. We must therefore see the origins of these primary settlement areas not in terms of Saxon invaders but in an

C

appreciation for good dwelling sites and farmland by their predecessors of a much more remote past.

Roman Cambridgeshire

Cambridgeshire is remarkably bare of obvious Roman sites. Apart from some of the great roads which have survived into the present century, either as busy modern highways or pleasant green lanes, there is little to see. But again this must not mislead us into thinking that the Romano-British people had no effect on the landscape we see today; indeed, it is probable that they played a vital part and may have literally laid the foundations of much of the modern landscape.

As a result of intensive archaeological work including excavation, field walking, air-photography and chance finds, hundreds of sites are now known and our knowledge of the location and types of settlement in the Roman period is large. There are, inevitably, gaps in our overall picture but the broad outlines are clear. In the south of the county the Romanised descendants of the earlier prehistoric people continued to live along the fen edges and in the major river valleys. The large number of sites known clearly indicates this and shows in a fair amount of detail the kind of settlement pattern there. On the whole it appears to have been dispersed, consisting of large numbers of single farms, hamlets or small villages, scattered along the river terraces or adjacent slopes often within two or three hundred yards of each other. Perhaps the term 'dispersed settlement' is not the correct one to use here for the pattern was not true dispersal as geographers understand it. The farmsteads and hamlets were fairly closely contained within the river valleys and along the fen edges (Fig. 2). However, it was certainly not 'nucleated', that is, made up of large compact villages as is the modern settlement pattern

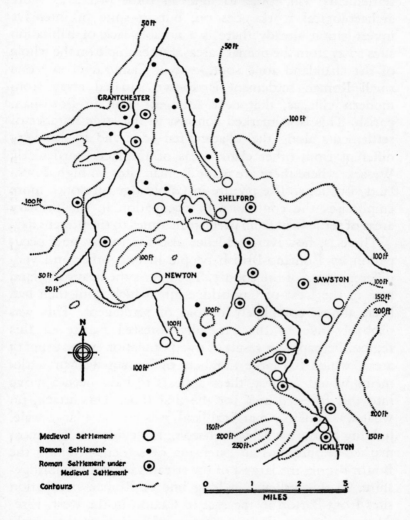

ROMAN AND MEDIEVAL SETTLEMENTS IN THE CAM VALLEY

GRANTCHESTER

SHELFORD

NEWTON

SAWSTON

ICKLETON

Medieval Settlement
Roman Settlement
Roman Settlement under
   Medieval Settlement
Contours

N

0   1   2   3
MILES

50 ft
50 ft
100 ft
100 ft
100 ft
100 ft
100 ft
100 ft
100 ft
50 ft
50 ft
100 ft
100 ft
150 ft
200 ft
100 ft
200 ft
150 ft
150 ft
200 ft
250 ft

Fig. 2

or as was the alleged medieval pattern. Outside these major areas, on the dry, open chalklands, Roman settlements appear to have been very rare indeed. No doubt settlements will come to light in these places as more archaeological work goes on, but in spite of intensive investigation already there is a notable lack of habitation sites away from the primary areas. For example on the whole of the chalkland zone south-east of Cambridge only one small Roman settlement is known situated away from modern villages, that near Allington Hill in Bottisham parish. This is in marked contrast to the large number of settlements along the adjacent fen edge and is also very different from other chalk areas of England, particularly Wessex, where there are many Roman sites on high downland situations. The picture in Cambridgeshire once more emphasises the continuity of occupation in the primary areas of settlement from prehistoric times to the present day.

There is, however, evidence also for totally new occupation by Romano-British people in two other and very different parts of the county. The first is the heavy clayland area in the west of Cambridgeshire which until then had been almost completely devoid of settlement. This was probably due to the generally forested nature of this region. Perhaps as a result of overpopulation in the primary areas, which the large numbers of known Roman settlements would suggest, there appears to have been a move into this forested area for the first time. This attack, on what was certainly marginal land, was not on a large scale, judging by the available archaeological evidence. The most marked feature was an extension of settlement along the Bourn Brook, the largest of the streams in west Cambridgeshire. In this valley is a long line of Roman occupation sites from Barton in the east to Caxton in the west. Elsewhere in the area finds are fewer and indicate perhaps only a scattered settlement within the forest.

This commencement of settlement and presumably the contemporary clearance of parts of the forest here is important, not only for the Roman period, but for the whole of its subsequent medieval history as we shall see later. It is notable that while this partial settlement of the west Cambridgeshire clay area occurred in Roman times it was not matched by a similar settlement in the south-east Cambridgeshire clay region. Apart from a concentration of Romano-British occupation sites around Linton and Bartlow along the Linton branch of the River Cam there is little evidence of Roman settlement in the south-east of the county. Again this is significant when we come to the later history of this area.

The other major area of new Romano-British settlement in the county was within the fens themselves, and this was largely related to the changing physical conditions here by the beginning of the Roman period. Around A.D. 50, as a result of a general relative lowering of the sea level, the north part of the county together with the adjacent areas surrounding the Wash emerged from the sea. What had been extensive tidal mudflats became low siltlands just above high-tide level. Tidal water was now confined to a multitude of winding channels traversing the former estuary, now shrunken seawards. The higher, dry levées or banks formed along these channels became suitable sites for settlement, while the rich siltlands were potential arable. The result was that within a few years Romano-British people started to move into this area, and between A.D. 100 and 150 there was a massive, and probably imperially organised, settlement all over the siltlands. Literally dozens of new villages, hamlets and farmsteads appeared, surrounded by their fields and paddocks. The majority of these are now visible only on air-photographs and very few have survived into the present decade. The destruction of the few remaining sites by modern agriculture is a major tragedy for both archaeologists and historians. It is a great pity that at least one or two could not have been preserved for posterity.

This massive settlement of the silt fens in the second century was not apparently a complete success. Many sites were abandoned by A.D. 200 and archaeological evidence indicates a constant battle against flooding and bad drainage which sometimes ended in defeat for the settlers. The remainder survived and continued to live there until at least the early fifth century and probably later. But with the collapse of the Roman imperial government and the local administrative framework necessary to carry out the drainage works there was a gradual abandonment of many of the settlements and much of the siltland became an overgrown and waterlogged landscape of choked drains and desolate, crumbling farmsteads.

But was all abandoned? The accepted story is that eventually all these Romano-British settlement sites decayed and that when the Anglo-Saxon invaders arrived there was little for them to take over. This may not be so. Although many of the Romano-British settlements were abandoned and much of the rich agricultural lands left choked with weeds and water, there are some slight indications that even on the silt fens the basic layout of the modern landscape owes something to our Roman predecessors. We shall return to this later.

Further south, the peat fens were also exploited during the Roman period though inevitably to a much lesser extent, due to the nature of the peat itself. This could not be settled directly and the occupation sites of the period that do exist are largely confined to the fen edges and the islands: that is, in the same general areas as the earlier prehistoric peoples, though not always on the same sites. However, there was certainly a marked increase in the number of settlements here, indicating a substantial population, with farmsteads, hamlets and sometimes small villages scattered over wide areas. Natural disasters in these southern peat fens took their toll of some of the more low-lying settlements and in particular there is a marked abandonment of settlement in the mid-third century which has been attributed to a major flood. Some of these sites were reoccupied and continued in use until at least the early fifth century. Once again the only traces of the majority of these settlements is either on air-photographs or as scatters of pottery lying on ploughed fields. However, at least two still survive, at the time of writing, as upstanding earthworks, both on the fen edge north of Cambridge, one at Cottenham (Plate 3) and the other at Chittering. To the unobservant eye the sites appear to be uneven grass fields, but with careful examination they can be seen as blocks of contiguous rectangular enclosures in which the houses stood, bounded by wide drainage ditches. It is these ditches, the most prominent feature of all the fenland Roman sites, which are the visual expression of the unrecorded and largely unknown struggles of the Romano-British peasantry to keep the waters at bay.

The generally 'dispersed' pattern of settlement, which we have noted as existing in the old primary settlement areas as well as in the newly reclaimed and cleared areas of west Cambridgeshire and the fens, is of considerable importance to the understanding of the medieval pattern of settlement. But the arrangement of villas, farmsteads and hamlets and their relationship to each other is also vital in this context. These facts are of course difficult to obtain, for they depend on detailed archaeological excavation and fieldwork of a kind which has hardly started in the county as yet. Thus our conclusions must be treated with a certain amount of care for the evidence is not as clear as that with which historians normally like to work. Nevertheless certain features are worth noting.

In the river valleys, and on the fen edges and islands, though the most common type of settlement appears to be a single farmstead or a small hamlet, there are also a fair number of sites which are known to be villas. These latter may be associated in some way with the more mundane farm and hamlet sites. There is every indication that the basic tenurial unit was an estate made up of farmsteads, scattered across a given area and controlled from a central villa. This together with earlier Iron Age material on or near Roman sites poses the question whether whole properties or estates passed into Roman hands or, more likely, remained in those of the Romanised descendants of Iron Age owners. There are even examples of a villa being associated with a Roman village as at Stonea in the fens, at Horningsea and Swaffham Prior on the fen edges and at Litlington and Barrington in the Cam valley. There are other possible examples and an archaeologist who recently pointed this out has said that "it is likely that this conjunction of *manor house and village* [this writer's italics], common in Gaul, was more often met with in Roman Britain than has usually been supposed". Certainly both the general distribution and the actual relationships of Roman settlement in Cambridgeshire have much similarity with what seems to have been the medieval picture.

Another major aspect of the Roman occupation is connected with the exploitation of the fenlands, that is the cutting of some of the many artificial canals which occur widely in the fens (Fig. 13). Some if not all of these were undoubtedly constructed to assist drainage but their main function was to enable water-borne traffic to cross the fens. The best known of these is the Car Dyke which runs north-west from the River Cam at Waterbeach to a point just west of Peterborough and then passes on northwards through Lincolnshire to Lincoln. For most of its length in Cambridgeshire it is now destroyed or mutilated but parts

Plate 1 The valley of the Ashwell Cam. The sheep in the foreground are grazing on the remains of the village of Clopton, finally swept away for their predecessors in the middle of the sixteenth century. The moat in the middle distance is the site of the manor house. Beyond is the wide, flat valley of the River Cam.

Plate 2 The northern silt fens. Here near Tydd St Giles is a patchwork of rectangular fields mostly of medieval date. The winding ditch in the foreground is the Shire Drain or Old South Eau, once a distributary channel of the River Nene.

Plate 3 Roman settlement, Cottenham. In a narrow, modern field, preserved by an accident of land-use, is one of the very few remaining Roman villages in the county. Tracks, paddocks and a curious form of cultivation are all still visible on the ground.

Plate 4 The Devil's Dyke. Though still undated, this gigantic defensive work, seven miles long, is the product of great effort and desperate need of people living in the dark centuries after the end of formal Roman rule. The mutilated bank in the foreground is the result of digging for road metal in the medieval period.

of it still exist for those who look. How many motorists driving north from Cambridge to Ely ever notice that the ditch on the north side of the road skirting Waterbeach airfield is abnormally large? Very few, one suspects, even see it, let alone realise that it is the Roman Car Dyke along which barges, loaded with wheat, hides and wool from the farms of the southern fens and uplands carried their cargoes to the Roman military establishments of Lincoln and beyond.

In addition there are other much shorter canals which linked Roman settlements along the fen edges to the nearest navigable river, and many of these have continued in use ever since. In the south-east of the county Reach Lode (Plate 32), a three-mile-long straight canal linking the River Cam to an important area of dense Roman occupation at Reach and Swaffham Prior, is definitely Roman and the two adjacent and parallel canals of Bottisham Lode and Swaffham Bulbeck Lode are probably of the same date. There are a number of other similar lodes or canals in the southern fens which have the same appearance and which may well be Roman, though there is no proof. Some of these still exist as major navigable waterways such as Soham Lode linking the Soham area with the River Cam, the so-called Navigation Drain which connects Swavesey with the River Ouse and the present artificial lower course of the River Lark between Isleham and Prickwillow which forms the county boundary with West Suffolk. Others are now minor drains or abandoned channels such as Landbeach Lode between Landbeach and the Car Dyke.

The problem of these lodes or canals is that they were all used intensively for water-borne traffic during the medieval period and much later. The result is that not only have they been often altered and realigned, but that absolute proof of their Roman origin is virtually unobtainable. The existence of Roman pottery which can be picked up along their banks, and which has often been taken to indicate their Roman origins, may not always be valid evidence. For example the existence of Roman pottery along the lodes in the south-east of the fens is probably quite misleading, for a detailed examination of nineteenth-century drainage board records reveals that the main clay-pit which provided the material for repairing the lode banks was cut through a Roman settlement. As a result large quantities of Roman pottery were dumped along the lode sides in the nineteenth century mixed up with the clay. Absolute proof of the Roman date of lodes is difficult. But it can be achieved, as at Reach Lode, where the fact that the late- or post-Roman Devil's Dyke was actually laid out to meet the lode clearly shows that the latter is of Roman date.

As well as these Roman navigation cuts there is another group of waterways in the eastern fens of fundamental importance in the way that they modify the natural drainage. In their original form all the rivers in the eastern fenlands drained into the Well Stream, predecessor of the Ouse, and thence via the Wisbech Estuary into the Wash. A system of artificial cuts such as the present Ouse between Littleport and Brandon Creek and the lower part of the Little Ouse from Brandon Creek up to Decoy Fen in Suffolk, results in the diversion of all the east fenland rivers and the River Cam drainage into the King's Lynn Estuary so relieving pressure on the Well Stream. If these cuts are Roman, and the archaeological evidence indicates that they are, they show a grasp of the basic principles of fen drainage on a large scale which was not to be repeated until the massive drainage works of the seventeenth century.

All these navigation and drainage works, together with the evidence of planned settlement and exploitation of the fenlands of the county in Roman times, are not only impressive but of considerable interest to the student of

Roman history. Beyond this, it is extremely important for the later landscape historian to realise how much of the modern landscape, even in an area such as the fens, is of Roman origin. We must not forget the great extent to which the developments and changes in medieval and later times were controlled by, and adapted to, the work of the Roman drainage engineers and countryside planners.

Thus it seems that the prehistoric and Romano-British peoples in Cambridgeshire played a major role in the making of the local landscape. When the Saxons arrived in the area towards the end of the Roman period, they were not moving into an untamed countryside and deciding which particular gravel terrace or spring-line position was most suitable for habitation, or which piece of open grassland or light scrub was ideal for ploughing up. They were coming into a fully occupied landscape, the most suitable parts of which were dotted with farmsteads, hamlets, villas and fields, already arranged and divided into estates or tenurial units whose origins lay back before the Roman period. We must bear this in mind when we examine the Saxon impact upon the scene.

SELECT BIBLIOGRAPHY

Chatwin, C. P. *British Regional Geology: East Anglia and Adjoining Areas* (1961).
Darby, H. C. (Ed.) *The Cambridge Region* (1938).
Fox, C. *The Archaeology of the Cambridge Region* (1923).
Hey, R. W. and Perrin, R. M. S. *The Geology and Soils of Cambridgeshire* (1960).
Philips, C. W. (Ed.) *The Fenland in Roman Times* (1970).
Proceedings of the Cambridge Antiquarian Society (in progress), hereafter *Procs. C.A.S.*, for many important excavation reports, notes and studies.
Royal Commission on Historical Monuments (England)

Cambridgeshire, Vols I and II (1968 and 1972), hereafter R.C.H.M. *Cambridgeshire*.

Steers, J. A. (Ed.) *The Cambridge Region* (1965).

Victoria County History *Cambridgeshire*, Vols I and II (1938 and 1948), hereafter V.C.H. *Cambridgeshire*.

Worssam, B. C. and Taylor, J. H. *Geology of the Country around Cambridge* (1969).

2. The English settlement

The arrival of the English. The shape of villages.
The coming of the Danes.

The arrival of the English

THE INTERPRETATION OF exactly how and when the
Old English took over control of Cambridgeshire is, as
elsewhere, one of the most difficult problems in English
history, and for the student of the English landscape it is
perhaps the most important and difficult problem of all.
Important, because if we do not assess the true impact of
the English on the landscape we are liable to see the whole
development of that landscape in the wrong perspective.
Difficult, because our evidence is sparse, hard to understand and often able to support very different explanations.
In this chapter we shall be concerned with one possible
interpretation of the evidence; that is the continuity of
settlement from Roman times into the medieval period. It
may not be readily acceptable, and is certainly not the only
explanation.

The old and still generally accepted picture of the Anglo-
Saxon settlers in Cambridgeshire is that they poured into
the region in the fifth century either along the fenland rivers
from the Wash or across Norfolk via the Icknield Way,
driving out or killing the older peoples and settling down
to produce the 'normal' medieval landscape of nucleated
villages with open or common fields around them. They
thus ignored or destroyed all that there was in the landscape
already. This view has always struck the writer as inherently

improbable for if history, or indeed prehistory, teaches us anything it is that one of man's greatest achievements has been that he has always taken over, moulded and adapted what his predecessors have left behind. He has rarely removed wholesale what has been handed down to him either by conquest or by inheritance. Perhaps one should except from this generalisation our own mid-twentieth-century generations who are seemingly bent on the complete destruction of their natural and historical environment; but even this is achieved only as a result of advanced technology. Earlier peoples, even if they wanted to destroy the past, were prevented from doing so by the limits of their technology which was rarely much more advanced than that of their immediate predecessors. The average Saxon farmer was little better equipped, if at all, than his Romano-British forebear, and is more likely to have taken over what had been left to him rather than embark on massive alterations of the landscape for their own sake.

The idea of the Old English peoples arriving in large numbers and removing all trace of earlier occupation has of course been queried by serious students of Cambridgeshire history in the past. Many, including Seebohm,[1] have tried to see a much earlier pattern of settlement and land-holding in the present landscape than the apparent Saxon one, and other historians and archaeologists have pointed to some inconvenient evidence which has to be explained away. It is not necessarily very easy to do, for the conflicting techniques and results of many disciplines such as archaeology, place-names, fieldwork and historical research must all be carefully examined and correlated.

The earliest and perhaps most tangible evidence that the Saxon peoples have left in the county is numerous burial sites. Large numbers of cemeteries with burials running into three figures as well as much smaller burial groups are

[1] F. Seebohm, *The English Village Community* (1883).

known and have been subjected to intensive study by archaeologists. If we eliminate those which are patently late in the Saxon period, such as the predominantly Christian cemetery at Burwell, we are left with a marked concentration of pagan-Saxon cemeteries and other burial sites in and around Cambridge and along the major river valleys in the south of the county in places such as Barrington, Foxton, Little Shelford, Sawston, Hildersham and Linton. There are also a few along the fen edge north-east of Cambridge at Little Wilbraham and Chippenham. It is at once obvious that these sites are all within what we have termed the primary areas of settlement in the earlier periods. These burials have often been regarded as evidence of early penetration of the area by Saxons coming up the fenland rivers from the Wash who conquered and drove out the Romano-British occupants of Cambridge and the surrounding area. The detailed analysis of the finds in these cemeteries, however, poses certain problems which are not explicable in terms of merely Saxon conquerors. Not only do many of these cemeteries start at a very early date, well within the fourth century A.D., but some seem to show evidence of intermarriage and presumably fairly peaceful co-existence with the Romano-British inhabitants. That is, they are not evidence of conquering warriors, but perhaps of invited guests or servants. In addition many of the cemeteries appear to have been abandoned by the late fifth century if not earlier and are hardly indicative of a massive and permanent conquest.

By far the most likely explanation for these early Saxon burials is that put forward by Dr Morris and others[2] who have suggested that they reflect at least in part the employment of Saxon mercenary troops in strategic positions by late- or sub-Roman rulers. The main point is that these

[2] J. Morris, 'Dark Age Dates' in B. Dobson and M. G. Jarrett (eds.), *Britain and Rome* (1966), pp. 145–85.

first settlers were accommodated alongside and with the existing Romano-British peoples. This phase of coexistence must have extended from about A.D. 380 to around 430, when various civil wars amongst the Romano-British led to a revolt by the Saxon mercenaries perhaps in A.D. 442. This resulted in a new influx of Saxon raiders and, in Cambridgeshire no doubt, a certain amount of destruction. It is in this phase that the abandonment of many of the small Roman farmsteads and hamlets took place. But, if we read the evidence aright, towards the end of the fifth century there was a re-establishment of Roman rule, albeit very different from the old imperial government. The majority of the Saxon raiders were driven out and a form of Roman administration organised. Certainly in Cambridgeshire, to judge by the archaeological evidence, some Saxons remained, living side by side with the Romano-British survivors in relative peace.

It is to this period that the four great linear dykes which span the chalklands of the south of the county perhaps belong, though this is by no means certain. Of these the most magnificent is the Devil's Dyke, a huge bank and ditch seven and a half miles long which extends from the fen edge at Reach, east of Cambridge, across the chalk to the forest edge near Woodditton (Plate 4). Though there are now many gaps in it, originally it was a continuous defensive work completely blocking access into East Anglia from the south-west. The bank still stands up to fifteen feet high with a deep ditch in front of it. Six miles to the south-west is another, the Fleam Dyke, also blocking the Icknield Way. This is smaller both in length and size, being only just over three miles long, lying between Fulbourn Fen in the north-west and Balsham near the forest edge to the south-east. Further south-west again is the Brent Ditch, now much damaged and ill-defined and only one and a half miles long near Pampisford. Finally a further six miles to the south-west again is the Heydon or Bran Ditch which extended from Heydon on the forest edge for three miles across the Icknield Way to a former mere, now drained, at Fowlmere. This has been almost completely destroyed.

The actual date of all these dykes or ditches has been a source of great speculation for generations of Cambridgeshire historians and archaeologists. There is no proof for any of the several suggestions put forward. All that is definitely known is that the Devil's Dyke was built after the third century A.D., and that the Heydon Ditch took on its present form between the early fifth and sixth centuries A.D. There is some slight evidence of Saxon warriors having fought at the Devil's Dyke and at the Bran Ditch archaeologists have found the remains of a savage massacre of at least fifty-six men, women and children. Whether these were Saxons or Romano-Britons is unfortunately unknown. Therefore the Cambridgeshire dykes remain an enigma. They probably do all belong to the early Saxon period but the exact date is not known. Nor is there any indication as to whether they were erected by Saxons or Britons. Both were capable of constructing such works. However, it is at least a possibility that they do belong to the mid-late fifth century and may be associated with the bitter fighting that resulted from the Saxon revolt of 442 and the re-establishment of Roman rule around A.D. 500.

By the end of the fifth century, then, some form of Romano-British control probably existed in Cambridgeshire and therefore though many of the Romano-British settlements had been abandoned others must have continued to survive in the old areas of primary occupation probably lived in by Britons and Romanised Saxons alike. Around A.D. 550 a new wave of Saxon peoples began and there does seem to be evidence of a more peaceful type of Saxon settlement at this time. These new settlers were

D

certainly led by warriors and there were probably many unrecorded fights and massacres as they gradually took over the land and homes of the Romano-Britons. But this new wave of people was primarily composed of farmers looking for land to cultivate and not soldiers of fortune bent on taking booty and slaves. As such, if we can trace the advance and settlement of these people in Cambridgeshire we shall perhaps understand more clearly the impact of the Saxons on the existing landscape and be able to see what part they played in the making of the present one.

The first point to emphasise is one we have already referred to but which must be stressed yet again. The archaeological evidence shows that by the end of the Roman period all the fen islands, fen edges and major river valleys had been intensively occupied by Romano-British peoples and in addition there was a considerable settlement in parts of the west Cambridgeshire forested area. By the sixth century some of these settlements had probably been destroyed and a number of Saxons were living in these areas alongside the Britons. In many cases no doubt the ownership of Roman estates had passed into the hands of Saxon lords but there is no need to think that the actual farmsteads and villages were occupied predominantly by Saxons. These were still probably in a minority. Therefore, when in the sixth century a new and larger wave of Saxon settlers moved into the county the amount of land available for settlement was considerably restricted.

One of the most telling pieces of evidence for the lack of land for the Saxons can be seen in the distribution of early Saxon place-names. These are not only remarkably sparse in view of the old idea of massive Saxon settlement, but they also have a very curious distribution. Haslingfield, just south-west of Cambridge, is the only large village in the primary settlement area with a clearly early name. Malton, further west along the Ashwell branch of the River Cam, is also early, but it is and always was a tiny place and lies on the edge of the River Cam well away from Orwell, the main settlement of the parish. By the normal rules of settlement patterns Malton should be regarded as a secondary or daughter settlement to Orwell. Apart from these, March and Mepal, both on islands in the fens, are probably early names, though neither can be considered ideal evidence of primary settlement. Finally Yen Hall, in West Wickham parish, is also a very early name. But this is the name given to a remote and isolated farmstead in the formerly forested south-east of the county, and one of a whole host of similar farms, all of which would normally be interpreted as very late settlements in woodland. Thus the evidence hardly reflects large-scale, early, Saxon settlement in the county. In fact there are probably more Celtic names in Cambridgeshire than definite early Saxon ones. Chatteris and Chettisham on the fen islands are both perhaps Celtic in origin, while other names, such as the lost Walworth near Ely (the 'enclosure of the Britons'), Walworth in Horningsea and Walworth Hill in West Wickham, are evidence of a British survival. There is also the possibility that the name Comberton, given to a village west of Cambridge, is not Cumbra's Farm as the place-name writers have suggested but the Cumbrians' *ton*, i.e. the farm of the Welshmen or Britons.[3]

There is a group of presumably early Saxon names which are noteworthy and require explanation. These are tribal names which have been given to villages and hamlets in the east and south-east of the county, as at Swaffham Bulbeck and Swaffham Prior (the Swabians' *ham*) on the fen edge, Saxon Street and Saxon Hall south of Newmarket, and Anglesey (the island where the Angles live), also on the fen edge east of Cambridge. It seems very likely that

[3] I am grateful to Professor Finberg for this suggestion.

these names were given to places where groups of people lived who were, or thought they were, Saxons, Swabians or Angles. But why was it necessary to distinguish themselves so carefully? If the idea of a massive invasion of settlers is a correct one, why should one group call its village 'the Angles' island' when presumably there were other Angles around them? The more likely explanation is that these names were given to these places because their surrounding areas were occupied by people who were not Angles or Saxons but Britons. If this is correct, these tribal names, together with some of the undoubtedly early place-names such as Malton and Haslingfield, represent small groups of Saxon settlers moving into the predominantly British areas of the county and settling down alongside the Britons.

The general picture of the sixth-century Saxon settlement in Cambridgeshire is then one of gradual infiltration of Saxon farming communities into the older British areas of settlement, perhaps spread over a considerable period of time. Eventually the number of Saxons was greater than that of the Britons, and this produced a basically English rather than Celtic place-name coverage of the county. But even then the existence of a purely Saxon place-name is not proof of complete Saxon occupation. Names such as Duxford (Ducca's enclosure) or Willingham (the home of the people of Wifel) reflect only the name of the local chief or leader at a certain date. Wifel's people could just as well have been Britons as Saxons, though a mixture of both is most likely. The Saxon chiefs no doubt eventually took over tenurial control of the villages and estates they found and settled some of their followers on them, but at least the possibility of a continuing element of British people living on in their old homes must not be discounted. Even Myres, who is no supporter of the idea of a British survival in eastern England, has pointed out that the Saxon royal family of East Anglia, the Wuffingas, whose territory included much of south-east Cambridgeshire, found it advisable to trace their descent from Caesar as well as from Woden.[4]

One possible exception to this slow infiltration by the Saxons of areas of Roman settlement is the forested area of south-east Cambridgeshire. Here there is singularly little evidence of large-scale prehistoric or Roman occupation. Yet the forest edge is lined with villages with impeccable Saxon names while within the forest are other villages and farmsteads including Yen Hall, one of the earliest Saxon place-names in the county. Some of these villages have particularly interesting names. They all lie on the west side of a forested area which extends south-east into Suffolk and Essex. Yet many of them have names which incorporate a 'West' element such as Westley Waterless, Weston Colville, West Wratting and West Wickham. It is hardly likely that these villages would have acquired such names if they had been settled by people coming down the Icknield Way from the north-east. It is more probable that they were settled by people from the east and south-east moving westward through the forest. Certainly West Wratting is explainable as a late settlement from the village of Great Wratting across the county boundary in Suffolk. Thus this south-east Cambridgeshire forest and forest-edge settlement can be interpreted as a late and secondary settlement by Saxons moving in from Suffolk to an area largely unoccupied by earlier people.

To summarise all this rather complex evidence and argument it seems that a case can be made out for the idea that the Saxon settlement of Cambridgeshire was by no means as massive or complete as we have often been led to believe. On the contrary it appears that the Saxon settlement

[4] R. G. Collingwood and J. N. L. Myres, *Roman Britain and the English Settlements* (1937), p. 390.

consisted mainly of slow infiltration into and between existing Romano-British settlements in most places and was only carried out on a large scale in those marginal areas which had been left largely unoccupied by earlier generations. This somewhat meagre evidence can be backed up to some extent by an examination of the so-called nucleated Saxon villages of the county to which we must now turn.

The shape of villages

Since the late nineteenth century, when the study of village shapes and forms really started, Cambridgeshire has been regarded as one of the classic areas in England of large nucleated villages. This apparently obvious feature of the landscape has been seized upon as giving added weight to the idea of large-scale Saxon invasions with the consequent destruction of any older pattern of settlement. Since the first work on village morphology was begun, no one has thought fit to query this. That there are now, and indeed were in the late nineteenth century, large nucleated villages over much of the county cannot of course be denied. The question is were such villages always characteristic of the region?

There is no doubt that some villages were always large and many had a compact nucleated form. Perhaps the best example, and certainly the one most often quoted, is that of Barrington, west of Cambridge (Plate 23). There the huge green, still largely surrounded by houses, with the church and manor house at one end, is a classic instance of a large Saxon village. And of course there are other examples in the county, such as Landbeach and Hinxton where the picture is not so obvious. However, this type of village is by no means the most common. The basic error in this idea

of large nucleated villages being the norm in Cambridgeshire is that students of village morphology have accepted
that the villages as they now are, or as they were eighty
years ago, had not grown or changed much for a thousand
years or more. Nothing could be further from the truth. A
glance at the nineteenth-century census returns from
Cambridgeshire shows that most of the county's villages
and indeed hamlets had at least doubled their population
between 1801 and 1851. This is confirmed by even a quick
examination on the ground. This population rise is still
marked by the existence of vast numbers of largely unattractive rural houses in standard Cambridgeshire white brick
or more crudely constructed dwellings of clay, chalk
blocks or timber framing. Thus the first students of
Cambridgeshire village shapes, even in the 1880s, were
looking at the results of near contemporary large-scale
growth, not at a medieval village.

This early-nineteenth-century rise in population was not
a new phenomenon. Work carried out by various local
history classes in the county has indicated that the population of many villages was increasing rapidly in the
eighteenth century as well. This work has been produced by
the laborious counting of births and deaths in parish
registers. The resulting figures are then turned into crude
population totals and checked against other sources where
available. The results are of particular interest for they
show by just how much villages have grown since the late
seventeenth century. For example the population of Great
Shelford was around 300 in 1700 and had been roughly the
same for at least the previous 150 years. It rose to nearly
600 by 1801 and then to over 1000 by 1851. Again, this
numerical growth can be seen on the ground by the careful
examination of the numerous small eighteenth-century
houses that remain in the villages. Estate, Tithe and
Enclosure Maps all also help to show by just how much

many of the county's villages have grown in the last 280 years.

It could still be argued that though villages were much smaller prior to the eighteenth century they have always been nucleated, and that even in the eleventh century from the evidence of Domesday Book it is clear that there were already relatively large and certainly nucleated villages. But is this so? Let us take one example, that of Bottisham, east of Cambridge on the edge of the fens (Fig. 3). The parish, before modern alterations, consisted of a long narrow strip of land extending across the dry chalk uplands to the south-east and well into the fens in the north-west. In the centre lies Bottisham village, a 'street' village nearly a mile long and lying on a slight ridge between two small streams. It is a typical Cambridgeshire village and one which at first sight is a 'normal' nucleated Saxon one with a perfectly normal Saxon name (Boduc's Farm). However, as Dr Hart[5] has recently pointed out, the name turns up in a will of 1043–5 as *Bidichseye* (the dry ground by the ditches) and this, while being an admirable description of the siting, is therefore not a Saxon habitative name.

Nevertheless the village is apparently a large nucleated one, and is listed in Domesday Book as a single ten-hide manor with a total recorded population of forty-nine. There seems every reason to assume that it has always been a single large village. But if we look beyond the village new problems emerge. Bottisham is not the only settlement in the parish. Along the fen edge, north-west of the village, are three other settlements, Anglesey, later the site of an abbey, Lode hamlet and another straggle of houses called Long Meadow. Anglesey is first mentioned in a document of 1213, Lode in one of 1154–89 and Long Meadow in one of 1260. In addition, fieldwork shows that in the park of Bottisham Hall, a mile north of the village and preserved

5 C. R. Hart, *The Early Charters of Eastern England* (1966), pp. 50–1.

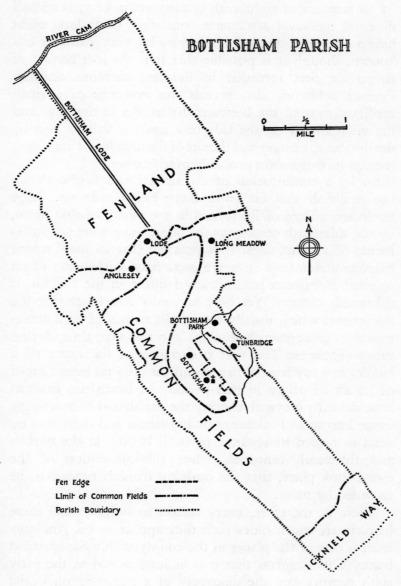

BOTTISHAM PARISH

RIVER CAM

BOTTISHAM LODE

FENLAND

0   ½   1
MILE

N

LODE

LONG MEADOW

ANGLESEY

COMMON

BOTTISHAM
PARK

TUNBRIDGE

BOTTISHAM

FIELDS

Fen Edge ....
Limit of Common Fields ———·———·———
Parish Boundary ···

ICKNIELD WAY

Fig. 3

57

by an accident of eighteenth-century emparking, is a small deserted medieval settlement consisting of at least eight house sites and moated platforms. Its very name is unknown, though it is possible that it is the lost hamlet of Angerhale first recorded in the late eleventh century. Further fieldwork also reveals the existence of a small medieval moated site between the hamlet in the park and the village itself on the side of a shallow valley. This by the thirteenth century was the site of the manor of Tunbridge, though its origins are probably much earlier.

So by a combination of documents and fieldwork we can establish that far from there being only one large nucleated village of Bottisham in the parish of that name, by the thirteenth century at the latest there were six settlements of various sizes. It is possible that all these minor hamlets and manor sites are secondary settlements of an original Bottisham set up away from it in the twelfth or thirteenth century. Yet here we must remember that the documents which usually record the names of such settlements only appear themselves for the first time during those centuries. The first occurrence of the name of a hamlet in a twelfth-century document is by no means proof of its actual origin in that period. At Bottisham from at least the early eleventh century the parish had been a single estate known as Bidichseye or Bottisham and there was no need to record its separate parts. It is only in the twelfth and thirteenth centuries, when sub-infeudation of the estate took place, that the outlying hamlets needed to be recorded by name.

There is, therefore, every reason to suppose that these hamlets are much older than they appear to be. Anglesey itself is one of the places in the county with a Saxon tribal name. This suggests that it is at least as old as the early sixth century and the discovery of a pagan-Saxon burial there probably of fifth-century date suggests an even earlier origin. Even more important is that the hamlet of Lode is situated at the end of, and indeed takes its name from, Bottisham Lode, a long artificial water-course which extends from the fen edge to the River Cam. The lode is certainly Roman in origin. Though later re-used as a canal in the medieval period, it was probably out of use between the sixth and thirteenth centuries. Thus Lode hamlet is not likely to have grown up to make use of the canal unless it was in existence at a very early date. At Long Meadow further along the fen edge the modern hamlet ends just one field short of a large Roman building or buildings. Roman coins and small quantities of Roman pottery have been found elsewhere in Long Meadow as well as at Lode and at Bottisham.

If we now turn to Bottisham village itself and examine more carefully the apparently long street, dating every house, noting every minor change in street alignment and combining this with a detailed study of old maps, the descent of manors and medieval landholding, another feature becomes clear. The village falls into two or perhaps three separate parts which were in the early medieval period physically and tenurially separate and which have only grown together more recently. One part is around the present church where the last fragments of an old green still exist in a widening of the village street. Another lies a quarter of a mile to the north-west, also apparently around the remains of a small green, while perhaps a third part lay at the south-east end of the present village almost half a mile away from the church.

Therefore, in a single parish with what appears to be a single nucleated village, detailed documentary studies and fieldwork reveal the existence of seven or eight medieval settlements scattered widely over a large area, all of which are of high antiquity and some of which possibly go back to the Roman period. This is a very different picture from the normally accepted one and here in one of our primary settlement areas there is a marked similarity between this dispersed medieval settlement pattern and that of the earlier Roman pattern in the same district. It is possible that the tenurial relationships of the main settlement with the outlying ones may have also once been similar.

This long and detailed analysis of one specific parish can be repeated again and again elsewhere in the county with very similar results. If we move away from the fen edge and across into the main Cam valley south of Cambridge we come to the village of Sawston. As a result of large-scale planned and unplanned development it is now one of the least attractive of all Cambridgeshire villages. Yet enough of the past still remains there for the observant fieldworker to learn a great deal. Once again we are at first sight faced with a large nucleated village lying along one main street, now over a mile long, set back from the River Cam on rising ground above the adjacent meadows. But the detailed published history of the parish[6] reveals that the complex description of Sawston given in Domesday Book is not related to the single nucleated village we see today. Domesday Book records the existence of three manors with a total recorded population of forty-one. But all these people were not living in the village that we know. Some were living in a hamlet one and a half miles away to the north-west around the present Durnford Farm[7] while others were living west of the village again close to the river at a place called significantly The Borough in later documents. In addition it is probable that there was at least a single farm if not a hamlet three-quarters of a mile north of the village on the edge of a marshy area now called Deal Grove. The remains of a later medieval house site still survive there. Again there appears to have been a type of dispersed

---

[6] T. F. Teversham, *History of Sawston*, Part I (1942).

[7] Durnford is actually first recorded in a charter of about 954.

settlement in the parish by at least the late eleventh century and the existence of a Roman villa just outside the present village and Roman pottery both at Durnford Farm and near The Borough suggests that a similar pattern existed much earlier.

Elsewhere in the same valley the picture is similar. Detailed work by a local history class at Great Shelford, north of Sawston, has shown that what is now a large nucleated village rapidly being submerged under Cambridge suburbia is made up of two small settlements which were still separate in the mid-nineteenth century and which can be identified as the two separate manors listed in Domesday Book for Great Shelford.

At Whittlesford, across the river from Sawston, the same pattern emerges. From the window of the room where these words are being written one can look out on to the street of a typical Cambridgeshire village. But across the fields a quarter of a mile away it is just possible to see through the trees a group of houses, some dating back to the fifteenth century and centred on an early and now abandoned medieval moated site. Both the main village and this outlying hamlet can be traced as separate physical and tenurial units as far back as 1086. And both parts were certainly occupied in the Roman period, for Sunday afternoon walks, with landscape-history always in mind, have produced Roman pottery from both places. So gradually a picture of a medieval form of dispersed settlement builds up. It is not a true dispersed pattern in that the various farmsteads, hamlets and villages are not scattered all over the parishes but are confined to the edges of the main valley or occasionally along minor tributary streams. But it is very different from the normally accepted picture of one large nucleated village per parish. And when the earlier dispersed Roman settlement pattern is superimposed on the medieval one the similarity between the two is striking

(Fig. 2). The possibility that both are related, while not proved or indeed provable, needs to be at least considered.

This concentration on the main Cam valley and the fen edge example of Bottisham does not mean that this dispersed pattern is confined to these areas. The same pattern seems to occur elsewhere though much documentary and field work would be needed to prove it. In the valley of the Ashwell Cam in the south-west of the county, villages such as Meldreth, Guilden Morden, Steeple Morden and Abington Pigotts not only have the appearance of former hamlets which have grown together, but some also have isolated farmsteads and hamlets which occur in documents as early as the twelfth century. For example Odsey, a hamlet in the remote south corner of Guilden Morden parish, is first recorded around 1150. In addition, in this same area there are a multitude of known Roman sites in and around the present villages. Indeed it was the village here at Litlington, with its curious rectangular layout and a large Roman villa in one corner, that Seebohm saw as a possible example of a Roman settlement which had never been abandoned.[8]

Moving north into the fens this same dispersed settlement pattern is again repeated, though here another and apparently later dispersal is also distinguishable. Even a large village such as Haddenham appears to have resulted from the growing together of at least three once separate parts, two of which are actually mentioned in a charter of 970 when King Edgar gave them to the monastery at Ely. Around Ely itself the existence of the hamlet of Chettisham, with a Celtic name, the lost Walworth ('the enclosure of the Britons'), and Braham Farm, recorded in the *Inquisitio Eliensis* of 1086, points to a very old dispersed pattern of settlement.

Further north again on the silt fens, where there was an

---

[8] F. Seebohm, *The English Village Community* (1883), p. 433.

intensive Romano-British settlement, when the medieval pattern of settlement first becomes clear from thirteenth-century documents it is certainly not a nucleated one. At Elm for example, though the village of Elm gives its name to the parish, by the thirteenth century there were at least four and possibly six other hamlets in the parish and four of these are on top of known Roman settlements. Here clearly the majority of the Roman villages were abandoned in the fifth century, almost certainly due to difficulties of drainage, but those on slightly higher and drier sites may have survived to become the centres of medieval manors.

So far we have concentrated on two major parts of the landscape, the main areas of settlement and the detailed pattern of settlement, in our examination of the continuity of occupation in the Cambridgeshire landscape. But there is another aspect to be considered, that of land units. In some parts of England attempts have been made to show that some medieval land units or, as we now call them, parishes are of considerable antiquity and perhaps go back into the pre-Saxon era.[9] On the continent too, work has shown that some parishes certainly go back to at least A.D. 400 to 500.[10] With this in mind, we need not be so sure that all our modern rural parishes are just the result of Anglo-Saxon land division. Some could well be much older, though the problems of proving this are immense.

Sometimes, however, there are indications and the best example in Cambridgeshire is just east of Cambridge in what we now call the parishes of Fen Ditton and Horningsea (Fig. 4). Most of the area covered by these two parishes is a long northward-pointing peninsula of chalk, bounded on the east and north by formerly undrained fenland and on

---

[9] C. C. Taylor, *The Making of the English Landscape: Dorset* (1970), p. 72; D. J. Bonney, 'Pagan Saxon Burials and Boundaries in Wiltshire', *Wilts. Arch. Mag.*, Vol. 61 (1966).

[10] W. Holmqvist, *Excavations at Helgö* (1961), pp. 25-8.

the west by the River Cam. There is no doubt that this area was an important one during the Roman period. The major pottery-producing industry of Cambridgeshire in the second to fourth centuries was located here; near Eye Hall there are two probable Roman villas, and at least two other Roman villages or hamlets and a further villa are known. That this land was also some form of Roman tenurial unit is suggested by the existence of a major linear defensive bank and ditch, now known as the north section of the Fleam Dyke, but actually having no connection with the real Fleam Dyke further south-east. This dyke cuts off the whole of the promontory from the land to the south and thus forms a large and well-protected land unit in which lie all the Roman settlements. The date of the dyke is not known with any certainty, but the discovery of pagan-Saxon weapons in the top of the silted-up ditch suggests that it is pre-Saxon. There is therefore every reason to see this promontory as a Roman and even prehistoric land unit. When the mists of the early Saxon period finally clear and documents appear, this land is still a compact estate of seven hides, which is recorded as being given by the newly baptised heathen to a monastery at Horningsea some time before A.D. 870.[11] After various vicissitudes the whole estate passed to the monastery at Ely and it remained in the hands of the Abbey and later the Bishops of Ely for centuries. The fact that this original estate is now two separate parishes need not cause us any concern. A glance at a map shows us that the boundary between the two parishes of Fen Ditton and Horningsea is extremely odd. One would immediately suspect that the two parishes were once a single unit. And indeed this is so, for the document recording the detailed layout for the division into the present parishes still survives in the Ely Bishops' Registers for 1412. We can see this area as perhaps a single Roman or

[11] Ely *Libellus* No. 237.

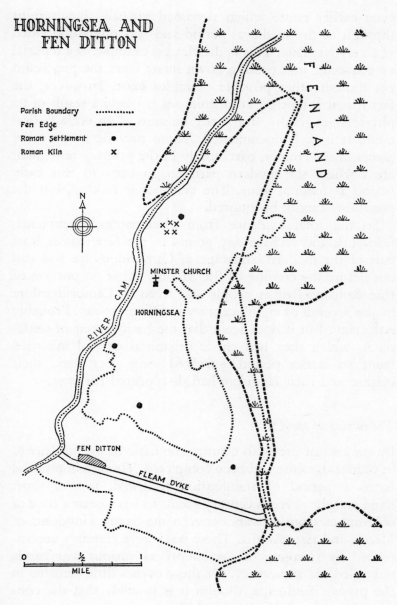

HORNINGSEA AND FEN DITTON

Parish Boundary ....

Fen Edge — — — — —

Roman Settlement ●

Roman Kiln ✕

N

F E N L A N D

R I V E R   C A M

MINSTER CHURCH

HORNINGSEA

FEN DITTON

FLEAM DYKE

0 ½ 1
MILE

Fig. 4

even earlier estate which remained virtually intact right through to the medieval period and was only subdivided at a very late date. This is the clearest example of a tenurial or economic unit passing down intact from the pre-Saxon era though other possible examples exist. However, the fact that it is so clear at Horningsea is partly a result of its physical geography and partly because as an ecclesiastical estate it is well documented. There may be many other places in the county, particularly in the primary settlement areas where the modern parishes go back to this early period as tenurial units. The evidence is lacking, but the possibility cannot be ignored.

So the total evidence from place-names, documents, fieldwork and archaeology points to the fact that at least part of the modern landscape of Cambridgeshire was laid out before the coming of the Saxons. What proportion of true Romano-British people still lived in Cambridgeshire by the seventh or eighth century is difficult to say. Probably not many. But it does seem that the basic layout of settlement, which they had either organised or had inherited from an earlier period, survived long after they, their culture and their language had disappeared for ever.

The coming of the Danes

By the end of the sixth century the basic Saxon settlement of Cambridgeshire had been completed. Though in political terms a period of stabilisation followed, it was short lived and the seventh century seems to have been a time of continuous frontier wars between the Saxon kingdoms of Mercia and East Anglia. These wars were certainly accompanied by ravaging of the county as various war bands struggled for supremacy. Of these events little remains in the present landscape, though it is possible that the construction, or at least the refurbishing, of some of the great linear defensive works in the south of the county, the Devil's Dyke, Fleam Dyke and the Heydon Ditch, took place at this time when the actual boundary between Mercia and East Anglia fluctuated along the broad chalk-land zone which was their common meeting ground.

While these savage wars were being waged and during the subsequent Danish raids and settlement of the ninth century more important and lasting events were taking place. These were the consolidation and continuous expansion of settlement, together with a massive extension of arable land. This was part of a process which was to continue until the fourteenth century. The actual details of all this and the problems of dating it will be dealt with in the next chapter. But it is important to remember that this expansion was taking place in these centuries. We can then see these wars and associated troubles more clearly. That they occurred there is not in dispute. That they were locally devastating is certain. At the same time people were continuing to alter the landscape in a more permanent way with the establishment of new villages, hamlets, farmsteads and fields. The wars, raids, massacres and so on, though they feature prominently in the political history of our county and though they brought hardship and tragedy to many, had but little impact on the slow development of the landscape.

One important event during this time was the Danish settlement of the ninth and tenth centuries, but even this had little overall impression on the landscape. The Danish raids along the east coast during the latter part of the eighth century gradually gave way to settlement and conquest. In the winter of 865 to 866 the Danes' Great Army established itself in East Anglia and this was followed by the general overrunning of the area, accompanied by the sacking of the early monasteries and other destruction. By the end of the century Cambridgeshire was under Danish control and so remained for nearly fifty years. This control was accompanied by Danish settlement but exactly how intensive is hard to estimate. The overall impression is that there was very little when compared with North-Eastern England where the evidence suggests whole new areas of settlement by the incoming Danes. No Danish burials are known in Cambridgeshire and though many finds of weapons and other objects have been made these do not imply massive settlement. A few villages have Danish names but both their etymology and their distribution are significant in pointing to the sparse nature of the Danish settlement. The villages of Conington, Croxton, Caxton, Bourn and Toft, all lie in the formerly wooded area of west Cambridgeshire outside the primary settlement areas, and Carlton in the south-east of the county is in a similar position. This indicates that such Danish settlement as existed was confined to the more remote and lightly settled areas. In addition, of these villages, only Bourn and Toft have real Danish names. Conington and Carlton are both basically Saxon place-names with a Danish pronunciation of the first element while Croxton and Caxton are only Danish personal names added to the older Saxon *-ton* or farm. The evidence suggests that all these villages were originally Saxon or earlier and were only perhaps taken over by Danes as at Toft or Bourn or merely acquired Danish overlords as a result of conquest as at Caxton and Croxton.

Elsewhere in the county there are many minor names of roads or fields such as Kirkgate in Tydd St Giles, Flag Fen in Whittlesey, Clipsall in Soham, Clint Field in Coton and Hobach in Wimpole and Whaddon which are either pure Danish or Anglo-Danish in origin. They seem to reflect a scattering of Danish influence and perhaps thinly distributed Danish settlement all over the county, but in numbers so small as to preclude any major landscape alterations by these Scandinavian people. The evidence of Sokemen in the county, listed in Domesday Book in 1086 and making up some twenty per cent of the population recorded at that date, has often been seen as the survival of a considerable number of Danish settlers. However, it is not certain that all these were necessarily the descendants of Danes.

SELECT BIBLIOGRAPHY

Hart, C. R. *The Early Charters of Eastern England* (1966).
Meaney, A. *Gazetteer of Early Anglo-Saxon Burial Sites* (1964).
Reaney, P. H. *Place Names of Cambridgeshire and the Isle of Ely* (1943).
R.C.H.M. *Cambridgeshire.*
V.C.H. *Cambridgeshire*, Vol. I (1938).

3. The medieval expansion

*New villages and farmsteads. The medieval fields. The
early Church and lords in the landscape.*

THOUGH WE HAVE seen how the Saxon settlers took over
the lands and habitations of their predecessors, this process
had been largely completed by the seventh century. When
we next see a reasonably clear picture of the landscape of
the county in 1086, as described in Domesday Book, it is
obvious that much had happened to that landscape in the
intervening 400 years. We must therefore use Domesday
Book and many other contemporary and later documents
to unravel the changes in the landscape during those
centuries, and this is not easy. Though the Norman
Conquest marks a major political and tenurial break in the
history of the county it is of little consequence in terms of
landscape history. Domesday Book is a useful product of
the political changes in the late eleventh century which
helps landscape historians, but it does not mark a major
break in the development of the landscape. Using Domesday
Book is like looking at one rather blurred frame of a cine-
film of the history of the landscape. We can see roughly
what the picture was like in 1086 and realise that much
went on before and after. The problem of sorting out
exactly how and when the changes that we see took place
is another matter.

In Cambridgeshire, Domesday Book is an invaluable
document if used with caution. It certainly shows that the
landscape had been greatly altered and modified in the

years following the Saxon settlement, but accepted at face
value it is misleading. Because it was compiled on a tenurial
basis, there are severe limitations on what it can tell us
about even the late-eleventh-century countryside and
even greater ones on what information we can gather for
the earlier centuries. We have already seen some of the
problems in the detailed study of Bottisham, where the
apparently single manor, village and parish, as recorded in
Domesday Book, was in all probability made up of a host
of separate hamlets, whose origins possibly lay back in the
Roman period. In fact Domesday Book, taken as it is
written, gives us the classical picture of large nucleated
villages arranged in much the same pattern that we have
today. Yet the reality was quite different. For example
Domesday Book does not record a number of villages which
one would expect to have existed by 1086. Fen Ditton is
one such and indeed it did exist and is recorded in a late-
tenth-century Saxon charter, while Newton, south-east of
Cambridge, whose name suggests a late origin, is also
recorded in a will of 975. Similarly, Coveney, on the fens,
is mentioned in a charter of about 1025 and was certainly a
settlement, for it was the place to which Aethelswyth, a
Saxon noblewoman, retired with her maidens to work at
embroidery and weaving. The village of Wimblington,
also on a fen island, is again not mentioned in Domesday
Book but was actually bought by the monastery at Ely
from Ramsey Abbey in the late tenth century. So we must
take great care when using Domesday Book to assess the
amount and type of settlement in existence by the late
eleventh century.

When we move into the period after 1086 we are
presented with an impression, based on a mass of documentary evidence, of a rapid increase in population with atten-
dant expansion of settlement into the marginal forested
areas and drier fenlands up to now left largely uninhabited.

This impression is probably misleading and Domesday Book and more particularly the massive twelfth- and thirteenth-century documentation give a totally wrong chronology of the development of the landscape. For it must never be forgotten that these documents, though they appear to record new settlements and land clearances at this time, themselves came into existence only in the twelfth and thirteenth centuries. Therefore the appearance of a farm-name in a thirteenth-century document may be leading us astray. It is more than likely that many such farmsteads are much older than their first record in a document.

That this is so can be seen by looking at the isolated farmstead of Yen Hall in West Wickham parish in the south-east of the county. It is only one of a whole host of similar farmsteads scattered throughout this formerly wooded area, most of whose names are first noted in twelfth-century or later documents. But Yen Hall, apart from having an unusually early name, actually appears by chance in a Saxon land charter of 974 relating to the adjacent parish of West Wratting. Not only is it certain that Yen Hall was in existence at that time, but part of the boundary of its land is defined. Thus we can be sure that Yen Hall was an inhabited place and an estate long before Domesday Book was written and where there is no reference to its existence. The chances that Yen Hall was the only farmstead in the woodland by the late tenth century are remote. Proof of its existence is an accident of documentary survival and there must have been other similar farmsteads and hamlets around it.

Therefore the problem in detailing the medieval expansion of settlements and fields in Cambridgeshire is to decide how much of what appears to be new in the post-eleventh-century landscape is really of that date and how much is actually far older. The answer is probably that, in spite of wars, raids, invasions and conquests, the development of the medieval landscape had started by the seventh century and continued until the fourteenth century at least.

New villages and farmsteads

The basis for all the growth of settlements and the establishment of new ones from the seventh to the fourteenth century was a continuing rise in population. There can be no doubt that the numbers of people in the county gradually increased, though we have no figures before Domesday Book to prove it. From 1086 onwards some general estimates are available, though they are by no means accurate or absolute, for the surviving statistics were gathered on very different bases and evasion and exemption occurred often on a large scale. Nevertheless some idea of the general increase in population is obtainable.

The eighty-nine surviving Hundred Rolls of 1279, which cover most of the county, list just over 8000 landowners and tenants. For the same parts of the county, Domesday Book in 1086 gives a recorded population of nearly 3100. These figures are not of course directly comparable, and what the actual total population was at either date is far from certain. Nevertheless the figures do indicate a substantial increase in the number of inhabitants of the county and it had been estimated that there were as many people in Cambridgeshire in 1279 as in 1801. We must now try to assess the effect of this population increase on the countryside of the county.

Within what we have termed the old primary settlement areas, that is the main river valleys in the south, the fen edges and fen islands, the evidence for expansion of settlement is hard to see. This is largely because of the difficulty, in most cases, of being sure which parts of the curiously dispersed pattern of villages, hamlets and farmsteads are of pre-Saxon origin, which are to be connected with the main Saxon settlement and which are the result of later expansion. In most places in these primary areas it would seem that the existing settlements, whose origins lay back perhaps in the Roman period, merely grew in size and that few new ones came into existence. At Great Shelford, in the main Cam valley, though the available statistics actually cover up the fact that there were originally two separate hamlets over three-quarters of a mile apart, they do indicate a substantial overall rise in population. The recorded population in 1086 is apparently thirty-four[1] while the number of tenants in 1279 is given as 137. Not only can we be certain that no new settlements in the parish accompanied this rise but we can still see on the ground where the increasing numbers of people were housed. Of the two original hamlets of Great Shelford, one lay by the River Cam, near the shallow ford which gave the village its name, while the other lay three-quarters of a mile away on the edge of a small stream. Between the two lay a broad, roughly triangular area of meadow and pasture with the arable fields around it. As the population increased people from both hamlets built their houses on the edges of this meadow and gradually both hamlets merged to form one village. The resulting plan was a large triangular village 'green', known as High Green, which existed until the middle of the nineteenth century, but its origins were not those of a normal village green. The actual date of the establishment of houses round this meadow is not known. It is unlikely to have started much before the eleventh century but was certainly complete by the fifteenth century to judge by the dates of some existing buildings there.[2]

[1] Absolute certainty is not possible as part of the village is combined with Little Shelford.

[2] C. C. Taylor (ed.), *Domesday to Dormitory* (1971).

This slow amalgamation of once separate hamlets into our 'typical' nucleated villages during this time of population expansion can be seen elsewhere. In the south of the county at Duxford there were originally at least four separate hamlets lying along the edge of the River Cam. Two of these, set fairly close together, grew rapidly in size during the twelfth and thirteenth centuries and soon became the compact village we see today. But the two very different parts are still visible to the observant historian. The south part of the present village is a long east–west street leading down to a ford across the river with its church, St Peter's, at the east end. North of this lies a very different settlement which, though now physically part of the first, still has its small, square green surrounded by houses with its own church, St John's, in one corner. In many other places we can see the marked pre-fourteenth-century expansion of population in terms of deserted house sites which have resulted from a later fall in population and contraction of the villages. We shall deal with this later.

As well as this enlargement of existing villages and the amalgamation of earlier dispersed hamlets, some definitely new settlements came into existence in the primary areas, though the actual date of their establishment is not known. One obvious example by its name and siting is Newton, south of Cambridge. Unlike its neighbours of Hauxton, Harston, Foxton and Little Shelford it is not on the edge of a river, nor, like Thriplow to the south, is it situated at a major spring-head. It lies on the edge of a small stream completely cut off from the adjacent river valley by low chalk ridges. Yet though not mentioned in Domesday Book it certainly existed before 1086, for it is recorded in a will of 975 when it was given to King Edgar. So 'new' it may have been by the standards of its neighbours but it is certainly a late Saxon settlement at least. Exactly how and when it was settled is of course quite unknown. The fact that the village is usually referred to in medieval documents as Newton cum Hauxton and indeed was given to King Edgar with Hauxton suggests that it may have originally been settled by people from that village. On the other hand, the parish of Newton is physically separated from Hauxton by Harston parish. So the details of its origin must remain lost in the mists of Saxon history.

Another probably secondary settlement of this type is the hamlet and parish of Westwick, between Oakington and Cottenham, north-west of Cambridge. Again its situation and name suggest that it was settled by people from Cottenham and originated as a *wick* or dairy farm on the side of a small brook at the far western end of Cottenham parish. Again, however, it is not a late settlement, for it is named in Domesday Book, albeit with a recorded population of only two.

Sometimes the pattern of medieval expansion is extremely complex and defies complete explanation. Such is Burwell, on the fen edge east of Cambridge. There was certainly a scatter of small Roman settlements in the area, two of which included large stone buildings. Near the site of one, on a low hill overlooking a spring, a Saxon village grew up which was probably protected by some form of fortification. The name Burwell (fort by the spring) suggests this and indeed the line of the encircling defences is partly preserved by the curving line of modern streets round the hill. A few hundred yards away to the north another Roman settlement appears to have developed into a long linear Saxon street village. The growth of population in the early medieval period resulted in the expansion of both villages until they formed one large one. In addition, a mile away across the fields and close to the fens there was in late-medieval times another village or hamlet known as North Street. This was certainly in existence by the early fourteenth century when it was first recorded, but it is probably much older. It has a curious sinuous street which lies parallel to and has the same shape as the headlands, still visible on the ground, of the medieval common fields which lay to the east of it. It looks very much as if the hamlet of North Street was developed within the existing common fields and used a headland between the strips as its main street. It is therefore unlikely to have been an early settlement and may have grown up relatively late in the medieval period as a result of increasing population. In addition, there is yet another settlement in the parish which lies between North Street and the northern of the two early Saxon villages. This is called Newnham and though it is not mentioned before the early fifteenth century it must be older than this. Its plan too is of particular interest for it takes the form of a neat rectangle of five narrow east–west lanes, bounded by two north–south lanes, the whole only 130 yards square. It looks rather as if it is a deliberately planned hamlet.

When we move out of the main areas of early settlement into other parts of the county we are faced with a somewhat different pattern of settlement, though still showing the result of large-scale population growth. As these other areas all have great differences in detail we must examine each in turn. First let us look at the great triangular area of boulder clay in the west of the county. Though this once largely wooded region was apparently sparsely occupied in prehistoric times, there are clear indications that during the Roman period there was penetration into it via the minor valleys and the beginnings of forest clearance here undoubtedly started then. The incoming Saxons certainly took over many of these clearings and settled within them. Therefore at an early date in the Saxon period and certainly by the seventh century at the latest there were lines of Saxon/Roman settlements around the edges of the wooded upland plateau and also within the main Bourn Brook valley which bisects it. Each of these villages had an area of land or estate, surrounding it and stretching back into the higher forested area. Some of these estates, but not all, are what we call parishes today. From this basic early Saxon or Roman layout, expansion into the forested area took place, marked by the establishment of new villages and farmsteads and accompanied by the gradual removal of the forest. The actual dating of all this expansion and its detailed chronology is beyond us but the general outlines are clear.

First, it certainly nearly all occurred before the Norman Conquest and the proof of this can be seen in Domesday Book itself. This upland area of west Cambridgeshire had once been thickly forested. We can be certain of this from the underlying heavy boulder clay and the occurrence of woodland place-names and topographical names. Domesday Book with its many entries concerning woodland here adds to the evidence. However, the entries in Domesday Book need to be looked at with great care. For though there are twenty-seven places in the area with woodland mentioned, the actual wording merely indicates the presence of sufficient wood for 'making fences' or for the houses or, in one entry, for fuel. The implication of all this is that by 1086 there was very little woodland left in west Cambridgeshire. With the undoubted evidence for occupation of this area having started as early as the Roman period it would seem likely that the clearance of the wood-land was well under way before the Saxon settlers arrived here and that they merely completed the process.

When we turn to the pattern of settlement in west Cambridgeshire the evidence for pre-Norman Conquest occupation and clearance of the woodland is the same, and we can even suggest a rough chronological development of the expansion into the forest. The first stage appears to be the establishment of new settlements well away from those along the edges and within the main valleys, on the flat plateau top. The villages of Eltisley, Graveley, East Hatley and Hatley St George are likely candidates. All have the characteristic -*ley* element in their names indicating that they could have originated as clearings in the woodland and two of them still retain triangular greens which may represent the original clearings. Eltisley has a superb triangular green, completely preserved and surrounded by attractive houses. As a result it is one of the most pleasing villages in the area. In sharp contrast East Hatley's green has been abandoned and built over so that the village now appears to be a normal single-street type. However, the observant fieldworker will quickly spot the boundaries of the original green, still lined with abandoned house and garden sites. Unfortunately, unlike Eltisley, modern 'developments' in the form of a scrapyard and what purports to be a 'church' have successfully ruined this tiny village. If we avert our eyes from the wreckage of the twentieth century and look beyond the village and even beyond the county we see that East Hatley, Hatley St George and the neighbouring Cockayne Hatley in Bedfordshire form a compact block of land which must represent late Saxon settlement presumably under some form of overall control which predates or ignores even the ancient county boundary. Whatever the date of the establishment of all these new upland settlements, and it is quite unknown, it certainly was before 1086, for all are listed in Domesday Book and Graveley is recorded in a document of 964 when it belonged to Ramsey Abbey.

In addition to these later upland settlements, and there are other probable examples at Papworth St Agnes and Longstowe, as well as more in the adjacent lands in Huntingdonshire and Bedfordshire, the earlier villages also seem to have produced daughter hamlets within the bounds of their own estates. A particularly good example is Grantchester, on the very edge of the west Cambridgeshire area. A glance at the map (Fig. 5) shows that Grantchester is the easternmost of a line of villages lying along a stream draining the interior of the clayland, whose estates or parishes extend from the stream to the ridgeway on the north. But Grantchester parish does not extend to the ridgeway. To the north of Grantchester lies Coton, a small village and parish occupying the valley of a tiny brook. Not only does it look from the map as if Coton parish has been cut out of a larger Grantchester parish which once extended north to the ridgeway, but there is documentary evidence that Coton was a parochial chapelry, dependent on the mother church of Grantchester until Henry III's reign, when it was granted full parochial status. The name Coton is also typical of a late secondary settlement. The village is not mentioned in Domesday Book, but this should not lead us to believe that it was not in existence by then. The chancel in the existing church is of twelfth-century date, and is hardly likely to have been built to serve a new village less than sixty years old.

Once the possibility has been established of identifying, from a map (Fig. 5) showing parish boundaries, the existence of daughter hamlets, one can see further examples elsewhere. West of Grantchester is the village of Toft which has a small rectangular parish. Immediately to the north of Toft parish and separated from it by a highly irregular boundary is Hardwick parish. This has undoubtedly been cut out of an original Toft estate whose boundary once extended north to the ridgeway. Though Hardwick is certainly a daughter hamlet of Toft it is an early one, for the village is recorded in a Saxon will of 991. Further west again both the name and the form of the parish boundaries indicate that Caldecote was also a daughter hamlet of Bourn and though in existence by 1086 has a church described as a 'capella' of Bourn in an early document.

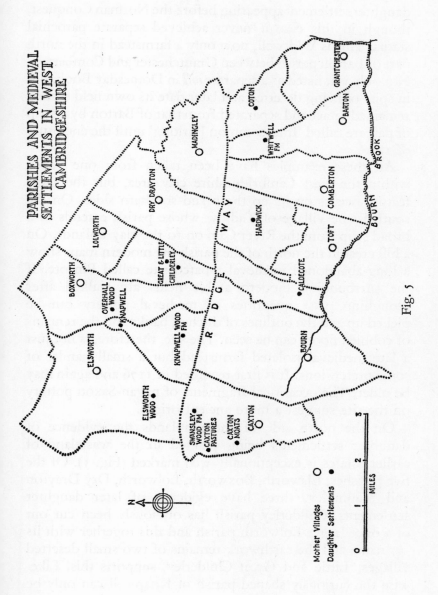

PARISHES AND MEDIEVAL
SETTLEMENTS IN WEST
CAMBRIDGESHIRE

GRANTCHESTER

BARTON

COTON

MADINGLEY

WHITWELL
FM

BOURN   BROOK

DRY DRAYTON

COMBERTON

LOLWORTH

HARDWICK

RIDGE   WAY

TOFT

BOXWORTH

GREAT & LITTLE
CHILDERLEY

CALDECOTE

OVERHALL
WOOD

KNAPWELL

KNAPWELL WOOD
FM

ELSWORTH

BOURN

ELSWORTH
WOOD

SWANSLEY
WOOD FM

CAXTON
PASTURES

CAXTON
MOATS

CAXTON

N

○ Mother Villages
● Daughter Settlements

0   1   2   3
MILES

Fig. 5

In this same valley there is yet another example of a daughter settlement appearing before the Norman Conquest, though in this case it never achieved separate parochial status. This is Whitwell, now only a farmstead in the north part of Barton parish between Grantchester and Comberton. Not only is it listed as a separate *vill* in Domesday Book, but in spite of being deserted at a later date its own field system remained intact and separated from that of Barton by a strip of pasture called 'Intercommon Furlong' until the enclosure of 1839.

All these examples have been taken from one valley within the west Cambridgeshire clay area, but the same feature occurs on its northern and southern sides. On the south is the village of Tadlow whose parish extends in a broad strip from the River Cam on to the clay uplands. On a hill crest in the north of the parish the modern maps show a long-abandoned medieval moated site called Pincote. If the surrounding modern arable fields are walked after ploughing, vast quantities of medieval pottery can be picked up and the outlines of ditches, banks and the remains of cobbled floors can be seen. The site, therefore, is not just a late medieval isolated farmstead but a small hamlet of some pretensions. It is first recorded in 1176 and again may be older. The occasional fragments of pagan-Saxon pottery on the site suggest a more ancient origin.

On the north side of these uplands the evidence of daughter settlements being planted in the wasteland of earlier estates is exceptionally well marked (Fig. 5). Of the five parishes, Elsworth, Boxworth, Lolworth, Dry Drayton and Madingley, three have evidence of later daughter settlements. Childerley parish has obviously been cut out of a once larger Lolworth parish and this together with its -*ley* name and the earthwork remains of two small deserted villages, Little and Great Childerley, supports this. Likewise the curiously shaped parish of Knapwell can only be explained by the fact that the village of Knapwell is a daughter hamlet of Elsworth.

Between Knapwell and Childerley the parish of Boxworth, though showing no evidence of subdivision, has the remains of a large moated site buried deep in Overhall Wood. This is the site of a medieval manor, well documented from the eleventh to the fourteenth centuries, which must have originated as a daughter farmstead of Boxworth village. In Elsworth too there is evidence of yet another secondary settlement in the south of the parish around Elsworth Wood. Not only does the Enclosure Map of 1803 show this area as 'old enclosures' surrounded by the former common fields, but our botanical colleagues tell us that part of the wood contains plants which are indicators of very old and perhaps primary woodland. Finally, there is evidence on the ground of abandoned paddocks, closes and a hollow-way indicating the former existence of a small farmstead. References to a Matheus *Atewode* living in the parish in 1279 and *Le Wodecroft* in the 1322 Court Rolls are probably connected with this place.

To show how complex this pattern of development can be, if we return to Knapwell we can find evidence of a daughter farmstead of Knapwell itself. Well to the south of the village in a remote part of the parish is Knapwell Wood which with three smaller adjacent fields totals just over fifteen acres. On one side is the modern Knapwell Wood Farm. Though by the eighteenth century this piece of land was completely surrounded by the common fields of the parish and thus existed as a tiny island of enclosed woodland and fields in a sea of strips, it must have originated centuries earlier as a single farm in the wooded waste whose fields were then formed by the clearance of that woodland. In 1311 the farm was occupied by one John *ad Boscum*, according to the Court Rolls of the manor, and is probably much older than that. Then as the common arable fields were gradually extended south from the village they completely surrounded the earlier assarts. Again botanical examination of the hedges here supports the idea that these fields are of great antiquity for they still contain plants such as Dog's Mercury and Herb Paris, both indicators of old woodland.

This example of secondary or daughter settlements themselves sending out further farmsteads is not the only one in west Cambridgeshire. In fact there are many. Most of these farmsteads are easily recognisable as being of medieval date by virtue of their surrounding moats, though, as will be discussed in detail later, this is not an indication of their original date. A typical one can be seen in Eltisley parish, where the village itself is a relatively late settlement in the woodland. To the north of the village and close to the edge of the parish is a single farmstead with an abandoned medieval moat nearby called Papley Grove Farm (Pappa's clearing). This farmstead is first recorded in the Hundred Rolls of 1279 where the Prior of Huntingdon is said to hold "one messuage called Pappele and sixteen acres of land, twelve acres of wood". This probably represents the farmstead and its land, a nice picture of the small size of these late woodland farms at this time. Once again the actual date of such a farm is difficult to ascertain. If we take the first recorded occurrence at its face value we might assume that the farmland was first cleared from the waste in the late thirteenth century. However, we know that the Prior of Huntingdon had purchased the farmstead and not made it and therefore it must be older than the thirteenth century.

Even more difficult to explain are the position and name of this farmstead and this involves the possible date of its establishment. As Papley Grove Farm is in Eltisley parish the obvious inference is that it was settled by people from Eltisley village. But the personal name Pappa occurs in the

two parishes immediately to the north of Eltisley, Papworth Everard and Papworth St Agnes (Pappa's enclosure).
Both these villages were certainly in existence by 1012 and
probably long before then. It may be that Pappa was one
man who gave his name to all three places, either because
he was responsible for their setting up, or because he held
the land on which they lay. Either way it means that Papley was established well back in the pre-Norman Conquest
period and perhaps before even the basic parish or estate
boundaries were finally fixed in that wooded area. Even
this single farmstead in a remote corner of an upland parish
is therefore probably of great antiquity and has no connection with any twelfth- or thirteenth-century agricultural
expansion.

The best example of one of these medieval clayland farms
is to be seen in Kingston parish at Kingston Wood Farm
(Fig. 6A). Here in a remote corner of the parish nearly one
and a half miles away from the village is a small circular
moat still surrounding a delightful early-sixteenth-century
house. The site was inhabited by at least the middle of the
thirteenth century and probably much earlier. However,
the setting here is all important for the farm lies within the
large Kingston Wood whose ragged and indented edges
still reflect the original clearing in the forest. To stand near
the present farmhouse with its home paddocks still largely
surrounded by trees is to be in a world of a thousand years
ago.

If we now cross the county and look at its south-east
corner we find a picture in some ways similar to, but in other
respects very different from, west Cambridgeshire. Here
again we are in a formerly forested area, based on the heavy
underlying clay, and again we see many small hamlets and
isolated farmsteads with names that suggest late forest
settlement. But the detailed picture and the chronology of
settlement are not the same. Unlike west Cambridgeshire,

UPLAND FIELD PATTERNS

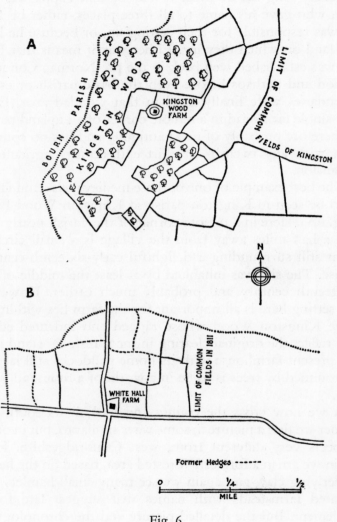

Fig. 6

there is little evidence of Roman exploitation of this area. The main attack on the forest seems to have been due almost entirely to the Saxons. As a result the clearance of the forest was considerably later in time than in the western part of the county and this can be seen in Domesday Book. Though there is evidence for little woodland remaining in the west of the county, in the south-east there still seem to have been considerable stretches left in 1086. There are fifteen entries in Domesday Book indicating woodland in this part of the county, mainly in the form of 'woodland for x swine' (*silva x porcis*). The numbers of swine recorded are as high as 450 at Woodditton and 511 at Camps (Castle and Shudy Camps). There are also two parks for wild beasts, that is deer parks, at Burrough Green and Kirtling. Although a large proportion of woodland still remained in 1086, and the process of clearing may have been slower here, the results are just as marked in the present landscape.

Once again this can be seen in both the layout of the modern fields and the pattern of farmsteads and villages within them. Most of the parishes consist of long strips of land extending from the chalklands in the north-west well into the claylands in the south-east, with their main village situated on or close to the edge of the clay and therefore on the boundary of the former forest (Fig. 7). They therefore appear to be neat estates or economic units which include all the necessities of a farming economy, that is pasture land on the upper chalklands, arable land around the villages and forest beyond. But in two places there appears to be evidence of the splitting up of parishes or estates as a result of later forest clearance and settlement.

The first example concerns the two modern parishes of Westley Waterless and Burrough Green. The boundaries of the two parishes at first sight seem to indicate that they were once one single unit based on the village of Westley

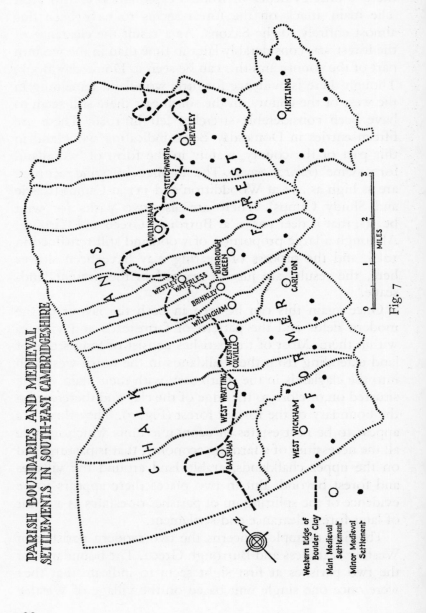

PARISH BOUNDARIES AND MEDIEVAL
SETTLEMENTS IN SOUTH-EAST CAMBRIDGESHIRE

KIRTLING

CHEVELEY

STETCHWORTH

DULLINGHAM

C H A L K   L A N D S

WESTLEY
WATERLESS

BURROUGH
GREEN

F O R E S T

BRINKLEY

WILLINGHAM

CARLTON

WESTON
COLVILLE

WEST WRATTING

F O R M E R

BALSHAM

WEST WICKHAM

N

Western Edge of
Boulder Clay   - - - - -

Main Medieval
Settlement   ○

Minor Medieval
Settlement   ●

0   1   2   3
MILES

Fig. 7

Waterless. This name incidentally means the opposite of 'waterless'. It is the western watermeadows, that is a well-watered place. The obvious interpretation is that Westley was once the main settlement and that later Burrough Green grew up within the forest, became larger than Westley and eventually acquired most of its land. The original triangular green cleared from the forest still survives at Burrough Green, which supports this idea. However, the complication is in the names of the two villages. First, Westley suggests that it is the western of two places and by analogy with elsewhere ought to be a secondary settlement of an earlier one to the east. The 'borough' element in Burrough Green means fort or fortified site and though no trace remains on the ground, the medieval moated sites there are later, it may be that the green in its original form was defended. In any case it would seem possible that the borough element indicates the mother village and Westley the daughter hamlet. If this is so it means that the normal pattern of settlement development from a forest edge into the forest has been reversed.

One instance of course is not enough for proof but additional evidence comes from further south in the parishes of Balsham and West Wickham. Again the two parishes appear to have once been one, and the very irregular boundary between the two supports this. The normal explanation is that West Wickham is the daughter hamlet of Balsham set up in the forest, but the name *West* Wickham suggests that it is the daughter hamlet of an earlier village to the east. This may be Withersfield across the county boundary in West Suffolk. Therefore, Balsham might be seen as the next stage in the expansion westward and be a daughter settlement of West Wickham. The existence of other west names such as West Wratting and Western Colville here indicate that the early Saxon settlement originated from the south-east in Suffolk and the evidence shows that perhaps it was of a fairly complex nature, spread over some time. Nevertheless, even with the evidence of forest still here in 1086, the setting up of these villages must have taken place early in the Saxon period. Mother and daughter hamlets alike, Westley Waterless, Burrough Green, Balsham and West Wickham all occur by name in tenth- or eleventh-century Saxon wills or charters.

Around all these hamlets and villages, scattered through the clayland, are a host of isolated farmsteads, many now surrounded by moats and most recorded in documents by the thirteenth century. Every parish in the area has them. In West Wickham there is Streetley Hall, which though not listed in Domesday Book is recorded in the *Inquisitio Eliensis* of the same date, the hamlet of Burton End first recorded in 1232, Hill Farm certainly occupied by 1350 and Yen Hall documented as early as 974. Further east, we can find places such as Ley Farm (1250) in Stetchworth, Mines Farm (1272) in Weston Colville, Barslead Farm (1298) in Kirtling and Derisley Farm (1239) in Woodditton. Even the parish names of Ashley, Silverley and Cheveley suggest clearance of woodland and all these were in existence by 1086 at the latest.

Finally in this examination of the development of Cambridgeshire settlement in the early medieval period we must move north on to the fens. Here again we can see the same picture of the massive expansion of farmsteads and hamlets into the wastes, though in a very different environment. The picture is somewhat blurred, for with the pre-existing scattered settlement on the fen islands and within the northern silt fens which, as we have seen, may date from Roman times, it is often impossible to see which settlements are early and which late. All one can say is that from the sixth to the thirteenth centuries there is a continuous development of farmsteads and hamlets all over the drier higher parts of the fenlands associated with a clearance of waste and drainage of fen. The magnificent surveys of the lands of the Bishops of Ely certainly indicate a rapidly rising population in the thirteenth century but lack of earlier documents prevents us from seeing whether this was a short-lived phenomenon or was the end of a long process of growth and expansion. The latter is more likely. The most important point to make is that the countless farmsteads and hamlets that we see dotted across the fen islands are probably much older than their first recorded occurrence in documents. Some of the farmsteads have names which suggest relatively late settlement. Bedwell Hay Farm, south-east of Ely, the 'enclosure by the spring in the hollow', is one, first recorded in 1302. Newnham, north of Ely, first recorded in 1195, is another. Both of these are on the fen island of Ely. Estover Farm and Westry near March, both documented from 1221 onwards, are also perhaps late hamlets settled, as their names suggest, from March which lies between them.

Further north again on the silt fens, a place such as Fitton Hall, in Leverington parish, was certainly settled by 1254 while the name Newton, now a village and separate parish in the extreme north of the county, probably means that it was a relatively late settlement on newly reclaimed land. The boundaries of the parish also indicate that it was once part of Tydd St Giles to the north and therefore can be seen as a secondary settlement of Tydd.

This detailed examination of all parts of the county has shown that the original dispersed pattern of settlement handed down to the Saxon invaders of the fifth and sixth centuries was expanded and consolidated in the following centuries as population increased and wood, waste and fenland were encroached upon. We can safely say that by 1300 the basic layout of settlement in the county was complete almost as we see it today, except for the relatively recent farms in the south, which followed the enclosure of the medieval fields, and those in the fens which appeared following the seventeenth-century drainage works.

The medieval fields

In most textbooks on medieval field systems Cambridgeshire is included in the part of England where the classic medieval open or common, two- or three-field system of agriculture was predominant until the late eighteenth and nineteenth centuries. While this is broadly true, there were also large areas with very different fields especially in the forest and fenland parts of the county. Even where the 'normal' common fields existed there were many complications and variations, many of which are still reflected in the present landscape.

Over most of our area the common field system in its fully developed form was in existence by the fourteenth century. Around all the major villages and even some of the minor hamlets there were broad open lands divided into two, three or more large fields, cultivated in common in the form of countless long, narrow strips. It used to be thought that this system of agriculture was introduced into this country by the Saxon invaders who by virtue of their vast numbers imposed it on the landscape, sweeping away all that there was before. Now we are not so sure. Dr Thirsk has suggested that intermingled strip holdings were the result of inheritance and partition and that common rotations were later superimposed over these and led to the emergence of the two- and three-field system.[3] If this is so, the original Saxon settlers had a very different type of agriculture which, in view of the evidence of settlement noted earlier, may well have been very similar to that of their predecessors. For if the Saxons took over many of the settlements of the Romano-Britons they could just as easily

[3] J. Thirsk, *Past and Present* No. 29 (1964).

have taken over their fields. Both the Romano-British fields
and the Saxon ones were in the same areas over much of the
county. The idea that the common field system of agriculture slowly developed in the subsequent centuries is quite
acceptable in Cambridgeshire.

Most students of the county's field systems have stressed
the existence by the thirteenth century of the normal two-
and three-field system and certainly these existed then.[4]
But occasionally there are indications of much more complicated agricultural practices in operation. The remarkable
work carried out by Mrs Spufford at Chippenham illustrates
this well.[5] In 1544 there were not two or three open fields in
the parish but eight, and far from this being the result of
recent subdivision following the introduction of new crops
it can be seen to be a tidying up of a much more complex
pattern. For in the thirteenth century there were at least
ten separate fields and there is certainly no evidence of the
equal distribution of tenants' strips within them. In fact
the reverse is true. For example, the eight-acre holding of
Nicholas Clericus lay entirely in the fields south and east
of the village and he held no lands in the fields to the north.
Therefore, though the fields were obviously worked in
common and had some form of rotation, the pattern is far
more complicated than we have been led to believe.

Though all these medieval common fields were finally
swept away in the eighteenth and nineteenth centuries,
mainly as a result of parliamentary enclosure, it is quite
wrong to assume that nothing now remains of them. Much
is left still to be seen by the careful observer. The most
marked relic of these fields in the landscape is of course
the ridges and furrows which can still be seen in places, in
spite of the enormous destruction by modern ploughing
(Plate 5). The long ridges, usually seven to nine yards wide

[4] W. E. Tate, 'Cambridgeshire Field Systems', *Procs. C.A.S.* (1939).
[5] M. Spufford, *A Cambridgeshire Community* (1965), p. 17.

and up to two feet high and separated by shallow furrows, are in part the remains of the actual strips of the medieval common field system and were formed solely by ploughing. They vary greatly in length from as little as twenty or thirty yards to as much as 200 to 300 yards and can be absolutely straight or markedly curved. Where the ridges meet existing hedges they usually pass under them showing that they are earlier than the modern fields.

Ridges do not in fact represent the actual strips held by individual farmers in the common fields. Each strip often comprised a number of ridges which probably varied in the course of time as they were sold, split up or amalgamated. This being so, it is obvious that the medieval strips, in Cambridgeshire at least, were not bounded by baulks or banks such as have been suggested as existing elsewhere. There were indeed pieces of land called 'balks' in some Cambridgeshire parishes but where it is possible to check these on the ground, for example in Wimpole Park where a particularly good area of ridge-and-furrow still remains, these turn out to be normal ridges which were apparently out of cultivation at the time when they were recorded in documents. This was pointed out even in the late nineteenth century by W. J. Corbett in an examination of baulks in Coton.[6]

This kind of detailed ground examination of ridge-and-furrow can tell us an enormous amount about medieval and later agricultural practices, none of which are recorded in documents. In Papworth St Agnes parish there is a group of ridges 550 yards long, a most unusual feature. But at three places along the length of the ridges they all rise slightly over an underlying feature running at right-angles and at the same point all have a marked change of direction in their plan. This indicates that originally there were four groups of ridges, or furlongs as they were known, lying

[6] W. J. Corbett, *Trans. Royal Hist. Soc.*, n.s. XI (1897).

end on to one another and separated by headlands on which the plough was turned. At some later period all four furlongs were ploughed as one and the earlier headlands were then ploughed over. This produced the marked rise in the ridges at this point while the changes of alignment are the result of the joining up of adjacent ridges. In Wimpole Park another group of ridges ends at a normal headland eleven yards wide, but a few yards in front of the headland is another narrower one overlying the ridges. This shows that two stages of ploughing have taken place here, though the reason for this is quite unknown. Elsewhere the roads and access lanes between the former strips can still be seen as slightly raised or hollowed-ways through the adjacent ridge-and-furrow.[7]

Ridge-and-furrow now exists mainly in the west and the south-east of the county and in a few places of the fen islands. Over much of the chalklands in the southern part of the county no ridge-and-furrow is visible even on air-photographs, but the remains of the common fields still exist there. These are long, low, sinuous ridges rarely more than one or two feet high, thirty yards wide and up to 500 yards long which can be seen in the modern arable fields during the winter and early spring. French geographers have recognised them on the continent and call them *crêtes de labor*, but we can more accurately term them headlands, which is what they are. The original strips or ridge-and-furrow between them have long since been ploughed away but these slightly higher headlands, where for centuries the medieval and later farmers turned their ploughs, still survive. In 1968 when a North Sea gas pipeline was driven across south Cambridgeshire the trench cut through a large number of these headlands and their origin as a result of ploughing was clearly demon-

---

[7] Much of this section is based on work carried out in west Cambridgeshire for the R.C.H.M. See R.C.H.M. *Cambridgeshire*, Vol. I (1968), pp. lxvi–lxix.

strated.[8] Elsewhere it is possible to correlate exactly the surviving ridges with the headlands shown on pre-enclosure estate maps which show the common fields. This has been done at Burwell where almost every headland shown on a map of the parish in 1808 is still visible on the ground.

One especially interesting example of the survival of these headlands is on the upper road between Duxford and Whittlesford. The straight road was laid out in 1830 when the common fields of Duxford were finally enclosed. Today there are still very slight but, for motorists driving fast, well marked rises in the tarmac. These rises can be seen to continue in the fields on either side of the road. They are of course medieval headlands, fossilised for posterity by the County Council Roads Department.

Much of this evidence for the former medieval common fields still visible in the landscape demands a trained eye and some documentary research. For those without the training or the access to documents a medieval common field system, albeit somewhat modified, still exists at Soham for all to see (Plate 6). North of the village on a large peninsula projecting into the fens is an area called North Field which is divided up into long curving strips with two smaller areas called Redland and Barecroft Fields on either side. No Act of Enclosure was ever passed for Soham and though much of the parish is now enclosed North Field is the last surviving remnant of the medieval fields. Naturally it no longer looks exactly like a medieval field system. The strips now grow a very mixed selection of crops. Nor of course is it farmed in common, but the general picture of long curving strips without any dividing hedges or baulks, arranged in curving furlongs, is the nearest we can now get to a true medieval common field system.

[8] C. C. Taylor, 'Archaeological Results from the North Sea Gas Pipeline', *Procs. C.A.S.*, Vol. LXII (1969).

After this digression into the remains of the common fields in the present landscape we must return to their development in terms of the medieval landscape. For, complex though the development of the tenurial and agricultural practices of this form of farming were, they were made even more so in the south of the county by the continuous growth of population. As this increase in the number of people went on the common fields were constantly being expanded to provide more and more food. What had earlier been waste and pasture was gradually taken into cultivation and often incorporated into the existing field systems. The evidence for this is twofold. First is the physical existence of the ploughing of apparently marginal land and second is the documentary evidence such as from maps. Unfortunately neither can be dated accurately.

The physical evidence takes the form of long, narrow plough terraces on relatively steep hillsides. These are the so-called strip-lynchets which are usually the result of the contour strip ploughing of marginal land when all other flatter and more easily worked areas in a parish were already under cultivation. These strip-lynchets, normally thought of as a Wessex, Cotswold and Northern England phenomenon, do exist in Cambridgeshire, though they are now being rapidly destroyed by modern ploughing. They occur typically on the margins of parishes wherever there are particularly steep slopes. What was once a splendid flight of these terraces, now sadly battered, exists on the east side of Copple Hill in the south of Ickleton parish while others can be seen on Anthony Hill in Heydon parish as well as in the adjacent Great Chishill parish. A good series can be seen buried under protective trees within Hill Plantation at Barrington and almost ploughed out on Rowley's Hill, Harston.

One of the best examples of strip-lynchets in the county

G

is at Great Shelford. Here in the remote northern corner of the parish on the rising land of the Gog Magog Hills is a fine beech wood which occupies a long, narrow strip of land. It is a very popular place for visitors, being close to Cambridge and open to the public. Many thousands of people must visit it every year. Yet probably very few ever notice that the trees are growing on a series of terraces, let alone understand what these terraces are. They represent the last push into the wasteland of the parish by the medieval farmers of Great Shelford, probably in the late thirteenth century when the population of the parish was greater than it was to be until the early nineteenth century.

A number of parishes in the south of the county had common field names which indicate intakes from the waste. At Sawston even by the sixteenth century the common field which lay furthest from the village was known as The Brack (or Breach Field), probably meaning 'land newly taken into cultivation'. Another field-name which often occurs in medieval and later documents is Stocking Field, meaning a place where there are stocks or tree stumps. When such field-names occur near the edges of parishes or close to woodland they probably indicate the clearance of trees to make new parts of the common fields. For example Stocking Field in Little Gransden parish lay in the extreme east of the parish adjacent to Waresley Wood in Huntingdonshire. The occurrence of the name here in a survey of 1222 indicates that the extension of common field arable to the margins of the parish had already taken place by this time. Occasionally we can get glimpses of what must have gone on for centuries. At Sawston, John de Sawston who died in 1270 is said to have "encroached on the common pasture of Dale Moor for a length of thirty rods, ten feet in width".[9]

9 *Hundred Rolls* (1279).

As well as the expansion of the common fields in the south of the county there was also a contemporary enclosure of waste to form fenced fields. In Burwell parish, an area of nearly 200 acres of enclosed fields on the northern edge of the parish called 'le Breche' existed quite separately from both the common fields and pasture from at least the mid-thirteenth century and some of these fields still exist on the ground today around the modern Breach Farm.

Moving now to the formerly forested areas of the county in the west and south-east we again find new fields associated with the spread of hamlets and farmsteads there. In west Cambridgeshire due to the very early clearance of the woodland there, which perhaps started in pre-Saxon times, the evidence both on the ground and in documents is not as clear as one would wish. In fact there are hardly any documentary references to the clearance of woodland in the area, but this is not surprising in view of the small amount recorded in Domesday Book. A recent study of the medieval woodland in west Cambridgeshire has shown that by the end of the thirteenth century there was a smaller acreage under trees than there is today. On the ground there is evidence which, though undated, shows that some at least of the isolated farmsteads set up in the wastes were surrounded by enclosed fields formed by the assarting or clearance of the forest. At Kingston Wood Farm (Fig. 6A) not only does part of the original woodland survive but the surrounding enclosed fields in an area which was never part of the common fields of the parish seem from their shape and general appearance to have originated from piecemeal assarting.

A similar example though not apparently associated with a farmstead can be seen in the south-east corner of Little Gransden parish. Here there still remains a piece of woodland called Hayley Wood whose name is first recorded in 1164. To the north-west of the wood is a roughly oval area bounded by thick and botanically ancient hedges which is the site of another piece of woodland cleared in the seventeenth century. Between the two are other hedges linking them and clearly defining the limits of a much larger wood. Work by Dr Rackham has shown that this original wood had already been reduced to its seventeenth-century state by 1251 at the latest. In a survey of that date in the Ely Coucher Book, not only are both woods listed, but the fields between them are recorded with almost the same acreage as that of the modern fields.

Further evidence of ancient clearance of woodland has already been described at Knapwell and Elsworth (see p. 83). These examples of enclosed fields produced by the assarting of waste or woodland, impressive though they are, are not in fact ubiquitous in west Cambridgeshire. Many of the isolated farmsteads there, at least in the relatively recent past, did not have enclosed fields around them but lay entirely within the common strip fields. The moated farmsteads of Papley Grove Farm in Eltisley and Swansley Wood Farm in Caxton are typical of this.[10] Elsewhere, though isolated farmsteads end up by being surrounded by enclosed fields, the evidence of the ground indicates that at an earlier period there were common fields around them. Thus the medieval farmstead at Caxton Pastures (Plate 10) certainly lay within a large area of enclosed fields by 1750, as a map of that date shows. A close examination of the shape of these fields indicates that they are generally of the long, narrow, curved type suggesting that they were formed by the enclosure of pre-existing common field furlongs, and the ridge-and-furrow which still survives in these fields, or which can be seen on air-photographs, supports this.[11] What does all this mean? It might be that these farmsteads were originally sur-

10 Tithe Map of Eltisley; Estate Map of Caxton (1750).
11 R.C.H.M. *Cambridgeshire*, Vol. I, Caxton (25).

rounded by enclosed fields which were later absorbed into the expanding common fields system as it reached them. On the other hand it may be that the owners of these farmsteads actually farmed their land within the existing common field system or in a way that could be developed into a later common field system. We do not know.

In the formerly wooded south-east part of the county the evidence for piecemeal clearance of woodland and the formation of enclosed fields as a result is much clearer in the present landscape. This may be due to the fact that the exploitation of this part of the county in agricultural terms was later than in the west and lay largely within the Saxon period. All the major settlements in south-east Cambridgeshire certainly had common field systems around them by the thirteenth century but these usually lay on the drier, lighter soils along the former forest edge. Further southeast, within the woodland, irregularly shaped fields and thick hedgerows are still characteristic of this part of the county. Also typical are small woods or copses with indented edges which seem to preserve the form left by the last onslaught of the medieval farmers as they reached the end of their drive for more arable land. Such fields and copses can be seen exceptionally well around Combers Wood in Stetchworth parish, at Harlocks Moor in Dullingham parish and especially between Bushy Wood, Osier Wood and Blackthorn Wood at the south end of Cheveley parish.

Sometimes we can identify not just the fields but the whole land worked by the occupants of these medieval woodland farmsteads in this part of the county. There is in the Cambridgeshire Record Office a splendid map of Carlton-cum-Willingham parish dated 1767. This shows a long, narrow, rectangular area of enclosed fields belonging to Lopham's Hall Farm which is first recorded in 1236. Modern farmers have removed many of the ancient hedges and only parts of the original boundary remain. Using the hedgerow-dating method devised by Dr Hooper, an examination of this boundary shows that it is at least 900 years old, that is nearly 300 years older than the first documentary appearance of the farmstead. Once again actual documentary evidence for this massive clearance of woodland is not very common and one can only suggest that this is because most of it took place at a time before the start of detailed records, that is prior to the twelfth century.

Sometimes in the remote corners of the county curious insights as to the actual agricultural practices in the medieval period come to light. In the south-west part of Castle Camps parish there is a typical woodland pattern of isolated farmsteads dotted about on the undulating clay-land. Many of these are clearly of high antiquity and Willesey Farm, for example, is first recorded in 1275. Yet instead of being surrounded by small irregular fields as one would expect, these farmsteads all have very rectangular fields looking surprisingly late, adjacent to them. These fields are indeed relatively modern and were formed in the middle of the nineteenth century. Our interest lies in what preceded these fields. For the Tithe Map of 1840 shows that far from there being older enclosed fields in this area there were seventeen separate common fields, many with as few as two, three and four strips in them and most inextricably mixed up with the scattered farmsteads. No doubt the 1840 picture is some way from the medieval one but it is obvious that the field system in the parish was by no means normal. Elsewhere in the parish there are the more usual irregular fields typical of south-east Cambridgeshire as a whole. One possible clue to some of the complexities is recorded in an Inquisition Post Mortem of 1372. There the lord's arable land is listed in four unequal pieces one of which was worth nothing as it was "fallow and in common". This suggests a fairly normal common field system, but in addition there is other arable land "lying newly broken and turned, value at times fifteen shillings per annum".[12] This emphasis on newly ploughed land *at times* worth fifteen shillings suggests that an infield-outfield system of agriculture was in existence, whereby certain areas were only occasionally brought into cultivation and then abandoned to recover their fertility. Whether or not this is the correct explanation the type of medieval agriculture in Castle Camps is a long way from the classic common field system which is usually said to be characteristic of this part of England.

Finally, in this review of the evidence of medieval fields and the expansion of farmland, we must turn to the fens. Here we are faced with a curious problem. Due to the fact that most of the land was held by great monastic houses or ecclesiastical lords, from the mid-thirteenth century onwards we have a vast amount of detailed documentation telling us where, when and how the development of new fields and their associated drainage works were undertaken. But when one moves into the landscape itself it seems at first sight that little or nothing can be identified of these works. Most of the fenland is criss-crossed by countless drains and the vast majority of the fields are rectangular in layout and bounded by narrow ditches instead of hedges. In addition, in view of the large amount of later drainage and reclamation which have constantly altered and still are altering the shape and size of fields, it might be thought that the actual areas reclaimed or assarted from the fens in the medieval period are impossible to recover. However, this is not so. If one adopts a different approach from that used on the uplands and, instead of concentrating on field shapes and sizes, looks at larger areas of land and takes

[12] P.R.O., C.135/222 (15).

note of general alignments and patterns of field arrangements, some at least of the medieval fenland fields are recoverable if only in outline.

Let us deal with the documentation first. Once again there is the very basic point which can never be stressed too often. The documents, however detailed and complete they may be, do not start until the late eleventh century at the earliest, and so are probably recording only the last 250 years of a process which had been going on for at least the previous 500 years and perhaps for much longer. We cannot overcome this difficulty but we must never forget that it exists.

Much of the evidence for the creation of new farmland in the fens comes from the splendid surveys carried out by the Bishops of Ely at various times in the Middle Ages. These give a picture of great prosperity and expansion culminating, in the thirteenth century, both in the peat fens of the south and the silt fens in the extreme north of the county. In the 1251 survey the manor of Downham has a list of thirteen new free tenants holding sixty-nine acres of reclaimed land at a place called *Apesholte*, while in the adjacent parish and manor of Littleport sixty new tenants were holding nearly 500 acres of similarly reclaimed land in the same area. Further north-west at Doddington, which then included the present parishes of March, Wimblington and Benwick, many new assarts are recorded in 1251 as well as 111 new tenants. All these areas of reclamation lay on the margins of the fen islands north of Ely. To the south the evidence indicates that there was considerably less assarting, but this might only mean that the greater part of the easily reclaimable land had already been brought into cultivation much earlier. At Haddenham, again in 1251, only a few *novi feoffati* are mentioned though assarts in 'Sephey' and a small new field called 'Snata' are recorded.

All these new lands lay on the peat fen, but further north

on the silt fens the same process was going on, though here recurrent flooding by the sea across the low-lying land caused considerable hardship and a great flood in 1236 a near disaster. There are constant references to land being inundated. In 1251 one of the two areas of marsh in Leverington was "overflowed and laid waste by the sea" and at Elm in the early fourteenth century, though one Edmond Peveral had 2400 acres of land, it was described as *"terra morosa et marisci"* and only 240 acres could be cultivated yearly.

Nevertheless, large areas of land were reclaimed and enclosed. In Leverington we read much about land in the new fields and the new purprestures. In Parson Drove parish, originally a chapelry of Leverington, the tenants of the hamlet of Throcenholt made an agreement with the Abbot of Thorney regarding shares in the new assarts they had made and in those that they were to make in the future. At Outwell and Upwell twenty-eight new tenants were recorded on the land of Ramsey Abbey in 1206–7 as well as many new purprestures, while at Tydd St Giles in 1251 it is stated that tenants could and ought to reclaim land towards the sea and marsh without increases in rent.

It is not always clear from the documents exactly what all this new land was used for, or indeed what form the reclamation took. Much of it certainly was the extension of the normal common field arable which existed on the fen islands, just as it did further south on the uplands. The actual system of agriculture is as mysterious as ever and particularly on the silt fens the common strips were often inextricably mixed up with the scattered pattern of hamlets and farmsteads there. As many as eight separate common fields are sometimes mentioned within a parish. The existence of one of these fields, New Field, in Leverington in the fourteenth century suggests that some of the expansion and reclamation was actually incorporated into the existing common fields. In addition, however, there were certainly piecemeal enclosures along the fen edges carried out by individual farmers living in farmsteads close at hand. Vast areas of land were also reclaimed for purely pastoral purposes. This was especially true of the northern silt fens where the danger of recurrent floods meant that little could be grown on the lower-lying ground. Here large pieces of marsh pasture or 'summer grounds' for grazing seem to have been the predominant form of reclamation.

This then is the documentary evidence for a massive extension of agricultural land into the fens during the medieval period. How much of this can we still see on the ground? Let us start where it is easiest and look at the silt fen parishes of Leverington, Newton and Tydd St Giles to the north of Wisbech (Plate 2). What one can generally call the main villages of these parishes lie well back from the present course of the River Nene and separated from it by wide flat land, some of it still marsh and rough grazing near the river but rich arable land closer to the villages. Between the river and the villages is a long continuous earthen bank, variously called the Sea Bank or Roman Bank (Fig. 8). It is not always easy to see, due to later destruction, but large-scale Ordnance Survey maps show its course clearly. The present road from Leverington to Newton runs on top of it as does part of the Wisbech to Long Sutton (Lincs.) road near Four Gates. Elsewhere it can be seen ten feet high wandering between modern fields. This bank probably marks the seaward limit of reclamation reached by the end of the medieval period. Behind it, that is to the west, are two low-lying triangular areas, one between Tydd St Giles and Newton and the other between Newton and Leverington. At first sight this land appears to be no lower than that where the villages are situated. In fact Tydd village is at about eleven feet above sea level, Newton between eleven and fourteen feet

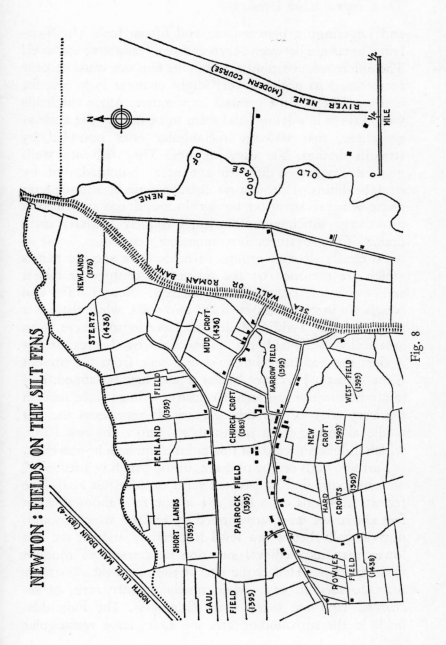

NEWTON: FIELDS ON THE SILT FENS

RIVER NENE (MODERN COURSE)

OLD COURSE OF NENE

NENE

SEA WALL OR ROMAN BANK

NEWLANDS (1376)

STERTS (1436)

MUD CROFT (1436)

FENLAND FIELD (1395)

CHURCH CROFT (1385)

KARROW FIELD (1395)

WEST FIELD (1395)

NEW CROFT (1595)

HARD CROFTS (1395)

PARROCK FIELD (1395)

SHORT LANDS (1395)

GAUL FIELD (1395)

ROWLES FIELD (1438)

NORTH LEVEL MAIN DRAIN (1831-4)

N

0   ¼   ½   MILE

Fig. 8

107

and Leverington between ten and fifteen feet. The 'low-lying' areas are between seven and five feet above sea level! The differences are minute, but in the fens one must become accustomed to noticing very slight changes in height for they are often of the greatest importance. Again the fields within these low-lying areas seem to be exactly the same as elsewhere, that is large rectangular ones bounded by straight ditches. Yet they are not. They fall into well-marked groups of fifty to 200 acres bounded, not by straight drains or droveways characteristic of a much later phase of fen reclamation, but by sinuous drains and curving droveways which are often cut obliquely by later main drains of the seventeenth to nineteenth centuries. Some of these clearly defined groups of fields have specific names which are recorded by the fourteenth century or earlier and some are of particular interest. New Crofts and Newlands in Newton parish are two such, while there is a New Field in Tydd St Giles. In Leverington there is an area called Sea Field, that is the field by the sea. It lies against the Sea Bank but is over a mile from the present Nene estuary. However, when it was first reclaimed, certainly before the fourteenth century, it must have lain on the very edge of the tidal estuary. It represents the last medieval intake from the mudflats before the Sea Bank, which bulges outwards at this point to include it, was built.

Further south on the peat fen, in the parish of Littleport, we can today find an isolated farm called Apes Hall. The farmstead stands on a low rise in the fens about thirteen feet above sea level surrounded by fenland which though now actually below sea level is certainly at least six feet lower than its medieval situation as a result of modern drainage. Apes Hall is the site of the medieval *Apsesholte* first recorded in 1251 when nearly seventy acres of reclaimed land are listed there (Fig. 9A). The individual fields in the surrounding area are again large rectangular

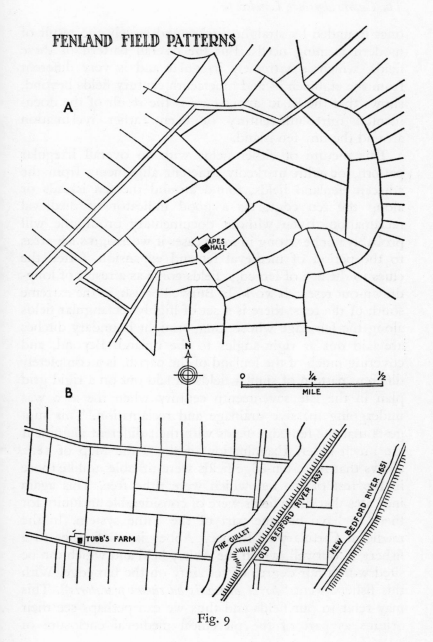

FENLAND FIELD PATTERNS

A

APES
HALL

N

0   ¼   ½
          MILE

B

TUBB'S FARM

THE GULLET

OLD BEDFORD RIVER 1637

NEW BEDFORD RIVER 1651

Fig. 9

ones bounded by straight ditches and largely the result of modern farming needs. But the overall pattern of these fields, which is extremely irregular and is very different from the eighteenth- and nineteenth-century fields beyond, shows that the basic layout here is the result of the documented thirteenth-century or even earlier reclamation around the tiny fen island.

This picture of either fields with an overall irregular pattern, or with markedly different alignments from the adjacent fenland fields, found around the fen islands or along the fen edges, is a good indicator of medieval reclamation. Even without documentary proof one will probably not be wrong in most cases if we assign such areas to the period of medieval fenland expansion. Often the clues to the age of fen-edge fields come as a result of long-drawn-out research work. In Burwell parish, in the extreme south of the fens, there is a set of highly rectangular fields along the fen edge whose long, straight boundary ditches are laid out at right-angles to the upland. Beyond, and covering much of the fenland of the parish, is a completely different pattern of similar fields all laid out on a rigid grid plan in the late seventeenth century when the area was undergoing massive drainage and reclamation. This suggests that the fen-edge fields with their different alignment are much older. Examination of the Tithe Map of 1842 shows that these fen-edge fields were tithable, unlike those in the rest of the fen which were tithe free. This again indicates that these fields were of considerable antiquity for them to have become part of the Tithe system. In the medieval Cartulary of Ramsey Abbey is a reference to a fishery in Burwell, which the Abbey held and which can be sited with a fair degree of certainty on the fen edge. With this fishery went *"terrae arrabilis ad civum piscatoris"*. This may refer to our fields and thus we can perhaps see their origins as part of the piecemeal medieval enclosure of the fen edge to provide food for the local manorial fishery.

The existence of all these fenland fields and pastures did not depend just on the momentary need of individual lords and peasants who first laboured to enclose them from the surrounding fen. Once made, generations of farmers had a long struggle to keep them dry and productive in the face of constant floods. Countless drains and ditches had to be cut and then cleared and recut again and again. The upkeep of almost every stream and ditch together with their adjacent banks was the responsibility of someone. Maintenance of these was a primary duty of every landowner. Landowners leased fenland on condition that ditches were kept scoured and there are many references to ditch-digging and cleaning being customary villein services on fenland manors. Much of this work involved great co-operative effort by all concerned and it is significant that much of the large-scale reclamation of the fens in the later medieval period was carried out by the great fenland abbeys such as Ely, Thorney and Ramsey. It was only perpetual corporate bodies such as these that could successfully undertake the reclamation and, more important, keep up the necessary drainage works. Even so, there were constant difficulties. In 1285 the lands of the Bishop of Ely's men at Elm, Wisbech, Leverington, Newton and Tydd were flooded by water but not as a result of a natural disaster. The floods were caused by the neglect of those whose duty it was to repair the banks and ditches "according to the custom of the fen".[13]

This long discussion of the expansion of fenland agriculture in the early medieval period must not mislead us into thinking that all of the fens were reclaimed at this time. In terms of total area only a small proportion of the

[13] P.R.O., Patent Rolls.

fenlands were affected by this work. Elsewhere, especially on the southern peat fens away from the edges of the islands and uplands, the meres, lakes, rivers and marshes remained as they were, valuable for fishing, reeds, sedge and peat as well as for wild-fowl and a host of other commodities. But even here there were large areas of relatively dry ground, 'summer lands' as they were called, which during the summer months and even in dry winters could be used for pasturing animals. This latter feature was particularly important on the drier silt fen parishes in the north of the county where the underlying soils produced a rich grassland which, unbelievably to the modern visitor who sees a totally arable economy, supported vast flocks of sheep. Even by 1086 very large numbers of sheep are recorded in the adjacent Norfolk silt fen parishes. For example 2000 are recorded at West Walton. Unfortunately we have no figures for Cambridgeshire and probably the development of large-scale sheep farms in the silt fens of our county came later. However, there is no doubt that by the fourteenth century the area was a major sheep-grazing region.

Elsewhere in the county too, sheep were a vital part of the economy, and though by the standards of the main wool-producing parts of England the numbers kept were not great, considerable flocks of sheep were kept on the chalk and boulder clay uplands as well as within the southern fens. This was certainly so by the twelfth and thirteenth centuries as can be seen at Chippenham. The 285 sheep of the lord of the manor in 1086 were increased dramatically within a few years, for by 1146 the de Mandevilles there granted pasture for 500 sheep to Chicksands Priory. In 1285 the Prior of Swavesey put a flock of 600 sheep on the commons of Dry Drayton and it has been estimated that there were probably at least 3600 sheep grazing within that parish between 1258 and 1315.

The early Church and lords in the landscape

When considering the impact of the Church and the upper classes of lay society on the medieval landscape we must remember that much of what they achieved has been described in the previous section. We have already stressed the part played by the great monastic establishments in the exploitation and reclamation of the fenlands. In addition much of the expansion of settlement and agriculture into the other marginal areas of the county was doubtless led by or carried out under the direction of many of the county's lords, though inevitably the detailed documentary proof has not survived. But these people and organisations also changed the landscape in other and varied ways, albeit on a smaller scale and at a more local level.

The two great fenland abbeys of Ely and Thorney have each left very different remains for us to see. Both were founded on remote fenland islands in the late seventh century and both were utterly destroyed in the Danish raids of 870. They were re-established in the tenth century and soon became not only important religious establishments but also, and more crucial from the point of view of the landscape, important economic centres. Ely, on a better site, better endowed and with the advantage of being a diocesan centre from 1108, not only became the greater of the two abbeys but also played a large part in the development of the adjacent town. Finally, when the monastery was dissolved, the existence of the abbey church as a cathedral protected it from large-scale destruction. Thus we have at Ely one of the great medieval monastic churches together with many of the conventual buildings still intact (Plate 35). The great cathedral is largely the result of the devoted work of the twelfth- and thirteenth-century builders. It was started in 1083 and by 1252 the whole cathedral was complete much as we see it today. Then on 22nd February 1322 the Norman crossing tower collapsed and had to be rebuilt. The result was not only a masterpiece of medieval engineering but one of the great glories of England, the Octagon designed by the then Sacrist Alan of Walsingham. With this unique piece of work, the major story of Ely Cathedral ended, but it still remains as one of the greatest achievements of English architecture as well as a permanent memorial to the glory of God lovingly erected by its medieval builders.

In sharp contrast, little remains of Thorney Abbey. On its much smaller fenland isle its surrounding village never became an urban centre, probably due to the proximity of Peterborough in a much better position. And with no bishop to protect it the Dissolution of the abbey resulted in its almost total destruction. Only the five western bays of the once-magnificent twelfth-century church now remain for the parishioners of the sleepy village. The battered west front and the blocked arcades are a poor reminder of what there once was.

Yet even here there is more than at most places of the religious houses of the county. Time on the whole has treated them badly. Nothing remains of the Benedictine priory of Chatteris, another pre-Conquest foundation on a fen island. Of the great Augustinian priory of Barnwell, only a much repaired fragment of the kitchen now remains hidden away in the nineteenth-century suburban sprawl of outer Cambridge. The sole remnant of the nunnery of Swaffham Bulbeck is a pasture field with some earthworks and a rather odd-looking eighteenth-century house which hides, though not very successfully to the observant field-worker, the fact that it stands on a beautiful thirteenth-century undercroft.

At Anglesey Abbey, near Bottisham, though the mutilated fragments of the original priory are now hardly

visible as a result of vast alterations and tasteless re-
modelling, in the surrounding gardens another aspect of
monastic life is wonderfully preserved. A complex series
of now-dry ditches and ponds, when carefully examined,
reveals a most interesting picture. We can see how the water
of a small stream was diverted through various channels
which first filled a series of broad rectangular fishponds
whose internal division banks and even the gaps for the
wooden sluices still survive. The water then passed along
other channels under the monastic site and out into the fens.
All these minor channels, including even overflow ditches
and storage reservoirs, are there to be seen today.

Perhaps the best monastic site in Cambridgeshire for the
fieldworker to investigate is Denney Abbey, in Waterbeach
parish, which has a particularly interesting history. For
a short while before 1170 the site was occupied by a small
community of Benedictine monks. Then it was transferred
to the Knights Templars who remained there until the
Order was suppressed in 1308. In 1342 it was taken over
by a house of the Franciscan Order of Minoresses, established by the widowed Countess of Pembroke, who held it
until the Dissolution. The existing building appears to be
mainly an eighteenth-century house surrounded by derelict
medieval barns. Closer examination shows it to be the
greater part of the original Benedictine twelfth-century
cruciform church to which the Templars attached what was
probably an infirmary in the thirteenth century. The whole
was altered in the fourteenth century by the Minoresses who
built a new church, now destroyed, and turned the old
church into a domestic dwelling for the Countess of
Pembroke. The surviving barns are in fact part of the
fourteenth-century refectory. The site is surrounded by
some fifteen acres of earthworks which include roads,
ditches, fishponds and particularly interesting, small half-
to two-acre garden plots each associated with a small

building platform. It has been suggested that these latter were used either by the individual nuns, or leased by them to local tenants. Either way, this kind of detailed fieldwork can throw much light on the use made of monastic land in the medieval period.

Turning now to the other aspect of the medieval Church in the landscape we come to the more familiar parish churches. In contrast to the detailed history of the development of the monastic establishments in the county, our knowledge of the growth of the parochial system and the setting up of parish churches is very limited. It is probable that in the early Christian period there were, in Cambridgeshire as in other areas, large 'minster' churches. Here semi-collegiate groups of priests lived who were jointly responsible for the spiritual welfare of large areas of land around these churches. However, evidence of such organisations in our county is lacking except at one place, Horningsea. A passage in the *Liber Eliensis* indicates that a minster church with a sizeable community of secular canons existed at Horningsea at least as early as the ninth century. In view of the topographical setting of Horningsea and its relationship to Fen Ditton, the northern section of the Fleam Dyke and the Roman settlement sites there discussed earlier (Fig. 4), it is of some significance that this should be the one place in the county with evidence for an early minster church. It is possible that the undoubted continuity here of a Roman estate into the Saxon period was an important factor in the establishment of a minster church. One other place that might be considered as a possible site of an early minster church is Doddington, out on the fens. Though there is no documentary evidence, the original parish, which included what are now the separate parishes of March, Benwick and Wimblington, covered nearly 38,000 acres, the largest in the county. The associated villages were all parochial chapelries of Doddington until the nineteenth century and the whole area might once have been a large minster parish based on Doddington.

Whatever the early Saxon ecclesiastical organisation was, by the tenth century individual parish churches began to be erected in the larger settlements. Outside the city of Cambridge no definite Saxon church survives, but late Saxon tomb lids at Balsham, Rampton and Stapleford indicate the probable existence of churches there. Domesday Book records churches at only three places, Meldreth, Shelford and Teversham, and priests are mentioned at Chesterton and Oakington. This is certainly not a complete list and just how many churches there were in the county by the late eleventh century is quite unknown. All one can say is that gradually each major settlement acquired a church and that by the thirteenth century the great majority of villages had one. Exactly when, and by whom, these churches were built is also a mystery. One can only guess that local lords, great ecclesiastical landowners or even groups of lesser mortals, from piety and pride, or merely as insurance for the hereafter, raised these often magnificent structures.

Usually each church was built to minister to the spiritual welfare of an existing settlement, or group of settlements, already recognisable as a compact economic or tenurial unit. These basic units then became the ecclesiastical parishes which of course often still exist today. However, it must be remembered that these parishes are, in the main, much older than the establishment of the churches, which merely used them as convenient units of ecclesiastical administration.

Occasionally individual piety or rivalry between local lords led to the setting up of more than one church within a land unit, and as a result the ecclesiastical parishes were hopelessly intermixed within that unit. This is adequate proof that the main parishes themselves are older than the churches. The best and most widely known example of this of course is at Swaffham Prior, on the fen edge east of Cambridge (Plate 7). Here on a high chalk ridge above the village are two churches in the same churchyard, St Mary and SS. Cyriac and Jullita. Who the original builders of these churches were and why they were put side by side is not known. Though this is now the only example of two churches side by side there was another at Fulbourn just south-east of Cambridge and also at Histon to the north-west of the city.

The part played by local lords in the establishment of parish churches may be reflected in the actual siting. They often stand close to the main manor house whose medieval occupier probably gave the land. The church at Shepreth lies next to one manor farm and opposite the former site of another manor house, while that of Abington Pigotts not only lies some distance away from the village centre but stands in the corner of the large Home Close of the manor farm. It is clear that the churchyard has been actually enclosed from this paddock. The proximity of church and manor house is seen at its best at Wimpole. Here the now tiny but beautiful church of 1749, on the site of a larger medieval one, stands a few yards from the magnificent Wimpole Hall (Plate 19). The present-day appearance is entirely of eighteenth-century date, but the setting reflects the original medieval arrangement of church and manor house. The same idea is perpetuated at Babraham where the pretty thirteenth-century church peeps out above the yew trees in a corner of the Hall garden.

Occasionally the siting of a church may reflect older and more mysterious ideas. At Comberton the church stands on a low hill away from the main village, and near a Roman villa. At March on the fens the magnificent church, though formerly only a parochial chapel, is oddly situated a mile south of the town centre in what must have been once a somewhat remote situation (Plate 14). At Tadlow in the west of the county, the church is set on a high spur overlooking the village and it has been suggested that this spur is the site of the original Taddas' burial mound whence the village gets its name.

Of the exact appearance of these early parish churches little can now be seen, due to constant rebuilding. Many must have been small, unaisled buildings with apsidal-ended chancels. The nearest one can get to this type of church is perhaps that at Hauxton. As fashion changed, prosperity increased and population grew, more elaborate churches appeared. Of the thirteenth-century churches, Histon and Cherry Hinton, both close to Cambridge, are the best. Many of the small early churches were altered and rebuilt in the late medieval period and often increased in size. However, it is noticeable that on the whole in the generally marginal areas of west and south-east Cambridgeshire and on the smaller fen islands the churches remained small, even after the rebuilding.

The great landowners then played a major role in the establishment of churches and their beautification. But they also left their mark on the present landscape in the castles and fortifications which for various reasons they found it necessary to construct. On the whole the county is poor in castles. None of the surviving sites is likely to attract the casual visitor. Nevertheless, what exists is of considerable interest, but once again it requires a deal of hard work to see and understand the most interesting facts. There are no known pre-Norman Conquest fortifications in the county, and the earliest castles are those which were built immediately after the Norman invasion. Of these the best known is the rather battered motte on Castle Hill in Cambridge. It was built soon after 1066 by William the Conqueror to control the town and the river crossing. It is now somewhat mutilated due to its adaptation in the seventeenth century to become part of a Civil War fortification and though easy of access is not a particularly fine example of its kind. However, at least it still remains. The other castle perhaps built by William at Wisbech to control the town there, which was apparently also of motte-and-bailey type, was utterly destroyed in 1794, though its layout is still preserved in the pattern of the streets there. A near-complete Norman castle remains at Ely, just south of the cathedral. This has a fine conical motte forty feet high with traces of a large square bailey to the south-east. Though not proved, it seems probable that it was built by William in 1070 after the final conquest of the Isle of Ely.

By far the best castle, though little known, is in the remote south corner of Cambridgeshire in Castle Camps parish. Here is the largest motte-and-bailey fortification in the county, built by Aubrey de Vere soon after 1066 as the centre of his extensive south Cambridgeshire and north Essex estates. It is sited on the end of a north-projecting spur and consists basically of a large motte with a semi-circular bailey to the north. However, if we look carefully at the remains we can see a very odd feature. Inside the bailey are the very reduced remains of a smaller bailey enclosing less than a quarter of the area of the main one. This indicates that the castle was greatly enlarged at some time, though when this was carried out is not recorded. Even more curious is that the present medieval parish church of Castle Camps, which stands within the outer bailey, lies on the line of the inner, earlier bailey; that is the church must have been erected there after the castle was enlarged. The church is almost entirely of the fifteenth century and therefore can hardly help in dating the extension of the castle. There is a reset thirteenth-century priest's door on the south side of the chancel, and this together

Plate 5 Ridge-and-furrow, Croxton. These remains of the medieval common fields are now becoming rare in Cambridgeshire. The typical interlocked pattern of ridge-and-furrow in the foreground was part of the common fields of Croxton until 1811. It has remained intact until today because the land was then taken into the adjacent park which dates from the sixteenth century.

Plate 6 North Field, Soham, a medieval field system still working. Though much altered, the curved strips of the common fields remain. At the bottom right, ridge-and-furrow of former strips continue the pattern.

Plate 7 Swaffham Prior. Here on a high ridge above the village stand two parish churches in one churchyard. They are probably the result of pious manorial rivalry in the eleventh century. In today's more materialistic world they pose a problem. One is now derelict and largely ruinous.

Plate 8 Burwell Castle. This remarkable air-photograph shows all the details of the unfinished castle. The uneven island is surrounded by the partially excavated ditch, while beyond the spoil heaps remain as they were left in 1144. To the right of the spoil heaps are the low banks and ditches which lay around the earlier gardens.

with a thirteenth-century font suggests the existence of an earlier church in the area, though not necessarily on the same site as the present one. It looks very much as if the de Veres built a new church within the confines of their castle. Just outside the outer bailey are the remains of the now long-deserted village of Castle Camps. Most of it has unfortunately been destroyed by modern ploughing though the careful plotting of the distribution of the medieval pottery which covers the adjacent fields can give us the exact area which the village covered. In one field there still exists part of one of the village streets, now a narrow hollow-way lined with the slight remains of a number of house platforms.

This is what we can see on the ground. What does it all mean? We must look at the whole parish and beyond to understand the true story. For in this remote and formerly wooded part of Cambridgeshire there were no true villages. Both in Castle Camps and in the adjacent parish of Shudy Camps most of the present settlement is in the form of scattered, isolated farmsteads and small hamlets most of which appear to have been set up in the newly cleared forest at an early date in the Saxon period. In any case the now-deserted village round the castle is in a very curious position on a clay-capped spur, in sharp contrast to the other hamlets and farms which lie mainly in the valleys. The most likely explanation is that the village of Castle Camps did not exist at all until 1066 and that the castle came first, built for military reasons on the spur. The village then grew up around it, largely dependent on it, and the parish church followed. When, towards the end of the medieval period, the castle fell into disuse and was abandoned except as a farm, the village too was deserted and the inhabitants moved away to the nearby hamlet of Camps Green which is now the main centre of the parish. Here, then, we can see how the establishment of a castle had a great influence on the development and abandonment of settlement in a remote corner of the county.

The next phase of military activity in Cambridgeshire, the mid-twelfth-century civil war between King Stephen and Geoffrey de Mandeville, has also left its mark on the landscape in a number of curious ways. In 1143 Geoffrey, one of the great lords of England, fell from power and rebelled against the king. He and his army marched into the fenlands and seized the Isle of Ely. From his base at Ely, de Mandeville devastated the surrounding countryside, and in an attempt to contain him in 1144 King Stephen ordered the construction of a number of castles along the fen edge. The sites of some of these are known and the one which survives the best is at Burwell (Plate 8). The remains are just west of Burwell church in a pasture field and to the untrained eye have little of interest. But again the practised fieldworker can unravel a fascinating story. The castle now consists of a rectangular 'island' surrounded by a wide, deep, dry moat. There are, however, a number of very strange features. The interior of the island is extremely uneven with mounds and hollows and with a gap in one side leading into the moat. In addition, on the north and west outer sides of the moat are huge uneven mounds of earth, higher than the interior island and completely dominating it. The bottom of the moat too is uneven with terraces and banks. With the information we can see there, together with the results of an old excavation on the site, it is possible to see that all this represents an unfinished castle. The interior island is a result of spoil being left in dumps prior to the construction of a full-sized mound, while the gap in the side is where the spoil was being brought out of the moat when the work stopped. The moat therefore was not completed which accounts for its appearance and so was never filled with water. Additional proof of this can be seen in the south-west corner where the dam which was to hold the water is an incomplete series of mounds. The great piles of earth outside the moat are spoil heaps and careful examination of these reveals the existence of individual tips with walk-ways along which the workmen carried the spoil.

Thus we can be absolutely sure that the castle was never finished and we even know why this was so. For while it was being constructed, de Mandeville attacked it and in the ensuing fight was mortally wounded. The whole rebellion then collapsed and the completion of the castle was therefore unnecessary. But even more can be learnt from looking at the site. When the island was dug into in 1935, the excavator found sherds of eleventh-century or early-twelfth-century pottery on the old ground surface under the spoil heaps. He did not then realise the significance of these but he recorded the fact. Now if we look in the field to the north of the castle we see a set of very low banks and ditches less than two feet high. They are the ends of a line of banked and ditched closes such as one finds on deserted medieval village sites. And these closes run down to the castle and disappear *under* the spoil heaps. The easternmost close passes round the castle and is therefore intact and at its end are the remains of a medieval house, thirty feet long and ten feet wide, bounded by a low grass-covered bank less than one foot high and clearly divided into two rooms by an internal cross wall still just visible. Beyond the house is a short stretch of slightly sunken road, or hollow-way, cut short by the ditch of the castle. These remains show that when the castle was built, far from being on an open piece of land it was raised on part of the village of Burwell and presumably a whole street of houses was demolished to make way for it. The pottery found by the excavator under the island was thus from these houses.[14]

[14] R.C.H.M. *Cambridgeshire North East* (1972), Burwell (132).

Though Burwell is the most interesting of these temporary eleventh-century castles along the fen edge, it is not the only one. Another similar though slightly smaller example exists at Rampton, known locally as the Giant's Hills. It too consists of an unfinished island, with a ramp leading up on to it from an incomplete ditch. There is also a large spoil heap on one side, and here again there are the remains of village closes passing under the spoil heaps. So we can be sure that here at Rampton, as at Burwell, part of the village was removed to make way for the castle which was then promptly abandoned unfinished. There are the remains of another similar castle at Swavesey further north-west along the fen edge and possibly another at Cottenham to the south-east, but both of these have been so mutilated by later quarrying and other activities that little can be discovered about them.

This line of royal fen-edge castles was not the only response to the threat of de Mandeville's rebellion. Other people too hurriedly attempted to protect their lands. One such was the Abbot of Ramsey in Huntingdonshire who gave orders for the defence of his manors. At Knapwell, a Ramsey holding, we can see the result (Plate 9). At the north-east corner of the medieval village, which has since moved away to the south, and guarding a long-abandoned crossing of a small brook is a small mound. It is only six feet high, with a thirty-foot-wide flat top and surrounded by a wide water-filled ditch. It appears to be of no military use whatsoever, but is in fact a tiny motte built to protect the village and, judging by the pottery found in it, built in the mid-twelfth century.

All these castles, interesting though they may be, are relatively rare in the county. But there is another type of semi-fortified site which appears in large numbers in the county. These are the so-called homestead moats which are common all over the Midlands and Eastern Counties of

England as well as elsewhere, the majority of which appear to have been built in the twelfth and thirteenth centuries. Exactly how many there are in the county is not known because many still remain to be discovered. Certainly there are at least 300. Dozens are marked on Ordnance Survey maps but this is probably only half of what still actually exists. They are to be found in almost every village and are also common around the isolated farmsteads in the south, east and west of the county.

These homestead moats vary considerably in form, but usually they consist of a rectangular or more rarely a circular island, surrounded by a water-filled ditch up to thirty feet wide (Plate 10). There are often outer enclosures or paddocks, sometimes bounded by similar ditches, but usually by no more than a low bank and shallow ditch (Fig. 10). Detailed examination can tell us a great deal about matters such as the construction of the dams which held the water in the ditches but it can also help us to understand what these moats were for. It is easy to jump to the conclusion that they were built primarily for some defensive purpose but this is not so. First of all the ditches are very narrow, never more than thirty feet wide and often considerably less, which hardly makes them formidable protection. In addition some moats have always had only two or three sides as at both those in Gamlingay parish. It is also very rare in Cambridgeshire to find moats with raised interiors which would give an additional element of protection. The interiors are usually level with the surrounding land. Many moats have entrances formed by permanent causeways across the ditches, again a weakness if defence was a priority.

It is often argued that moats were primarily a protection from wild animals, but not only is it extremely doubtful that there were any wild animals left in the largely cleared and cultivated countryside of the thirteenth century,

MOATS AND GARDENS

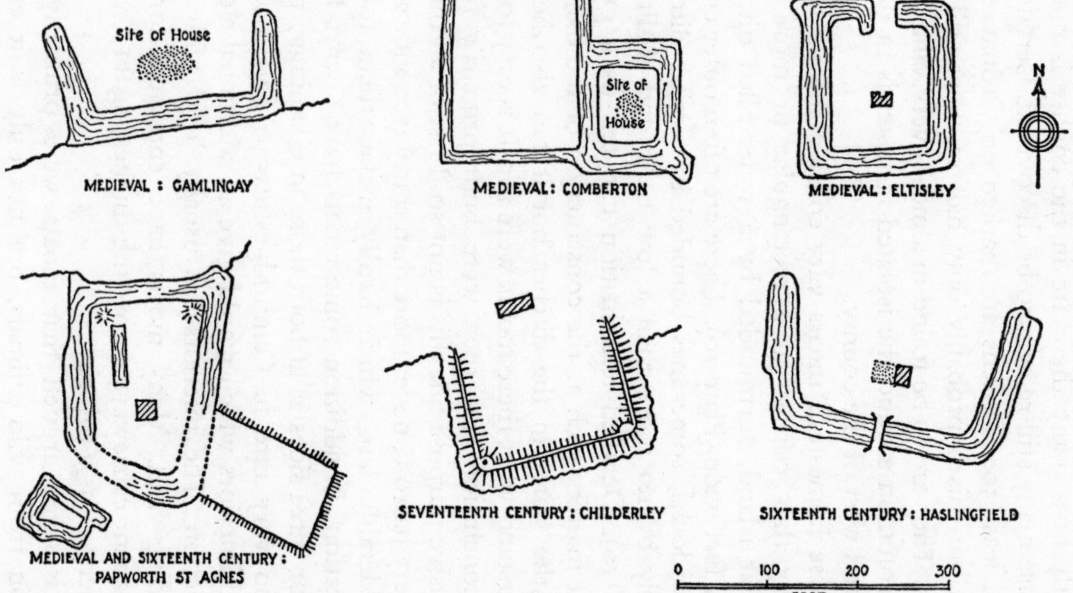

MEDIEVAL: ELTISLEY

SIXTEENTH CENTURY: HASLINGFIELD

MEDIEVAL: COMBERTON

Site of
House

SEVENTEENTH CENTURY: CHILDERLEY

MEDIEVAL: GAMLINGAY

Site of House

MEDIEVAL AND SIXTEENTH CENTURY:
PAPWORTH ST AGNES

N

0   100   200   300
FEET

Fig. 10

at most moated sites the stables and stockyards which would need protection were outside the main moat and bounded only by hedges and fences. Finally a statistical analysis of Cambridgeshire moats has shown that the larger and most formidable moats lie in the main villages and that the smaller and more ill-defended ones lie away from the villages. This is quite the reverse of what one would expect if they were mainly for defence.

It is also often suggested that moats were for fishponds, water supply, fire protection or drainage. Yet all these functions could have been achieved by constructing less complex forms of ditches. In most cases simple ponds would have done admirably and indeed many Cambridge-shire moated sites are associated with such ponds. As regards drainage it becomes clear after only the briefest examination of moats in the county that a large number were deliberately sited so that water ran into the ditches from outside. Many lie in valleys either near or actually within the beds of streams. Elsewhere complex waterworks were constructed to carry water into the moats. This can be well seen at Bottisham Park where there are four moated sites arranged in a line on the side of a narrow valley. Due to an accident of preservation these moats still retain a wonderful system of ditches by which water was taken from the stream to fill each moat in turn and then returned to the stream (See also Fig. 12). Therefore, drainage cannot be the answer to the question of why moated sites were built.

What then were these moated sites made for? Why was it that in the twelfth and thirteenth centuries some, but by no means all, local lords and wealthy farmers went to the trouble of digging wide ditches around their homes? The only answer is that it was the fashionable thing to do, a human trait of which we in the twentieth century are perhaps only too well aware. Moated sites presumably

127

reflect the general prosperity of their owners and the desire to show off this prosperity by imitating the moated castles of the higher ranks of contemporary society. It is not always easy to see the types of people who constructed these moats for the detailed documentation has not survived, even if it was ever written.

Sometimes one can get a glimpse of these people. An example is at Burrough Green parish in the remote southeast of the county where there are three simple moats, one in the village, the other two standing alone well away from all other habitations. The one in the village was the site of the main manor which was held from the eleventh century by the de Burgh family. Until the early fourteenth century this family was little more than local farmers, but they then, in common with many similar people, started to improve their social position. One Thomas de Burgh became involved in public life and represented the county in Parliament and his second son, another Thomas, certainly spent money on his estate. In 1330 this Thomas obtained a licence to make a deer park at Burrough Green and almost certainly built the moated site which lies within the park at Park Wood. The moat around the manor house was probably constructed at the same time.

The third moat in the parish was the site of an old woodland farmstead of considerable antiquity. By the thirteenth century it was the centre of a small manor held in 1234 by William de Bretton. This man started life as a small independent farmer, but ended his days as one of the King's Justices. He gradually acquired small pieces of land in a number of counties but always lived in his farm at Burrough Green. By the time he died in 1261 he had founded a county family and his son John de Bretton continued to increase the estates. It seems likely that either William or John de Bretton was responsible for the moat around their home. These examples of moat-builders are not perhaps typical of all those who constructed similar moated sites. Many must have been small farmers whose activities or indeed names were never recorded. But at least from such examples one can begin to see some of the aims and aspirations behind the appearance of the ubiquitous moat.[15]

One final feature of the medieval and modern landscape which the prosperous medieval lords constructed for their pleasure, convenience and perhaps prestige was the deer park. We have already seen that Thomas de Burgh obtained a licence to make a deer park at Burrough Green in 1330. Thomas was merely one of a number of medieval lords who did this. These deer parks were not the gracious landscaped parks of the eighteenth century, but basically areas of waste or marginal land usually bounded by a massive bank with a fence on top together with an internal ditch to prevent the deer from escaping. Such parks provided a store of fresh meat for the owner and a breeding place for deer which could be let out when desired and hunted for sport across the surrounding land. There were a number of these parks in the county and most can still be identified. The appearance of 'park' names on maps usually gives a clue and then further map examination often gives suggestive continuous lines of modern hedges which indicate the boundary. Then fieldwork to discover the actual boundary bank and ditch will finally confirm the discovery.

Lords both great and small had these parks and some were made at quite an early date. Even in Domesday Book parks for 'wild beasts' are recorded at Kirtling and Burrough Green. The latter must be the one which Thomas de Burgh altered or restored in 1330. There was another medieval deer park at Gamlingay by 1289 for in that year it is recorded that "certain evil doers unknown entered by night

[15] C. C. Taylor, 'Moated Sites in Cambridgeshire', in P. J. Fowler (ed.), *Archaeology and the Landscape* (1972) and R.C.H.M. *West Cambridgeshire* (1968), pp. lxi–lxvi.

the park of Gamenegeye . . . and killed a deer".[16] This park can, with the help of a superb map of the parish made for Merton College, Oxford, in 1601, be identified exactly on the ground as a roughly oval area of some 250 acres bounded by a continuous hedge, still on a large bank, lying to the west of the village. Another deer park is documented in Eltisley parish and though its exact site is not recorded, a glance at a large-scale Ordnance Survey map indicates its position. South of the village a large area of woodland, Eltisley Wood, and a group of adjacent fields to the south are bounded by a continuous curving hedge line. The Enclosure Map of 1864 confirms that this area was probably never part of the common fields of the parish, as does the lack of ridge-and-furrow in the same place. Finally, on the ground the massive bank of the park pale can be seen defining exactly the suggested boundaries of the park. Another medieval deer park which can be easily seen even on the map is that at Little Downham. It was a favourite retreat for most of the medieval Bishops of Ely, the fragments of whose palace still stand to the north of the village. Not only do we know there was a deer park there (it is mentioned in 1250–1), but its boundary is still preserved as a continuous hedge line enclosing some 300 acres of land on the fen edge with the Bishop's Palace in the centre.

SELECT BIBLIOGRAPHY

Darby, H. C. *The Domesday Geography of Eastern England* (1957).
Lethbridge, T. C. 'Excavations at Burwell Castle', *Procs. C.A.S.*, Vol. 36 (1936).
Miller, E. *The Estates of Ely* (1951).
R.C.H.M. *Cambridgeshire*.
Steers, J. A. (Ed.) *The Cambridge Region* (1965).
V.C.H. *Cambridgeshire*, Vol. I (1938) and Vol. IV (1953).

[16] *Cal. Inq. Misc.*, Vol. I (1219–1307), No. 1478.

4. Decline and recovery, 1300–1600

The landscape in 1300. Decline and disaster. The start of the new prosperity. Buildings in the landscape.

The landscape in 1300

SO FAR WE have been following the development of the Cambridgeshire landscape in terms of a continuous expansion of settlement and agriculture, from prehistoric to medieval times. But many reverses due to economic, political and military circumstances probably occurred which are undocumented. The overall picture nevertheless of the main features of the county's landscape being laid out before 1300 as a result of steady expansion is probably near the truth. By the end of the thirteenth century every part of the county had the imprint of man's hand upon it. Even on the higher chalklands sheep grazed continually and the plough was still making inroads into the remaining grassland. The forests had all gone and been replaced by countless farmsteads, hamlets and villages, each surrounded by their varied fields. Large areas of fenland, it is true, remained undrained and apparently unused. But even here the fen edges had been reclaimed and sheep and cattle were grazed on the parts which were reasonably dry in summer. Elsewhere the marshes, lakes and meres were being used by the fen people for fish, peat, rushes and wild-fowl, and water-courses and ditches were being constantly cleaned and re-dug. Much remained to be done before the landscape was to take on its modern appearance, but the outlines were fixed and most of the county was being exploited to the full within the limits of the medieval technology.

Around 1300, however, there was a cessation of this development due to complex economic factors which were not confined merely to Cambridgeshire but were country-wide and indeed on a continental scale. The reasons for these economic changes are not known with certainty and economic historians themselves are not all agreed on the real answers, but these problems are beyond the scope of this book. Here we will be concerned only with their effect on the landscape of the county which, when combined with other events such as pestilence, put a stop to the development of the landscape for a short while and then set it off again along new lines.

Decline and disaster

There is no doubt that towards the end of the thirteenth century a period of stabilisation sets in. Where the details are best documented, on the great manors of the Bishops of Ely, it is clear that the continued expansion of demesne land stops and references to reclamation and assarting of fenland dry up. Part of this may be due to natural disasters which are known to have occurred at this time. The massive reduction of the amount of land at Haddenham farmed directly by the Bishop, noted in 1356, was said to have been caused by floods and at nearby Stretham at the same time twenty acres of 'fennemedwe' were described as flooded and worthless. Damage from floods is recorded at Wisbech in the same year when several hundred acres of land were left unvalued *"quod superfluitas aquarum fene omnibus annis totaliter superfluit"*. Yet there had been dreadful disasters and floods earlier which did not stop the work of reclamation. Now economic recession was setting in and the recurring floods merely emphasised this and made it more difficult to keep in good heart the land which had been reclaimed, let alone take in more which was now not needed.

The documentary evidence for an agricultural recession at this time is not confined to the fenlands. Work carried out by Dr A. R. H. Baker on the *Nonarum Inquisitiones* of 1342 has indicated that arable land was also being abandoned in the south of the county. The record is not as complete as one would wish but it is estimated that nearly 5000 acres of land are listed as having gone out of cultivation in the previous half-century. This is almost certainly a hopeless underestimate for it includes 1000 acres flooded in Newton and Tydd St Giles in the northern fens and this is all that is listed for the fenlands. We know from other sources that much fenland elsewhere was being abandoned at this time and so we cannot rely on the figures absolutely. Nevertheless, they do indicate that much land in the clay areas of west and south-east Cambridgeshire was being left untilled. This is what one might expect as the relatively lately cleared marginal lands were abandoned. Places such as Croxton, Eltisley, Madingley and Kingston in west Cambridgeshire and Shudy Camps, Horseheath and Dullingham in south-east Cambridgeshire are all recorded as having former arable land uncultivated. But such land was not confined to the marginal areas. At Bassingbourn in the main valley of the Ashwell Cam, 400 acres lay untilled because of the tenants' impoverishment, while at nearby Melbourn, a large village even then, other land had been abandoned. In the valley of the Linton Cam, Bartlow, Hildersham and Linton itself are listed as having land uncultivated, as are Swaffham Prior, Great Wilbraham and Bottisham on the fen edges. At Impington, north of Cambridge, 200 acres of arable and 100 acres of pasture were recorded as having been laid waste by flooding.

Various explanations for the contraction of arable lands are given in the *Nonarum Inquisitiones*. Frequency of recent taxation is given for Kingston and Swaffham Prior, flooding and failure of the harvest are noted elsewhere, but again these are only immediate reasons and the general economic decline lay behind all.

On top of these economic difficulties, in 1348–50 came the terrible Black Death, which in fact returned again and again to Cambridgeshire in the later fourteenth century, albeit in a less severe form. The result was a dramatic fall in population. It has been calculated that there was as much as a thirty-nine per cent fall in the county's population between 1279 and 1377,[1] and detailed figures confirm this. On the Abbey of Crowland's manors at Oakington thirty-five out of fifty tenants died, at Dry Drayton twenty out of forty-two and at Cottenham thirty-three out of fifty-eight. At Soham the boon-works of thirty-four tenements were in default by reason of the pestilence and at Woodditton nine tenements had reverted to the lord of the manor by the death of the tenants. Institutions of new clergy, too, show the extent of the disaster. In the three years before 1349 the average number of new clergy instituted in the diocese of Ely was nine. In 1349 there were ninety-two such institutions. Likewise a commission of 1350 set up to enquire into the values before and after the plague of the advowsons of churches belonging to the Priory of Lewes recorded that at Caxton the value had fallen from nearly thirty pounds to just over nineteen pounds.[2]

Not all places were affected by the plague. At Whaddon, the value of the rectory was virtually the same in 1350 as it had been in 1348, while detailed records at places such as Great Shelford and Elsworth show no trace of the pestilence. However, Shelford appears to have suffered greatly from a second outbreak of the disease in 1361, for it was then recorded that no crops had been reaped and little

[1] C. T. Smith, 'Settlement and Population', *The Cambridge Region* (1965).
[2] *Cal. Inq. Misc.*, Vol. III (1348–77), No. 43.

sown. Elsewhere the plague came more than once and at Soham there is a reference to twenty-six shillings and eight-pence rent being in default 'since the last pestilence' while fourteen pounds and thirteen shillings was still in default 'since the first pestilence'.

While the effects of the Black Death were not as permanent as used to be thought, combined with the continuing economic difficulties it certainly changed the tenurial and social organisation in the county and so ultimately affected the landscape. These economic disasters and the accompanying disease left their mark on the countryside for us to see. On the agricultural side this is somewhat limited, for later waves of agricultural expansion have obliterated and removed the traces of derelict lands. However, sometimes one can see this. For example there are in one or two places in the county patches of permanent grassland which have medieval ridge-and-furrow on them and which botanists regard as important because of their vegetational content. The richness of their flora shows that they have not been ploughed for many centuries and they may well represent land which went out of cultivation in the fourteenth century and has not been ploughed since. Elsewhere fieldwork can show land which was perhaps abandoned at this time. In west Cambridgeshire there are patches of woodland which on close examination reveal ridge-and-furrow in them, indicating that they were once under cultivation. Some of these woods are certainly of considerable age and may have grown up naturally when the land was left un-tilled. In the south of Wimpole parish, near the banks of the River Cam, is a group of fields which, though now modern arable, show traces of ridge-and-furrow within them. The present use as arable fields is very recent, and before 1950 they were, and had been for centuries, permanent pasture. Indeed, they are shown as such and are called the Rhee pasture on an estate map of 1638 while the name Common

Rhee referring to this pasture can be traced back as far as 1512 in the Wimpole papers in the British Museum. There can be little doubt that the ridge-and-furrow in these fields represents the final expansion of medieval agriculture and its contraction in the fourteenth century. In the south of the county many of the strip-lynchets or cultivation-terraces on the hillsides, which are now slowly being ploughed away, were probably abandoned in the fourteenth century too when it was no longer either profitable or necessary to cultivate steeply sloping ground. Certainly some were not under cultivation in the seventeenth and eighteenth centuries, as estate maps indicate.

The clearest evidence of fourteenth-century recession is, however, that of the contraction of settlement. With the dramatic fall in population which was not to be made up until the nineteenth century many villages and hamlets were reduced markedly in size and some farmsteads were deserted. Much of the evidence for this was destroyed in the nineteenth-century expansion of the villages and more is going every year as new housing estates and individual houses grow up. Yet much still remains to be seen by this generation, if not the next. One of the best examples of evidence for the contraction of settlement is the village of Longstowe in west Cambridgeshire. There is no doubt that the village declined in size during the fourteenth century, even before the onset of the Black Death, for in the *Nonarum Inquisitiones* of 1342, not only is a great part of the parish recorded as being untilled but even many of the houses had been abandoned: *"plura messuagia existunt vacua"*. If we go to Longstowe we can still see this description for ourselves (Fig. 11). The village, as its name suggests, is strung out for just over a mile along a winding lane. At the north end is the church, hall, rectory and a few cottages, but the other habitations consisting of less than twenty houses and farm-steads are scattered along the main street often separated by

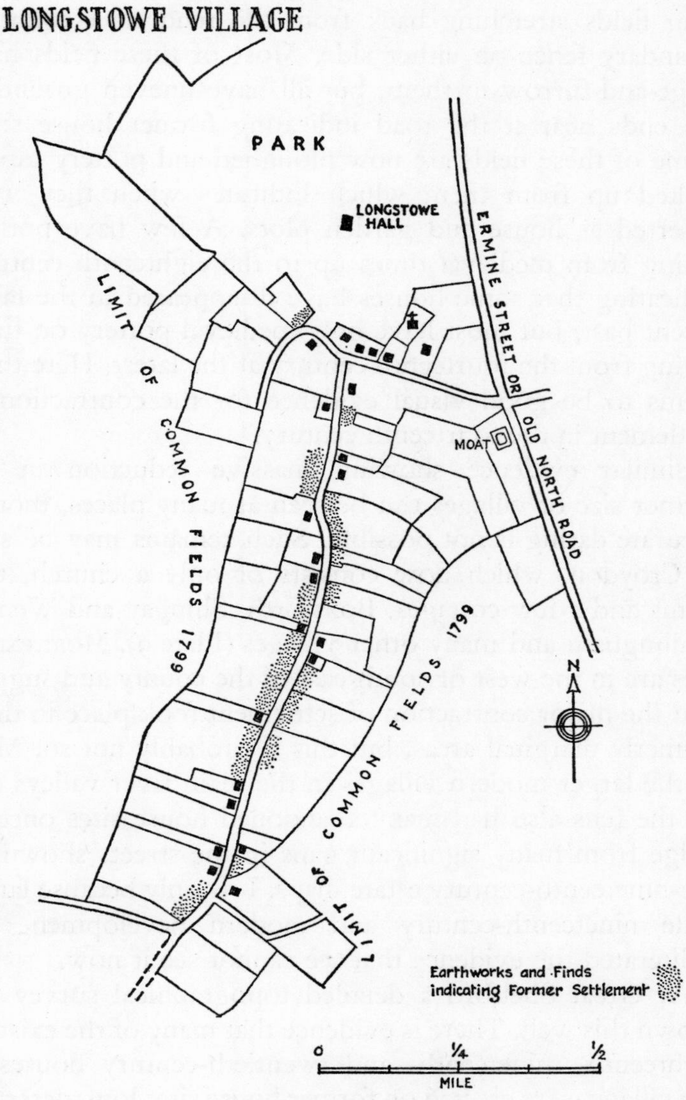

Fig. 11

distances of as much as 230 yards. Between the houses are long fields stretching back from the road to a common boundary fence on either side. Most of these fields have ridge-and-furrow in them, but all have uneven ground at the ends nearest the road indicating former house sites. Some of these fields are now ploughed and pottery can be picked up from them which indicates when they were deserted as house and garden plots. A few have pottery dating from medieval times up to the eighteenth century, indicating that some houses have disappeared in the fairly recent past, but most have only medieval pottery on them dating from the fourteenth century at the latest. Here there seems to be good visual evidence for the contraction of settlement in the fourteenth century.

Similar evidence showing massive reduction in the former size of villages can be seen at many places, though accurate dating is not possible. Such remains may be seen at Croydon, which now consists of only a church, two farms and a few cottages, Boxworth, Shingay and Wendy, Dullingham and many other villages (Plate 9). Most examples are in the west or south-east of the county and suggest that the major contraction of settlement took place in these formerly marginal areas, but this is probably not so. Most of the larger modern villages in the main river valleys and on the fens also had many abandoned house sites once to judge from many significant gaps in the streets shown on pre-nineteenth-century estate maps. It is only because large-scale nineteenth-century and modern development has obliterated the evidence that we cannot see it now.

At Great Shelford a detailed topographical survey has shown this well. There is evidence that many of the existing eighteenth-, nineteenth- and twentieth-century houses in the village were erected on former house sites long deserted. Occasionally where modern development has been slow or restricted by the planners the remains still exist. There is a splendid set of abandoned house sites at Whittlesford in the south of the county, while recent housing development in Swaffham Bulbeck has also produced pre-fifteenth-century pottery from former house sites near the village centre. At Chippenham in the east of the county Mrs Spufford has found extremely good evidence of a similar decline. "Even at a conservative estimate the population must have fallen by over half in the century between 1279 and 1377", and a remarkable survey of 1544 still described whole streets as "clere decaied" and every other house missing. The jurors of the survey were able to describe sixty-four crofts as sites where houses had once stood and yet, as Mrs Spufford points out, the fifteenth-century tax reliefs for poverty "treat Chippenham as if it had not suffered at all badly. . . . If the judgment of the assessors of the reliefs is to be trusted, the disappearance of half a village was so commonplace an affair in an area as thickly populated as Cambridgeshire that it called for no special action."

A number of smaller settlements and hamlets seem to have almost disappeared at this time. The hamlet of Whitwell, whose position shows it to be a daughter settlement of Barton, is now reduced to a single farmstead and a series of indeterminate mounds in a pasture field. It was probably always small, but the economic recession rather than the Black Death finally killed it and it was reunited with its mother village ecclesiastically just before 1300. Likewise the hamlet of Pincote in Tadlow parish, which as we have seen is now only a moated site and a scatter of pottery on the hillside, was probably deserted at this time. The vast bulk of the pottery is of the fourteenth century or earlier, and very little exists of a later date. Other villages such as Clopton and Childerley were also probably much reduced in size at this time and here the virtual desertion paved the way for a very different form of land-use at a later date (Plate 1). We shall return to these later.

On the fenlands, too, some villages seem to have been reduced in size at this time. An example of this may be seen at Wentworth, on the Isle of Ely. It is a very small village with only a church and two or three farms. Yet in Domesday Book it is given a recorded population of thirty-eight, which probably means a total of between 100 and 150 inhabitants. In 1428 the Feudal Aids list only nine parishioners. Here again are the house sites still remaining to show visually what the documents tell us.

This reduction in population and the abandonment of houses was not confined to villages and hamlets. Some at least of the outlying farmsteads in the marginal areas were probably deserted too. Here we have no direct evidence for the documentary record is not full enough to give us the history of individual farms. However, the large number of uninhabited moated sites which exist in the claylands of the west and south-east of the county may be connected with this period of agricultural recession. This cannot be proved and indeed some of these farmsteads were probably left much later on when improved agricultural techniques and land-transfers made them unnecessary, but some desertion of farmsteads perhaps occurred at this time. We still lack good modern excavations of Cambridgeshire moated sites which would tell us for certain. As it is we are reduced to using scraps of pottery thrown up by the modern plough as it destroys these moats, or more happily rely on what badgers, foxes and rabbits bring up out of their burrows. This evidence, slim and unreliable though it is, does indicate some abandonment of moated sites in the fourteenth century. The date of the pottery from the moat in Overhall Wood at Boxworth runs from the eleventh to the fourteenth century, while another site at Wimpole has pottery extending up to the same period.

Clearly much more fieldwork, excavation and documentary research still remains to be done but in outline our ideas are probably correct. The economic decline and the recurrent visitations of disease in the fourteenth century wrought great changes in the county's landscape.

The start of the new prosperity

These economic and natural disasters had other more lasting effects which though not always directly related to the landscape were to affect it in the end. One of the most important of these was the growth of a largely new rural class of yeoman farmers who owned or leased their land. These men took advantage of the economic situation of the period to free themselves from their medieval peasant status and their descendants were able to use the later prosperity to further their positions. The origins of this class lay back in the thirteenth century, but the great increase in their number was mainly the result of the economic difficulties of the fourteenth century. Detailed documentation shows that many major landowners at this period were forced to lease or sell their land. As a result, intelligent peasants were able to take the opportunity of becoming independent farmers in their own right.

At Chippenham in the late fourteenth century go-ahead farmers were accumulating what had been fifteen-acre peasant holdings of the century before. In 1384 John Lenote took two fifteen-acre holdings, another in 1392, one more in 1399 and yet another in 1400. This accumulation of land produced problems when the new farmers laid common field strips together and, again at Chippenham, there is evidence that the lord of the manor tried to prevent it. This amalgamation of common field strips into larger units can be seen physically on the ground at times if the fieldworker looks carefully at the ridge-and-furrow that remains. A relatively common occurrence, in west Cambridgeshire at least, is that of areas of ridge-and-furrow where the width of ridges varies considerably. In most ridge-and-furrow the ridges are between seven and nine yards wide but often groups of ridges have different widths. Typically there are five to ten ridges of perhaps six yards width and then five to ten ridges eleven yards wide. Where a map showing common field strips survives, these variations can usually be shown to be connected with land ownership, as at Lolworth where the Tithe Map of 1841 makes this clear or, much earlier, at Wimpole on a map of 1638. Where there are large blocks of similar-width ridges all held by one man, it suggests that amalgamation of strips was followed by alterations in ploughing techniques.

Many of these new rising yeomen actually enclosed some of their common field land where this was possible. Usually this was land close to or adjacent to their farmhouses. In the Court Rolls of Sawston there are a number of references to illegal enclosure of strips being carried out in the immediate vicinity of the delinquents' homesteads.[3] These no longer exist on the ground, due to modern development, but at nearby Great Shelford similar enclosures can still be seen. Behind a line of farmsteads on the edge of the former High Green there is a series of long, narrow, curving fields. They have been cut by the later railway and much mutilated by modern housing but they can still be recognised. Their form indicates that they were once normal curved strips in the common fields. There is no documentary proof of the date of their enclosure but an examination of the botanical content of the remaining hedges bounding them, by the method invented by Dr Hooper, suggests that they were enclosed at least 500 years ago.

This growth of the new class of yeoman farmers was accompanied in the fourteenth century by other social changes. Naturally not all the older landlords failed to survive these times. Many adapted themselves to the new

[3] T. F. Teversham, *A History of Sawston*, Part II (1947), pp. 72–3.

conditions and flourished, and they were reinforced by other men who had made money in commerce in the towns and who were acquiring landed estates in the country. The history of most of these men is as yet unknown but some details are recoverable. By the late fourteenth century sheep farming had become extremely profitable and more of the larger landowners moved into the sheep business. Wool reached its maximum price between 1450 and 1550 and if possible landlords converted arable land into pasture for sheep. Many of these certainly made a great deal of money out of it and one such was John Pygot of Abington Pigotts. The family which gave its name to the village was the major landowner there from 1427, but, though it later became a minor county family, there is no doubt that its early wealth came from sheep. John Pygot is specifically described as a Woolman in 1461 when he was involved in large-scale land transactions.[4]

Even more interesting is the story of the village of Clopton, now in Croydon parish (Plate 1). The village was one of a line of similar settlements along a spring line above the marshy valley of the Ashwell Cam. Though details of its population are difficult to unravel as its records are always combined with those of the adjacent East Hatley, the village had probably never been very large and it certainly shrank in the fourteenth century. By the late fifteenth century most of the land in the parish was in the hands of the Clopton family who later went bankrupt. They finally had to sell their land in 1489 to John Fisher, a lawyer. Fisher was a man with new ideas and saw the advantages of producing wool rather than corn. He therefore at once enclosed all the arable land in the parish, an area of around a thousand acres, and laid it down to pasture. The new fields still exist today as generally rectangular areas of some ten to fifteen acres. Violent protests arose as a result of this

[4] *Cal. Ancient Deeds*, Vol. I, C.706.

enclosure, particularly from the Clopton family, who had continued to hold the manor house, and the Rector, but there is no record of any smaller tenants objecting and it may be that by this time there were none. This is the most likely explanation for the enclosure and we may see Fisher as an astute lawyer taking the opportunity to buy out the impecunious owner of a deserted village with the deliberate intention of making money out of sheep-farming.[5]

By the sixteenth century enclosure became common in the upland parts of the county. The surviving evidence is scanty, and this has led to suggestions that enclosure was on a small scale. Compared with the Midland counties perhaps it was but it certainly made a lasting impression on the landscape. Some evidence is contained in the 1517 Inquisition on Enclosure though the records of only a part of the county have survived.[6] Nine villages are listed, namely Cheveley, Childerley, Cottenham, East Hatley, Gamlingay, Longstowe, Malton in Orwell, Shingay and Steeple Morden, as having land enclosed between 1485 and 1517 and this totals no more than 1422 acres. Yet this is by no means a complete list, for Clopton which has already been mentioned as having at least 1000 acres enclosed in 1489 is not included. In addition there is circumstantial evidence based on the existing field shapes, ridge-and-furrow and later maps, that parts of the parishes of Tadlow, Croydon and Arrington were also enclosed at this time.[7] Most of this land was apparently put down for pasture and sheep-farming may be seen as the cause. However, it is also important to note that of all these places, Malton, Childerley and Clopton were already largely deserted by this time and Longstowe, Arrington, East Hatley, Tadlow, Croydon, Cheveley and Shingay all show either on the ground or

[5] W. M. Palmer, 'A History of Clopton', *Procs. C.A.S.*, Vol. 33 (1933).
[6] I. S. Leadam, 'The Inquisition of 1517', *Trans. Royal Hist. Soc.* (1894).
[7] R.C.H.M. *West Cambridgeshire* (1968), p. lxix.

from documents evidence of massive shrinkage. It seems, therefore, that large-scale enclosure was perhaps only possible where even the most ruthless landowner had a limited number of tenants to deal with.

Even in flourishing villages, however, trouble was caused by the demands of enclosing landlords. From Landbeach on the fen edge north-west of Cambridge we have the best evidence of this type of enclosure. Richard Kirby, a typical member of the new gentry and lord of the Manor of Brays, was the culprit here. His origins are not known with certainty, but his father had come to Landbeach from London and may have been in commerce. In 1549 there was dissension in the village as a result of Kirby's activities and the complaints listed by the villagers clearly show what had been going on: "1. He and all his predecessors hath letten all his tenements fall down to the number of fourteen of which divers were standing within the mind of man and some of very late days decayed. 2. Likely he intendeth the destruction of the rest of the town for he wishes there were no more houses in the town but his own and no more." When the villagers describe Kirby's holding as "whereupon there is at this present time no habitation or dwelling house remaining but only the chief mansion house wherein the said Richard Kirby inhabiteth himself" we can see exactly what he had been doing. The decayed house sites still exist in the centre of the village around the now-abandoned moated site where Kirby's house once stood. They remain as eloquent testimony to the truth of the sixteenth-century tenants' complaints. The results of Kirby's efforts led to violence in the village which was only stopped from becoming much worse by the intervention of the Master of Corpus Christi College who organised new rules for the stocking of sheep and cattle in the parish.[8]

This deliberate attempt at the creation of pasture land for

[8] J. R. Ravensdale, 'Landbeach in 1549', *East Anglian Studies* (1968).

sheep out of former house sites is to be compared with the work of another new landowner at Isleham on the fen edge north-east of Cambridge. The evidence is preserved in the Court Rolls of the village in King's College Archives. Here the villagers complained about the enclosure of twelve acres of common field arable which was the lord's own land. They were concerned about the loss of their common grazing rights over this land. The jury said that the villagers had always had these rights until 1574 when the lord, Robert Payton, enclosed the land and expelled the tenants. At both here and Landbeach the evidence suggests that landowners were prepared at least to try to enclose land even where the villages were still well populated. Taking into consideration all the available evidence and accepting its defective nature it seems likely that a great deal more enclosure took place on the uplands of Cambridgeshire in this period than has been hitherto realised.

On the fenlands, too, enclosure was going on apace at this time and sheep were probably the prime cause. This was particularly true of the northern silt fens. The long series of fourteenth- and fifteenth-century bailiffs' accounts of the Manor of Wisbech Barton show not only that sheep were always important but that they gradually took over from grain as the basic agricultural produce. Particularly interesting is the evidence from the fourteenth century onwards for the rise of large numbers of 'manors' all owned either by exceptionally gifted yeoman farmers, or members of the new gentry and these were greatly increased by the breaking up of the great monastic estates in the mid-sixteenth century. Many of these manors were primarily sheep farms and associated enclosure was common. It is extremely difficult to identify these enclosures with certainty on the ground today, partly because of the lack of detailed research, but more particularly because of the amount of seventeenth-century enclosure in these areas which confuses the picture. Even on the peat fens to the south sheep were important, though cattle were pastured in great numbers as well. At the small village of Witchford there is evidence of a thriving trade in wool in the fourteenth century, when two rich East Anglian merchants often mentioned in the Ely Accounts at this time were buying large numbers of sheep skins. At nearby Wentworth there is evidence of fifteenth-century enclosures probably as a result of the undoubted depopulation there.

A remarkable picture of enclosure on the fen islands at this time has been detailed by the late Dr Palmer.[9] The documents he examined were part of a mass of evidence collected for an enquiry into the enclosure of arable land for pasture in 1548. Here we have a detailed record of what went on in the late fourteenth and early fifteenth centuries on the Isle of Ely which we can still relate to the modern landscape. However, it must be noted that the enclosures recorded are not only usually very small but there is no evidence for extensive sheep-farming here. It is probable that they were used mainly for dairying or cattle-raising. This is important, for sheep were not the only stock reared on the fens. Cattle, often brought in from elsewhere to be fattened on the rich fen pastures, were an extremely valued source of revenue for fen farmers both large and small and there are many complaints about overstocking the commons with cattle at this time.

Of these enclosures one of the largest was that held by Robert Hargase called Bedwelhaye (now Bedwell Hay Farm, south of Ely). The farmstead itself was established in the early medieval period on the fen edge and probably always had some enclosed fields around it. The document of 1548 records that 120 acres of land near the farmstead had been enclosed in the reign of Henry VIII by one John

[9] W. M. Palmer, 'Enclosures at Ely, Downham and Littleport in 1548', *Trans. Cambs. and Hunts. Arch. Soc.*, Vol. V (1936).

Bulweyer. In 1548 it was still enclosed and the inhabitants of Ely said that they had formerly had common rights over it after harvest. This sounds as if the land, prior to enclosure, was part of the common fields of Ely which perhaps by then was held by Bulweyer as a compact block. That this is probably so can be seen on the ground today. Bedwell Hay Farm lies on the eastern edge of a block of fields which are probably the original medieval enclosures. To the east of the farm is another block of modern fields, covering about 120 acres. One of these fields has a reversed-S curved boundary, reflecting its origin as part of a curving common field furlong and thus these fields must be the ones enclosed by Bulweyer. Indeed, to the north the modern Ely Fields Farm indicates that the common fields of Ely lay near here and the Parliamentary Enclosure Award of 1848 proves this. So here on the fen edge we can actually still see the sixteenth-century enclosures of a single farmstead. Similar fields west of the hamlet of Chettisham which are still long and narrow with reversed-S hedgelines are probably part of the fifty-four acres of land listed as being recently enclosed in 1548.

Not all the enclosures at this time were for either sheep or cattle. In the same document Bishop West of Ely is said to have made a park of 180 acres called Chettisham Bushes at this time, and he had done this shortly before he was appointed a commissioner to stop such enclosures. The boundaries of this park can still be seen lying between the Ely–King's Lynn Road and the fen edge east of Chettisham. The only place where there was serious enclosure for sheep was at Stuntney, a small fen island to the south-east of Ely. Here the landlord is represented by the 1548 jury as a grasping and tyrannical man. He was said to have made farming for his tenants so difficult that they were forced to sell out their copyholds to him with the result that he held the whole area in his own hands. Whatever we might think

of his methods the resulting enclosures are still partly there
to see today south of Stuntney hamlet, in the form of
modern fields with curving sides and sharply indented
borders.

This detailed analysis of the agricultural and social
changes which resulted from the growth in prosperity after
the Black Death has involved us in an examination of only
part of the landscape. These times were marked by other
major changes which can still be seen. These are the buildings and associated features which the new yeoman farmers,
the new country gentry and the older landowning families
erected for their own convenience or to the glory of God.
To these we must now turn.

Buildings in the landscape

From the late fourteenth century we begin, for the first
time, to see exactly how all but the lowest orders of society
lived by a detailed examination of what still remains. The
fact that this is possible is partly due to the economic and
social changes which we have discussed earlier. Before the
fourteenth century in a rural area such as Cambridgeshire
there were few houses, outside the palaces of the great lay
and ecclesiastical landowners, which were more than crude
timber buildings. Certainly the great bulk of the population
lived in what we should term hovels as the earthwork
remains at places such as the deserted villages of Childerley
and Clopton indicate. With the appearance of new independent and prosperous yeoman farmers higher quality buildings were erected which have sometimes lasted into the
present century. These were inevitably crude imitations of
ideas of architecture and living conditions which gradually
filtered down from higher up the social scale. In addition,
the influx of new landlords, who having made their money
in commerce, government and the law, desired to become

country gentlemen and to found county families, has not only left its own mark on the landscape but it helped to change the aspirations of the yeoman farmers below them. These new social classes when combined with the older long-established landowners produced a fascinating confusion of dwelling places. The outlines of its development can still be seen today.

Of the great medieval landlords it is the Church which has left most for us to see. The remains of the monastic houses, with the exception of those at Ely and in Cambridge, have been swept away. However, because the Bishops of Ely were independent of the abbey there we do have the remains of some of their palaces which did not disappear at the Dissolution. One of the best is the so-called Biggin Abbey, at Fen Ditton north-east of Cambridge. By today's standards it can hardly be called attractive, for its huge, grey-plastered stone walls and solid square appearance are perhaps not to our taste, but this is the result of constant adaptation and alteration by later generations. Beneath it all is a remarkable late-fourteenth-century building which was one of the homes of the medieval Bishops of Ely, though there is little more than the large buttresses to give us the clue. It does, however, represent the ideal type of dwelling of a great lord of the period, and contains a fine hall where the Bishop and his retainers lived.

Very different but well illustrating the changing fashions of the period are the battered remains of another palace of the Bishops of Ely, that inside the medieval deer park at Little Downham. It was built between 1486 and 1500 by Bishop Alcock in the then advanced material of brick and in appearance must have been very different from Biggin Abbey. Yet, though the remains are difficult to interpret, it seems that as a dwelling it was still very much within the medieval tradition. Again there was a large open hall.

The idea of a main open room wherein most of the

household activities were concentrated was common to all ranks of society at this time and is reflected in a number of Cambridgeshire houses of this period, built by lesser lords and even prosperous farmers. The difficulty for the landscape historian is that later alterations and adaptations to bring them up to date and make them acceptable for new and constantly changing standards of living make them very hard to recognise from the outside alone. The majority today look delightful 'period' buildings with an appearance often identical to seventeenth-century and later houses. However, these medieval houses do exist. A house at Barrington underneath its pretty white-painted and plastered exterior is a fourteenth-century open aisled hall, with a kitchen wing at one end and a parlour with a bedroom above at the other (Plate 11). Nothing is known of its builders but it was probably erected by a small but wealthy farmer. In layout and room arrangement it is identical to the contemporary palaces of the great.

By the early sixteenth century new ideas of design and living conditions were coming into fashion and this affected all new buildings and especially those at the higher levels of society, though they soon filtered down the scale. The two most important factors were the desire for symmetrical elevations, especially to the front of a building, and the change from one main living room, the hall, to a multiplicity of rooms for special purposes. These ideas, combined with a rigid conservatism which tried to retain at least part of the old medieval arrangement, is often met with. It is perhaps best seen at Madingley Hall just west of Cambridge (Plate 16). The house was built by John Hynde, a wealthy lawyer, and later King's Sergeant and a Justice of the Common Pleas. He bought the property in 1543 and began building the present house. It was largely completed by 1547 though further work took place between 1591 and 1596. Though somewhat altered and partly rebuilt in the

151

late nineteenth century it shows all the aims and ideals of a new wealthy county family of the sixteenth century. There is still the great hall with a screens passage separating it from a kitchen range beyond in the true medieval tradition, but instead of being open to the roof there was an upper hall. At the north end of the hall the normal parlour range was designed to take a long gallery, then particularly fashionable, above a set of private rooms. All this had to be given an up-to-date symmetrical front, which was virtually impossible. This was made worse by the fact that the kitchen wing had to have an octagonal stair turret on the corner and there had to be a main entrance porch and a fine oriel window to the hall. Further, as the long gallery wing of necessity projected forward there could be no balancing turret at this end. The architect was therefore forced to put in a curious three-sided projection in the angle between the wing and the main range to give an appearance of symmetry.

A very similar house as far as we can see is that now known as Kirtling Tower in the south-east of the county, built around 1530. The house itself was pulled down in 1801 and only the gatehouse still stands. From old engravings of the house it is clear that it had an elaborate symmetrical elevation with much Renaissance detail, but there was still a large hall with wings at each end in the medieval manner. The magnificent red brick gatehouse which remains is a large crenellated structure with polygonal outer turrets. At first sight, as one approaches from afar, it appears to be a huge defensive structure, but a closer look reveals it to be a delightful piece of nonsense. The splendid first-floor oriel window, jammed rather unsatisfactorily between the turrets, gives the game away. All this was the work of the first Baron North, the son of a successful London merchant. He rose to become Chancellor of the Court of Augmentations, a body which dealt with the

Plate 9 Knapwell village. A typical example of massive shrinkage. The church stands alone surrounded by banks, scarps and ditches of former houses, gardens and lanes. The remaining buildings too are separated by abandoned house sites. In the bottom left-hand corner is a tiny castle mound built to protect the village in the mid-twelfth century.

Plate 10 Caxton Pastures Farm, Caxton. The farmhouse and buildings lie within a large medieval moat which has been carefully sited in a shallow valley in order to keep the ditch filled with water from the stream which now passes through it.

Plate 11 House at Barrington. The generally seventeenth-century appearance of this pretty building hides the largely complete remains of a fourteenth-century open hall, undoubtedly built by a rich yeoman farmer.

Plate 12 Pigeon House, Grantchester. This building is the one probably recorded as the 'Great Duffhouse' in 1467. It was erected by the lords of the manor to keep pigeons in. In the nineteenth century, as the pressure of population increased, it was converted into two dwellings.

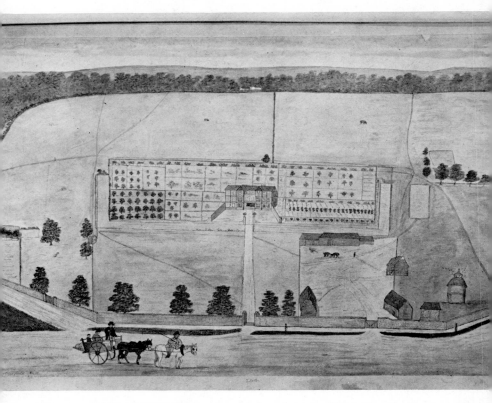

Plate 13 Haslingfield Hall in 1814. At that time the Elizabethan house was still complete, surrounded by its formal gardens and set within a three-sided 'moat'. Beyond is the small walled park, a farmyard and a pigeon house. Today only part of the house remains and the park has largely disappeared under modern housing.

spoils of the monasteries, and this enabled him to become exceedingly rich. He was also politically astute for he remained in favour with Somerset, Queen Mary and Queen Elizabeth in quick succession. Kirtling Tower, fragment though it is, is a splendid monument to a successful middle-class family who moved into the aristocracy.

On a smaller scale, but still reflecting the same desire by successful men to become landed gentry, is Haslingfield Hall (Plate 13 and Fig. 10). Again it is now only a fragment of what it once was and originally it consisted of a large hall with cross wings, and with balancing turrets to give an impression of symmetry. It was built by Thomas Wendy, physician to Henry VIII, soon after he bought the property in 1541.

None of these houses of course stood alone. Just as important as the house, by this time, was its setting and all had gardens around them. None survives as a garden in the county but careful fieldwork can reveal a great deal about the settings of these houses. A number of them were erected on the sites of older houses, which in the tradition of the thirteenth century were surrounded by moats constructed as we have seen largely for status purposes. At Kirtling, for example, the house was built inside an existing medieval moat, and the moat therefore became an integral part of the mock defensive appearance. Elsewhere new moats were actually constructed for this purpose. At Haslingfield Hall the approach to the house is across a deep moat on a pretty brick bridge. The moat does not go all round the house but is on the front and along part of the sides. Here the whole object is to provide an imposing approach to the house with a trace of medieval baronial pretension.

Even more splendid, though now sadly neglected and mutilated, was the water arrangement around the manor house at Papworth St Agnes (Fig. 10). Here again the old medieval manor house was surrounded by a normal rectangular moat. When the house was rebuilt to lavish modern designs, albeit on a medieval plan, in the late sixteenth century, the old moat was radically altered. To the north of the house which lay at the south end of the moated enclosure a long pond was dug and mounds, probably to take summerhouses, were erected at the corners of the main moated enclosure. This presumably was the basis for an elaborate garden to be viewed from the north window of the parlour. To the east of the house a section of the old moat was filled in and a new embanked garden was laid out across the adjacent fields, while to the south-west of the house a balancing, but this time moated, garden was laid out beyond the old medieval moat. All this can still be seen around the manor house today.

The new ideas of house design and layout came down to the new yeoman farmers and lesser gentry. On the whole the same local building materials were used and the result is the typical timber-framed and plastered houses, often with thatched roofs which are such an attractive feature of the county today. To the unobservant they all look much the same, but it is the layout of the house which is important. If we look carefully we can see how changing ideas of living conditions altered the homes of middle-class farmers.

Before the late fifteenth century most of these people built themselves normal medieval houses. That is they usually had a large hall, open to the roof, with a kitchen wing at one end and a parlour wing at the other. Then as the idea that a number of rooms provided more privacy, and a higher standard of living reached these people by example from above, they started to build houses with one or two ground-floor rooms on either side of a great internal chimney stack and with first-floor bedrooms above. Rather than rebuild all the older houses, many people merely adapted them to fit their new ideas. The result was that many of the old open halls had ceilings inserted into the upper parts and huge brick chimneys built up through the centre. Both types of houses, those built from the beginning with first-floor bedrooms and the older ones which were modified to this layout can be seen in many places, though externally they all appear to be very similar. Of the first type Avenalls Farm, Gamlingay and Manor Farm, Great Eversden, both late sixteenth century in date, are good examples. Of the older modified houses, Burgh Hall in Swaffham Bulbeck, built around 1500, and Rectory Farm in Great Shelford, of the late fourteenth century, both altered in the sixteenth century, are worth noting.

With this great development of homes went a contemporary one connected with the churches of the county. However, in many respects this is not so clearly defined as the changes in house types nor is it so marked as in many other areas of this country. It is not at all easy to pick out major periods of building in the churches of Cambridgeshire and one cannot easily relate changes in ecclesiastical architecture to economic decline and prosperity as can sometimes be done elsewhere. For example there is no lack of early- and mid-fourteenth-century church building and alteration in Cambridgeshire, though one might expect this from the story of the dire economic distress and pestilence of the period. Some villages which were always small, or which were affected badly by the troubles of the fourteenth century, apparently were never able or never needed to enlarge or rebuild their churches and these remained fairly small and simple. Mepal and Coveney churches which are small and almost entirely thirteenth-century are two examples, while that at Witcham nearly all dates from the late thirteenth and fourteenth centuries. St Michael's, Long Stanton, is another small church mostly of about 1230. Elsewhere churches were continually modified and altered throughout the fourteenth century. Sometimes the whole church was rebuilt, as at Little Eversden where the tiny unaisled nave and chancel are entirely of this date. On a very different scale, but of the same period, is the large and ambitious church at Swavesey which is mainly of the early fourteenth century. At Fen Drayton, the construction of the church-tower there in the early fourteenth century was the beginning of an almost total rebuilding which went on for over a century and the same is true of Comberton church.

From the late fourteenth century onwards there is plenty of evidence for new work in most churches and it is tempting to relate this to the prosperity of the times. Most Cambridgeshire churches have some late-fourteenth- and fifteenth-century additions to them, some of them extremely fine. The best are truly remarkable. The vast Perpendicular glasshouse of Burwell, on the south-east fen edge, dated 1464, must represent to some extent the great prosperity of the period. The church of Wisbech St Mary, with evidence of continuous building from the late fourteenth century to nearly 1500, is an indicator of the economic wealth of the silt fens at this time as is the remarkable west tower of St John's, Parson Drove. Even on the less prosperous peat fens there are some magnificent churches. The spire of St Mary's, Whittlesey, one of the best in the county, was built in the Northamptonshire style around 1450 and at March, the fifteenth-century additions to the existing fourteenth-century church are sumptuous and include the most splendid timber roof in the county of the double hammer-beam type (Plate 14).

Though these magnificent churches stand out even to the casual visitor, far more commonplace in the landscape is the evidence for fifteenth-century work on a smaller scale. Dozens of Cambridgeshire churches have expensive and fashionable additions of fifteenth-century date. These range from fine towers to the insertion of one or two Perpendicular windows, and the construction of clerestories is a particularly marked feature at this time. At Little Chishill in the south of the county many alterations were carried out to the church in the fifteenth century. At Kennet in the east, the largely thirteenth-century church had a new tower added in the fifteenth century; Great Abington church, south-east of Cambridge, though mostly thirteenth- and early fourteenth-century had many of its windows rebuilt in the Perpendicular style, while at Girton the clerestory and south porch were added in the fifteenth century. The church at Wicken, way out in the fens, had most of its windows renewed at this time and the small tower is of the same date.

The importance of all this late-fourteenth-century and fifteenth-century rebuilding is normally said to reflect the great prosperity of the period. While this is probably true to a certain extent, there are other factors to be borne in mind. First we must remember that there was a considerable amount of work going on during the immediately preceding years when prosperity can hardly have been a factor. Further, much of the new work, though obviously based on wealth, is also a reflection of architectural fashion which was continually changing. As a result, necessary repairs and alterations were carried out in an up-to-date design rather than in the old style. This is often forgotten today with our emphasis on restoration rather than alteration. Nor must it be forgotten that the fifteenth century was the last period of large-scale architectural change for churches and therefore the remains of that period have survived better than the earlier ones. The most important factor, however, is that much of this new work in the county's churches reflects a different form of piety. Earlier generations often expressed their belief in God or attempted to prepare for the hereafter by giving money and land to the great monastic houses. By the late fourteenth century new religious ideas and outlooks were coming in and people tended to give money to individual churches for chantry chapels and other more mundane rebuildings and alterations. It is perhaps this change in religious ideas as much as the economic background which is the reason for our fine late medieval ecclesiastical architecture.

This can be seen if we look specifically at some of the people who rebuilt and altered churches in Cambridgeshire at this time. At Orwell, west of Cambridge, there is an extremely beautiful late-fourteenth-century chancel added to the earlier church (Plate 15). This was erected around 1398 at the expense of Richard Anlaby, a Rector, to the memory of Sir Simon Bury, formerly lord of the manor and tutor to Richard II, who had been impeached and executed in 1388. This type of memorial is not likely to have been constructed at an earlier period.

At Little Shelford, not only was much of the church repaired and altered in the fifteenth century, but an attractive little chapel was added to the south side. This, to judge by the fine brasses in it, was all done by members of the de Freville family who were lords of the manor here from the twelfth to the early sixteenth century. They had been responsible for many of the earlier fourteenth-century alterations to the church and the later work was doubtless meant to be a final memorial to the family.

In the far east of the county in the tiny parish of Landwade is another church almost entirely of the fifteenth century which was built around 1445 for Sir Walter Cotton. The village of Landwade had always been small and by the early fifteenth century was virtually deserted. The land there was bought by Walter Cotton, a rich London mercer, who as usual founded a major county family which remained there until the nineteenth century. Walter Cotton rebuilt the church as a burial place for his family and this was its sole purpose until recently. The interior is crowded with some of the best and most remarkable tombs in the county and these together with the church itself now stand as a silent memorial to the new aristocracy of the fifteenth century.

SELECT BIBLIOGRAPHY

Baker, A. R. H. 'Evidence . . . of Contracting Arable Land in England during the Early Fourteenth Century', *Econ. Hist. Rev.* (1966).

Darby, H. C. *The Medieval Fenland* (1940).

Palmer, W. M. 'A History of Clopton', *Procs. C.A.S.* (1933).

Pevsner, N. *The Buildings of England, Cambridgeshire* (1970).

R.C.H.M. *Cambridgeshire*, Vols I and II (1968 and 1972).

Spufford, M. 'A Cambridge Community', *Leicester University Occasional Papers*, 20 (1965).

Steers, J. A. *The Cambridge Region* (1965).

V.C.H. *Cambridgeshire*, Vols II and IV (1948 and 1953).

5. The uplands, 1600–1900

Buildings in the landscape. Changes in the farming pattern, 1600–1900. Private and parliamentary enclosure.

Buildings in the landscape

FROM THE EARLY seventeenth century the history of the landscape of the northern fenlands and the southern uplands is so different that it is more convenient to deal with them separately. Both areas, however, were affected by what was going on in the other, and along a broad zone in the centre of the county the fen-edge villages looked both to fen and to upland. It is important to realise that on the larger fen islands the landscape changes of the seventeenth to nineteenth centuries were more like those of the uplands at the same period, and in many respects very different from the surrounding fens. On the uplands the general prosperity, which we have noted developing during the fifteenth and sixteenth centuries, continued, and this was reflected in the landscape. New ideas of architecture, living conditions, garden design and agricultural techniques continued to arrive and many of these can still be seen today.

Particularly important are the larger houses which were erected, for they intensified the move towards different living conditions and house appearance which soon moved down through society. In the early part of the seventeenth century most of the new houses of the gentry were still being built in the medieval tradition as we noted above. This type of building went on well into the seventeenth century and may be seen at Bourn Hall (1602), a fine brick mansion with basically a central hall and cross wing, and Elsworth Manor House, also of brick and with the same plan.

By the middle of the century the first classical houses appeared. By this we mean that the elements of layout and appearance which were due to medieval traditions were finally abandoned and the more logical double-depth house with symmetrical elevations appeared. This type of house was a completely new concept at that time. Before this all buildings were merely ranges of single room width, and size was increased by extending the range or by adding wings. The appearance of these double-depth houses, and their gradual adoption by successive levels of society in the next 250 years is of outstanding importance, not only to the landscape historian but to the student of architectural and social history as well.

Amongst the earliest of these new-style houses are Wimpole Hall, built *c.* 1640 for Thomas Chicheley, a keen supporter of the Crown by whom he was suitably rewarded, and Hatley Park, built at the same time for Sir Henry St George, Garter King of Arms. Both were later altered out of all recognition, though the original structures still exist. These new ideas soon reached the lower orders of society and by the late seventeenth and early eighteenth centuries many smaller landowners were erecting this type of house, though naturally architectural embellishments had changed by that time. Conington Hall is an especially fine example of one of these smaller houses, apparently erected by one of the Cotton family (Plate 24).

As the eighteenth century progressed, more and more houses were erected with neat symmetrical elevations. Upland Cambridgeshire has few large country houses, but it has a host of smaller ones. These are largely products of local landowners all aspiring to become county gentlemen living in the gracious style reflected in so much

L

contemporary literature. The architectural details which interest the art historians continually changed and many older houses were adapted and altered to new fashions, but the overall picture is of a prosperous squirearchy living quietly in pleasant surroundings. One of the joys of exploring the upland areas of the county is that of discovering small eighteenth-century country houses set in tiny parks or large gardens hidden in remote villages or tucked away in areas of often contemporary woodland. None perhaps is of great architectural merit. Of the many, Tetworth Hall in Gamlingay is of particular interest, built in 1710 for John Pedley, MP for Huntingdonshire 1706–8, and enlarged in the later part of the century (Plate 17). It is a fine square brick house on a sloping site with extensive views. Stetchworth House, a rather gaunt heavy-weight built in 1786, Brinkley Hall, a much prettier house of the same date, and Tyrells Hall, Shepreth, of about 1750 though much enlarged, all set in small parks, are other typical examples. This pattern of small, neat country houses continues into the nineteenth century.

Once again these houses were associated with gardens and parks of one form or another and though today the majority have small parks around them, it is often possible to see the remains of earlier garden layouts which went with the original houses. For example at Childerley Hall, northwest of Cambridge, all Ordnance Survey maps mark a three-sided moat south of the house. In view of the fact that a deserted medieval village lies adjacent to it, it would be easy to assume that the moat is the site of the medieval manor house. But a close inspection of the site immediately reveals that the 'moat' is not a moat at all (Fig. 10). It is a large bank or terrace enclosing a small square garden with low mounds on the corners which presumably supported summerhouses or seats. From these one could view both the neat rectangular formal garden within or the natural landscape without, an aim frequently advocated by writers on gardening design in the late sixteenth and early seventeenth centuries. This garden was probably constructed during the reign of Charles I by the fifth Sir John Cutts whose family lived in the hall.

Sir John's efforts to improve the appearance of his house were not apparently confined to his garden. He seems to have laid out a large deer park around the hall and garden. Part of the boundary, a large bank and ditch, can still be traced as can the embanked ponds within it. However, in order to produce the deer park Sir John had also to remove the few remaining inhabitants of the already declining village of Childerley which lay immediately to the east of his garden. This he successfully did and now only the deeply worn hollow-ways of the streets and the grass-covered sites of houses and closes remain for the field-worker to see.[1]

Much more interesting are the remains of the gardens of Wimpole, where the full story of what rich and prosperous landowners could do is stamped on the landscape. Today Wimpole Hall is surrounded by one of the finest parkland areas in the country, produced by the efforts of almost every major garden designer since the early eighteenth century (Plates 18 and 19). Before that, however, the mid-seventeenth-century house was surrounded by an elaborate formal garden with typical rectangular areas of flower borders, arbours and glades, whose details were recorded for posterity in one of J. Kip's magnificent engravings. Today if we walk carefully across the great parkland near the house we can see slight ditches and tiny rises in the grass which can be correlated with the paths, hedges and walls shown by Kip. As we walk, however, there are other more prominent earthworks to be seen. Scattered across the park and surrounded by ridge-and-furrow of medieval

[1] F. A. Walker, *Some Account of the Parishes of Childerley* (1879).

date are deep hollow-ways, passing through areas with house sites and associated banks and ditches. These are the remains of the once-flourishing village of Wimpole. As was suggested in Chapter 2 many Cambridgeshire villages were not originally nucleated at all but were made up of a series of hamlets. At Wimpole we have a fine example. Not only were there once houses round the present church and hall as one might expect, but the remains in the park show that there was another group of houses 300 yards to the south-west of the hall, another 400 yards to the south, a further one well to the north and one more over half a mile away to the north-east outside the present park. All these hamlets still existed in the early seventeenth century and are shown complete on a map of 1638. Indeed, it is possible to identify all the roads, houses and gardens shown on the map almost exactly with the remains on the ground. The removal of these scattered hamlets took place gradually as the gardens and park were enlarged and extended over the next 200 years. The houses near the hall itself were demolished soon after the new hall was built in the middle of the seventeenth century to make way for the new elaborate formal gardens with avenues of trees.

In the 1730s Edward Lord Harley, son of the first Earl of Oxford, who then owned Wimpole, brought in Charles Bridgeman the garden designer. The result of his work was that the formal gardens round the house were altered to suit the then new fashion and a rigidly formalised parkland of 200 acres with avenues and rectangular ponds was laid out around it to the south-west. The present east and west avenues in the park providing long tree-lined vistas from the formal gardens north of the hall are part of this work. The eastern avenue in typical Bridgeman fashion was nearly a mile long and projected far beyond the park itself. But the finest piece of work at this time was the magnificent south avenue over two miles long which still extends from the southern edge of the park across the Cambridge–Bedford Road to a huge octagonal basin fed by the River Cam, and then on across the southern part of the adjacent parish of Whaddon. This work certainly resulted in the removal of the two parts of the village south and south-west of the hall.

In 1740 the estate passed to Philip Hardwicke, Lord Chancellor Hardwicke, later Earl of Hardwicke and Viscount Royston, who further enlarged the hall. In 1752–4 a general landscaping north and west of the house was started. The formal gardens were destroyed and a small inner park bounded by a ha-ha, which still marks its line, replaced them. Most of the work was done by Robert Greening, though the designer William Shenstone was also probably involved. Between 1762 and 1772 the second earl brought in Capability Brown to extend and landscape the park in the most up-to-date way. This time the park was extended to the north on to the rising ground. It was bounded by long belts of trees with characteristic clumps of trees dotted about and some of the old rectangular ponds were united to form a large serpentine lake. A splendid 'Gothic tower' was placed on the hill above the hall at the end of the park. This general landscaping resulted in the removal of yet another part of the old village, that to the north of the hall. The third earl continued the work of improving the park and in the early nineteenth century engaged Humphrey Repton, another great landscape gardener, to make further extensions. A new small formal garden was added to the north side of the hall, and the park itself was extended eastwards where new tree belts and drives were laid out. The most important element was a long tree-lined winding approach from Cambridge, over a mile long, which lay entirely outside the main park. Further work later in the nineteenth century included the extension of the park to its now present size of some 600 acres.

Finally, around 1850, as if to make up for the gradual destruction of the medieval village of Wimpole over the previous 200 years, the then owner of the hall, Admiral Sir Charles Philip Yorke, erected twelve new semi-detached houses, all in the Tudoresque style but of various designs, along the Cambridge Road south-east of the park (Plate 20). This was then called New Wimpole and so remains today a splendid example of a nineteenth-century estate-village. This long description of Wimpole Park has been given not only because it is one of the most magnificent pieces of landscaping in the county but also because it shows so well how both documentary research and ground observation can unravel the detailed making of a piece of the best of the English landscape.[2] However, though Wimpole over-shadows all else, other smaller examples are there for the landscape historian to study.

At Gamlingay, west of the village, on a broad piece of open land, there is no fine house or park to be seen, only a series of curious uneven terraces, banks and depressions across the fields. These are the remains of a magnificent house and garden constructed for the third Sir George Downing in 1712 and demolished in 1776. Though no standing structure remains it is possible, with the aid of a contemporary plan now in Downing College, to see a complete early-eighteenth-century garden design unaltered by later additions. The site of the house with its wings enclosing a circular sunken lawn is visible near the present road. Then to the north is a series of large terraces, with the sites of arbours or summerhouses on them, dropping down the valley side into what is now a huge trapezoidal field bounded by massive banks. This is all that remains of a large lake whose waters once lapped the lower terrace before flowing east of the house to a series of long rectangu-

[2] The full details are in R.C.H.M. *West Cambridgeshire* (1968), Wimpole (2), (15) and (21).

lar ponds which are still there. To the west and north-west of the house long straight ditches, only a few inches deep, mark the positions of former enclosed gardens, while unbelievably the tiny sinuous grassy bank, literally only about six inches high, can be identified on the map as a gravel path passing between flowerbeds.[3]

Larger landowners made an even greater impression on the landscape. In 1696 Edward Russell, later Lord Orford, bought up a large estate at Chippenham in the east of the county. In a letter to King William, Orford wrote that he "has a seat called Chippenham Hall . . . about which he is desirous to make a park". As Mrs Spufford has said, "His action probably did more to change the landscape of the parish than any other." The new park included most of the southern part of the medieval village and licence to block off the relevant streets was obtained in 1702. By 1712 almost all the houses in the southern half of the village had been removed and the park was being laid out. In addition a small part of the common fields as well as a large area of common land were taken. The remains of a street, bounded by the low banks of the former gardens and house plots, can still be seen in the present park south of the village. Unlike the position at Wimpole, Orford seems to have taken some trouble to compensate the villagers for their loss. He granted them rights for pasturing cattle on other land he owned and of the twenty-five families whose homes were demolished, nine were rehoused by him. At least six new houses were built in Vicarage Lane and probably more on land which up to that time had been empty of houses. Some of these new buildings still survive today and represent a fine example of the work of an early-eighteenth-century benevolent landlord. The village continued to be fortunate in its owners. In the late eighteenth century John

[3] R.C.H.M. *West Cambridgeshire* (1968), Gamlingay (61) and Plates 3 and 28.

Tharp altered the hall and redesigned the park to more modern ideas, with a lake which still survives. He also provided new houses for his tenants and at least one terrace of cottages, and a group of eight pairs of semi-detached cottages, all dating from about 1800, still remain.

Other villages were not apparently so fortunate. At Madingley Hall the Cotton family, who had enlarged their park and gardens in 1743–4, commissioned Capability Brown to carry out further work in 1756–7. Brown put in the usual serpentine lake, belts and clumps of trees and a sham bridge. He also extended the park eastwards from the house to produce a long tree-edged vista still called 'The View'. This involved the demolition of a group of houses on either side of the main street and, to ensure that the prospect from the hall was uninterrupted, the ground nearest to the hall was raised slightly. This meant that the old street, still inevitably used, was hidden from view by being in the bottom of a form of ha-ha. As a result the village was cut into two parts with the church and some cottages at the south end being quite separate from the remaining part of the village to the north. The sites of the demolished houses can still be seen in the park on the east side of the road but there is no evidence that the displaced inhabitants were rehoused.

The removal of houses to make way for new landscaped parks went on into the nineteenth century. At Croxton, in the west of the county, the late-sixteenth-century house lay in one part of a typically dispersed village whose other half lay nearly half a mile to the north-west. Its contemporary formal gardens can still be seen in the present park west of the hall as low banks and ditches in the grass. In the adjacent village all the houses, streets and the church remained south-east of the hall and are shown in detail on the Enclosure Map of 1811. A few years later the park was enlarged to its present 300 acres and landscaped with trees, and the

Plate 14 St Wendreda's church, March. It stands some distance from the town centre, in a formerly remote situation, and perhaps on a much older sacred site. The present structure which is largely of fourteenth- and fifteenth-century date reflects both the wealth and changing religious ideas of the fenlands at this time.

Plate 15 Orwell church. Here the external appearance alone shows the constant alteration and rebuilding which is so typical of many Cambridgeshire churches. The lower part of the tower is twelfth century, the upper stage thirteenth century. The nave and aisles are of the early fourteenth century with windows inserted 100 years later. The chancel was built in 1398 as a memorial.

Plate 16 Madingley Hall. Built in the mid-sixteenth century for John Hynde in a basically medieval form, but reflecting the new ideas of architecture, room arrangements and living standards of its age. The result is a rather muddled, but undoubtedly attractive, building.

Plate 17 Tetworth Hall. This gracious building was erected in 1710 for John Pedley. It is typical of the small country house of this period.

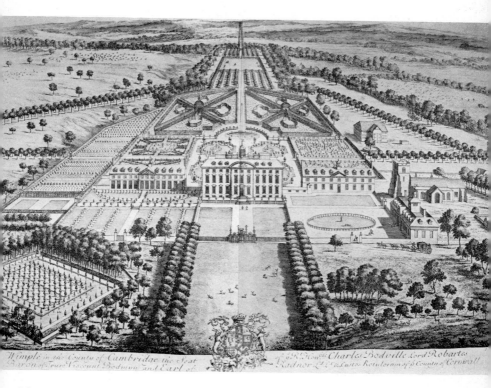

Wimple in the County of Cambridge the Seat of y^e R^t Honble Charles Bodville Lord Robartes
Baron of Truro Viscount Bodmin and Earl of   Radnor L^d L^t & Custos Rotulorum of y^e County of Cornwall

Plate 18 Wimpole in the early eighteenth century. Most of the village has already
disappeared although a few houses remain, hidden in the trees at the top right. The
great house stands in its formal gardens with the medieval church alongside it.

Plate 19 Wimpole today. The great house and its magnificent park stand as the end product of over 300 years of aristocratic aims, ideals, wealth and domination.

village near the hall bodily removed except for the church. All the house sites and streets are still visible in the grass-land and especially interesting is the old main road which now, as a deeply cut hollow-way, swings past the hall, down the hillside and disappears under the waters of a large nineteenth-century triangular lake.

The impact of all these country houses and their parks on the uplands of the county was considerable and is still well marked today. But just as marked is the result of the changing ideas and aspirations of the lower classes of society and especially their rapidly rising numbers after 1700. In the early seventeenth century Cambridgeshire, as elsewhere, was affected by what Dr Hoskins has termed 'The Great Rebuilding'. Almost all the county's older and more picturesque small houses either date from this period or were radically altered at this time. Amongst the richer farmers who already lived in substantial timber-framed medieval houses, the tendency to insert floors in the original open halls and to provide individual living-rooms and bed-rooms went on apace. Far outnumbering these, however, were new houses, built from the start to the new fashions. Perhaps the most common type which can be seen all over the county is one that consists of three ground-floor rooms, kitchen, living-room and parlour, with bedrooms above, and with one large internal chimney-stack serving two of the ground-floor rooms (Plate 21). The front door of this type of house is almost always opposite the chimney-stack. Some of these houses, timber-framed and often thatched, are a constant delight to even the unobservant visitor, but many others are not so obvious as a result of later encasing in brick, reroofing with tiles or slate and even subdivision into two or three tenements. Yet the clues to their age and origins are still clear from the three ground-floor windows of the rooms, their great chimney-stacks of patently old brick and the original door opposite this stack. For example, at Ickleton, a beautiful village full of pretty houses, one of the least attractive dwellings stands on the corner of Church Street. At first sight it seems to be a pair of late-nineteenth-century brick cottages, but closer inspection reveals that it is a standard seventeenth-century timber-framed house, with just a front elevation of yellow brick added on. And though there are now two front doors, the larger one opposite the huge red-brick chimney-stack can be seen to be the original. This type of house continued to be built well on into the eighteenth century and by then was often constructed of brick or chalk blocks (clunch) as well as of timber-framing.

By the middle of the seventeenth century the general economic prosperity of the times enabled less wealthy people to build new houses and they erected a different type of house which is also readily recognisable today in spite of later alterations and additions. These consist of only two ground-floor rooms with a single central chimney between them. One of the earliest is Upper Farm at Bourn, dated 1664, though its nineteenth-century porch may confuse people. This kind of house had a basic symmetry which was acceptable to eighteenth- and nineteenth-century fashion and thus continued to be built widely all over the county until relatively recently. By the end of the seventeenth century the increasing use of brick and tile as well as chalk blocks and even clay enabled other changes to take place in small houses. From the visual point of view the most important of these was the replacement of the large multiple internal chimney-stacks by single external chimneys on the gable ends and this kind of arrangement became common throughout the eighteenth and nineteenth centuries in farmhouses and labourers' cottages alike.

By the early nineteenth century the idea of double-depth houses, which we have mentioned earlier, reached the middle of the social scale. A few were built before this, as at

Little Eversden where the rectory was constructed around 1730 to this form by the then rector. After 1800 the bulk of the parsonages, mansions and farmhouses were all of this type, many of the latter erected following the enclosures of the common fields.

Also by the nineteenth century, rural upland Cambridge-shire, and indeed the fens, were starting to feel the impact of population pressure. The population of the county rose from nearly 90,000 in 1801 to over 185,000 in 1851. In more local terms, in a village such as Over on the fen edge north-west of Cambridge, the number of people increased from 689 in 1801 to 1256 in 1851, while at the hamlet of Knees-worth in the south-west of the county the 120 inhabitants there at the first census had risen to almost 300 fifty years later. These large numbers of people had to be housed somewhere, even if the standard of building declined. This resulted in the vast expansion of almost every village in the county, producing the characteristic yellow and pink brick dwellings which are by no means the most attractive feature of the Cambridge landscape. At the same time more tradi-tional building materials continued to be used such as timber-framing, chalk blocks, chalk rubble and lumps of clay. Many of these are now greatly sought after as 'period' dwellings to which owners and estate agents give a highly dubious antiquity. A cottage in Swaffham Bulbeck, care-fully dated 1737 over its front door, is in fact a crudely built timber dwelling erected about 1820 for labourers.

Even all these new houses were not sufficient to cope with the increasing numbers of people in the early nine-teenth century and many were housed by splitting up older buildings into two or more tenements. Again this is a marked feature of many Cambridgeshire villages today, although with increasing prosperity, newcomers are now turning these houses back into single occupation. Even so the visual remains of this early-nineteenth-century population explosion are still with us. Countless seventeenth- and eighteenth-century houses, originally built for one owner, have two or more front doors, added chimneys on the gable ends, lean-tos attached at the rear and extra windows of early-nineteenth-century date. They reflect, as much as the slums of our industrial cities, the problems associated with the rise in population during the nineteenth century.

One particularly curious feature of this problem, frequently met with in the county, is the adaptation of old pigeon houses or dovecotes. These structures, mainly of seventeenth- or eighteenth-century date, are relatively common and can easily be recognised by their square plan and curious hipped gable in which there were holes to allow the pigeons access. Inside were hundreds of nesting boxes. These buildings were often turned into dwellings in the early nineteenth century by inserting floors and chimneys and cutting openings for windows. The best example is a very large one at Manor Farm, Grantchester (Plate 12), but others exist, as at Granham's Farm, Great Shelford, and on Barrington Green.

From 1600 onwards the churches in the Cambridgeshire landscape were not on the whole altered to any great extent. Once again this is not because of any lack of prosperity, but merely reflects changing religious ideas and outlooks. A few churches were enlarged or altered in the seventeenth and eighteenth centuries but this was often done as part of larger schemes for beautifying houses and parks. Thus Sir John Cotton spent £300 in 1770–80 on rebuilding the chancel of Madingley church, but by that date it lay within the gates of his park where it still forms part of the overall landscaping. At Wimpole, in keeping with the vast emparking, the old medieval church was pulled down in 1748, except for its fourteenth-century north chapel, and replaced by a small brick one designed by Henry Flitcroft in the height of fashion. The old chapel was used as a burial place for the successive owners of Wimpole Hall.

Some other churches were also improved or embellished by local lords, but on the whole Cambridgeshire had to wait until the late nineteenth century before it received new churches, and few of them were of any great merit either visually or architecturally. Even then the influence of the local 'squarson' was paramount and the roughly 'Decorated' church of Papworth St Agnes, built by the local squire and incumbent the Rev. Sperling around 1850, is typical.

The religious fervour and ideas of the great mass of the people were, from the seventeenth century, channelled along different lines. These were the various Nonconformist movements, always strong in Cambridgeshire. The county is dotted with numerous chapels mostly of the mid- or late nineteenth century and almost without exception dull or worse to modern eyes. They often have older origins but were constantly enlarged or rebuilt and the result is usually rather depressing in visual terms. But, they still mark an important aspect of English social and religious history which is perhaps reflected better in the landscape than in the hopes and aspirations of the descendants of their builders.

Changes in the farming pattern, 1600–1900

Many of the changes in the buildings which we have catalogued earlier in this chapter depended to a large extent on the agricultural prosperity and changing techniques over the same three centuries. Until the late nineteenth century there was a general economic prosperity for all but the lower ranks of rural society, with some relatively short-lived depressions, and this was accompanied by a steady development of farming methods and practices. As a result, changes in the rural landscape gathered momentum and have continued ever since. Most contemporary visitors to the county commented on this prosperity. Camden, writing in the first half of the seventeenth century, said that in upland Cambridgeshire "the most part or all of it rather is laid out into corne fields and yieldeth plentifully the best barley; of which . . . they make store of mault: By renting and sending out whereof into the neighbor-counties, the Inhabitants raise very great gaine." Morden in 1700 described the county as abounding "in corn of all sorts, chiefly Barley that has the reputation of being very good".

Many eighteenth-century topographical writers continued to emphasise the importance of barley. Together with wheat and rye this crop was the major agricultural product in these years and no doubt made it considerably easier to maintain the old common field system over much of the county. But cereals were by no means the only crop grown. Saffron, produced for dyeing, was also very important in the seventeenth and eighteenth centuries and was grown both in the common fields and in small enclosed fields around the villages. What Dr Kerridge has termed the Agricultural Revolution of the seventeenth century also affected Cambridgeshire and there are records of other crops such as rape and turnips being grown in the uplands of the county by the late seventeenth century.

Livestock was also important. In 1753 Carter said that the uplands had "good pasture ground which produces excellent cheese and butter" and some parishes in the valley of the Ashwell Cam, namely Shingay, Wendy and Whaddon, were called 'The Dairies' in the eighteenth century. Sheep, as always, were important at this time. In the early seventeenth century the higher chalklands of the south part of the county were described as providing "sustenance to many thousand sheep".[4] These animals were kept as part

4 *The Beauties of England: Cambs.* (1610), p. 19.

of a sheep-barley practice and continued on from the great era of late medieval sheep-farming which we have noted earlier. As always, however, the numbers of sheep were limited by the lack of winter and spring feed on the relatively dry uplands of the county. This problem was solved by sending the sheep into the fens when feed was in short supply on the uplands, but another solution was introduced in the late sixteenth century with the development of watermeadows.

The method of 'floating' watermeadows was to run water over and across alluvial land in the spring to produce an early frost-free pasture for sheep. By this means farmers were able to keep far more sheep than would otherwise have been possible. The classic form of watermeadows with 'water carriages' or long ridges with channels down their spines are rare in this county though common in the south of England.[5] In Cambridgeshire we can still see the remains of a different and less sophisticated form of these meadows. This was achieved by running a leat or channel from a dammed stream along the valley side. By lifting hatches or sluices set along this leat water then ran across the meadows back to the stream in great floods, so producing the necessary grass growth. Such meadows were introduced into Cambridgeshire in the sixteenth century by Horatio Pallalvicino, the owner of the manor of Babraham, south-east of Cambridge, and a number of these can still be seen on the ground today, though their actual date is unknown.

The best are at Swaffham Bulbeck, north-east of Cambridge. Just north of the church is the wide shallow valley of the Gutter Bridge Brook (Fig. 12). On the south side of the meadows there is a long water channel now disused which runs from the brook to the side of the valley and then runs parallel to it for 300 yards or so. At intervals

[5] C. C. Taylor, *The Making of the English Landscape: Dorset* (1970), pp. 130–2.

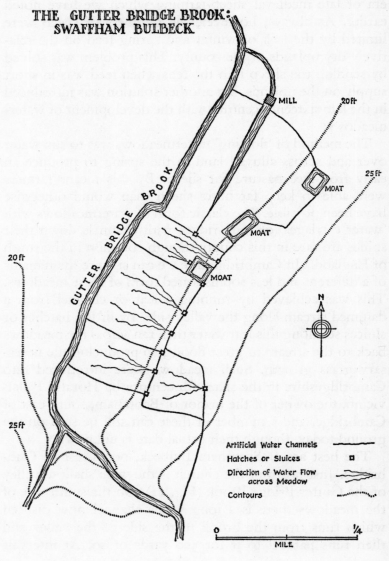

THE GUTTER BRIDGE BROOK:
SWAFFHAM BULBECK

MILL

20 ft

25 ft

MOAT

MOAT

GUTTER BRIDGE BROOK

20 ft

MOAT

N

25 ft

Artificial Water Channels ————
Hatches or Sluices ▫
Direction of Water Flow
across Meadow
Contours ·········

0   ¼
MILE

Fig. 12

176

along the channel are the remains of small wooden hatches or sluices set in seventeenth- or eighteenth-century brickwork and through which the water was released to flow across the lower meadows back to the brook. The casual visitor may not notice this or dismiss it as of no interest, but the keen landscape historian can recognise it as the remains of a vital part of seventeenth- and eighteenth-century sheep-farming in the county.

There is just one place in Cambridgeshire where the more sophisticated watermeadows of the Wessex type can be seen. This is in the valley of the River Cam between the villages of Duxford and Hinxton and within the parish of the former. It provides a good example of how even the trained eye sees only what it expects. Because it is usually asserted that such watermeadows were never constructed in the county one is not prepared to look for them. The writer travelled regularly past these watermeadows by train for almost four years before he noticed them. Yet once seen, it was clear that they had all the characteristics of classic watermeadows with channelled ridges, sluices, head mains and so on. They presumably date from the seventeenth or eighteenth century but so far no indication of this has been discovered.

Private and parliamentary enclosure

Alongside all these changes in the farming scene went another which had a much greater impact on the landscape. This was the enclosure of the common fields and wastes by Act of Parliament. This took place on the fen islands as well as on the uplands from 1750 onwards. However, the great age of enclosure had its beginnings much earlier than this, and though the county as a whole is often regarded as a classic area of late parliamentary enclosure, this needs to be seen in perspective.

In the previous chapter we have already looked at the evidence for fifteenth- and sixteenth-century enclosures of the county's fields and this process continued throughout the seventeenth century. Enclosure was usually carried out by the larger and more enterprising landowners who had the power, money and opportunity. This was particularly true in parishes where there was only one owner, or where there was a very small population. In the west of the county where both these factors existed complete enclosure of the old common fields was achieved in a number of parishes without any recorded disputes or opposition. The new owners of Wimpole Hall, the Chicheleys, as well as rebuilding the house and beginning the development of the park, enclosed all the common fields of Wimpole sometime between 1638 and 1686 to judge from surviving estate maps. They apparently did the same in the adjacent parishes of Wendy and Arrington which they also owned and where there were very few people. At Arrington the common fields were certainly still there in 1546 when a terrier lists individual strips as being in High Field and Low Field, but they had all disappeared by 1700 and had been replaced by the existing hedged fields. At Childerley the common fields went some time in the seventeenth century, presumably after the final depopulation of Childerley village by the Cutts family. At both East Hatley and Hatley St George the common fields were enclosed in the same century by the St George family who owned most of both parishes, and the common fields at Tadlow suffered the same fate between 1650 and 1750. Most of these parishes still retain the characteristic field shapes of this form of enclosure. Unlike the generally irregular outlines of the early medieval fields cut from the waste and woodland, and the rigidly geometrical fields of the later parliamentary enclosure, these fields tend to be rectangular but with slightly sinuous boundaries. These were usually the result of putting the new hedges around furlongs or blocks of pre-existing common field strips, and so fossilising the curving form of these strips in the new hedges. In some places it is clear that these new fields were promptly cultivated by ploughing them in the old-fashioned way with ridge-and-furrow. In parts of Arrington, Tadlow and in the sixteenth-century enclosed fields of Croydon-cum-Clopton we can see ridge-and-furrow identical to that of the old common field type except that it always lies inside the fields and has headlands inside the hedges.

As well as this large-scale enclosure of whole parishes there was a certain amount of enclosure of wastes and commons on a comparatively small scale. Dr Rackham, working on the history and botany of Hayley Wood in Little Gransden parish, has been able to prove that during the second half of the seventeenth century a detached part of the wood, covering some forty-four acres, which had been left when the surrounding land was cleared from the forest before the Norman Conquest, was finally removed and the area enclosed. Or as a survey of about 1670 has it, "Memoranda that little Hound wood new stubbed is lett . . ." The site of this wood is still clearly visible as an irregular heart-shaped area bounded by a thick hedge and divided into three roughly rectangular fields. In the same survey there is another note: "Item 60 acres of pasture being divided into 3 sev'all closes . . . adioying upon Great Wood." These sixty acres were and still are to the north of Hayley Wood. Before the rest of the parish was enclosed in 1826 these fields lay on the southern edge of Cow Common, the parochial waste from which they had been taken. Shortly after their enclosure a new farmstead was built in the centre and this, now called Gransden Lodge and dating from the late seventeenth century, still stands there.[6]

Both large and small farmers were also involved in the

[6] I am grateful to Dr Rackham for allowing me access to his work.

piecemeal enclosure of the common fields themselves. Much of this is completely undated, but the existence on many Enclosure Maps of isolated enclosed strips within the common fields as well as around the villages shows that many people found it convenient to take pieces of land out of the communal rotation system and cultivate it separately. At Great Shelford the Enclosure Map of 1834 shows a small enclosed piece of land lying in the open Causeway West Field. It is clear from its shape that this plot had once been part of the adjacent open field but a documented date for its enclosure is not forthcoming. However, enough remains of the original hedges to carry out a botanical analysis. This has revealed that they are approximately 300 years old and suggests that the plot was originally taken out of the common field in the seventeenth century.

The same feature can be seen elsewhere. At Croxton the Enclosure Map of 1811 shows two isolated old enclosed fields, long and narrow in shape, in the corner of the common Woodway Field, both belonging to the rector. Here again both fields still remain on the ground today. Also at Croxton, in the north-west corner of the parish, is a 120-acre block of land divided into twelve rectangular fields each between six and twenty acres (Fig. 6B). All must have once been part of the former common fields and the reversed-S curved boundaries of some of them show this. At what date these fields were enclosed is not known, but they certainly predate the parliamentary enclosure of the parish. The fact that they are called White Hall Closes on the Enclosure Map of 1799 and that White Hall Farm which still stands on the south side of them is a house of the early eighteenth century suggests that the whole scheme was contemporary with the construction of the farmstead.

Before the end of the eighteenth century, another form of enclosure was taking place in the uplands of the county. This, probably connected with the increasing number of sheep, was the breaking up and enclosure of parts of the higher chalk downlands. Arthur Young in his *Annals of Agriculture* (1805) describes the paring and burning of the 'dry heaths' before cultivation. One of the places he specifically mentions is Dullingham in the south-east of the county and there we see the results. On the Enclosure Map of Dullingham, made in 1807, a large area of the north-west end of the parish on the dry chalkland is shown as already enclosed and described as 'Late Heath' with two farmsteads, the present Lower Hare Park and Lordship Farm in existence. These farmsteads and the surrounding fields must date from the late eighteenth century. Further east at Cheveley the same picture is repeated. On the draft Enclosure Map of 1816 a large area of land between the edge of the then existing common fields and the open downland of Warren Hill is shown as divided into enclosed fields. The fields are still there, now part of the fashionable racehorse training area around Newmarket.

By the time these downland enclosures were being laid out, more important enclosure was taking place elsewhere. From the late eighteenth century onwards parliamentary enclosure started to sweep away the common fields of the county. The first Act of Parliament authorising the enclosure of common fields and waste in the upland parts of the county was passed in 1770 and concerned the parish of Abington Pigotts. Five years later an Act for the enclosure of Knapwell parish was passed and in 1777 a similar one for Weston Colville went through Parliament. There was then a lull for almost twenty years, but in 1794 Charles Vancouver published his *General View of the Agriculture of the County of Cambridgeshire* for the Board of Agriculture. Vancouver estimated, perhaps inaccurately, that of the 147,000 acres of arable land in the county 132,000 acres lay in common fields and he considered that no improvement was possible until the enclosure of these fields had taken place. Enclosure appeared to be 'indispensibly necessary' and 'urgent'. His views were apparently supported by the majority of the larger farmers and it is perhaps no coincidence that within two years of Vancouver's book appearing a flood of Enclosure Bills started to go through Parliament.

Between 1796 and 1850, ninety-five parishes in upland Cambridgeshire were enclosed by Act of Parliament and four others by private agreement. This involved approximately 160,000 acres of former common fields and open pasture land. Never before in the history of the county had there been such a rapid alteration of the upland landscape. In just over fifty years the old common fields and the open grassland pastures were swept away and replaced by the modern geometrically shaped fields and isolated enclosure farmsteads we still have today. Even now, with our present speed of change, it is difficult to imagine the impact of the enclosure movement on the landscape. In less than a lifetime the greater part of the Cambridgeshire uplands were altered out of all recognition. After 1850 enclosure tailed off, as most of the work had been done, and between then and 1889 when the last parish, Hildersham, was enclosed, only six parishes, involving some 7000 acres, had Parliamentary Acts passed.

It is this enclosure landscape which is naturally most marked today in southern Cambridgeshire (Plate 22). Everywhere we see the huge fields, bounded by angular hedges, all rigidly laid out by a professional surveyor. Large isolated farmsteads of white brick dot the countryside and all the lanes, characterised by wide verges, cut straight across the landscape. To many the result is a dull countryside with little to see, yet the keen observer can find much to interest him. Even without a map it is possible to interpret much of this landscape. If one travels to the village of Coton from Grantchester one passes along a typical straight lane with normal small quickset hedges. Then suddenly the verges disappear, the lane narrows and at the same point tall thick hedges run back from the road across the fields. This spot is where the common fields originally started. The straight wide lane is the enclosure surveyor's replacement for an old medieval trackway, laid out in 1800. The narrower lane is the old medieval track passing between the enclosed paddocks around the village and the thick hedges mark the ancient boundary between these paddocks and the former common fields.

Elsewhere other fragments of the past can be seen. On the otherwise straight road between Fordham and Chippenham there is a sharp change of alignment about halfway along it. This coincides with the parish boundary and marks the point where the enclosure surveyor, who laid out the new roads and fields in Fordham just before 1820, had to join his new road with one which a colleague had laid out in Chippenham in 1791. A similar slight kink, resulting from the same difficulty, can be seen on the land between Milton and Impington, north of Cambridge, and in many other places as well.

The cost of enclosure and the heavy works involved in it are often forgotten when looking at this landscape. On the dry open chalkland, the cost of planting quickset hedges was probably cheap, but many parishes also had low-lying ground along the fen edges or in the river valleys which needed considerable work carried out on it. A Sunday afternoon's walk along the footpaths of many south Cambridgeshire parishes makes this very clear. One constantly notices deep, straight ditches and crumbling white-brick bridges and culverts, all dating from the period after enclosure and all of which cost the enclosing landlords a great deal of money. A document in the Ely Diocesan Archives in the Cambridge University Library shows this well. It lists work done on the Dean and Chapter's Estate in Great and Little Wilbraham parishes after the enclosure of 1797.

The various works cost well over £800. They included erecting and painting fences, ditching, stopping up old culverts and constructing new ones, building bridges of brick and timber across new ditches and supplying gates. One particularly interesting item is a bill for employing two horses and a man for one day "to plow the road on the common". This is how many of the enclosure roads were originally laid out. Straight furrows were ploughed across the open land to fix the line of the new roads.

Another example of the cost of enclosure is recorded in the muniments of St John's College, Cambridge. Amongst the many items in the accounts are £950 for fencing and building new farmsteads at Horningsea in 1804, £393 for the Fordham enclosure in 1814 and another £369 in 1820 for the same parish. Partly as a result of these high costs, the actual establishment of the post-enclosure landscape sometimes took many years to complete. Often a considerable time elapsed between the actual Enclosure Act and the final layout of the new hedges. At Fulbourn, where the Act of Enclosure was passed in 1805, a memorandum dated 1813, concerning an estate in Fulbourn in the Trinity Hall Archives, records an agreement "to continue the Quickwood on the north side of the grass enclosure . . . and to fence same with old Battens from the New enclosures and to plant both enclosures with elm".

Many of the farmsteads which were built in the newly enclosed fields were often erected long after enclosure and certainly it must not be assumed that they all date from immediately after enclosure. The actual dates of construction are usually undocumented, but a careful analysis of the standing buildings can tell us a great deal. In Swaffham Bulbeck parish, where enclosure was completed by 1801, of the three outlying farmsteads within the new enclosures on the chalklands, two were built soon after 1801, but the third, New England Farm, is dated 1833. In the adjacent

Plate 20 New Wimpole. These houses in 'Tudor' style were built between 1840 and 1855 for workers on the estate.

Plate 21 House at Comberton. An example of the standard type of timber-framed seventeenth- and early-eighteenth-century house in the county. This one dates from around 1650. Though once a single farmhouse it is now two dwellings, having been subdivided in the nineteenth century when the population of the village increased rapidly.

Plate 22 The landscape of parliamentary enclosure. Here, in south-east Cambridgeshire, the rigidly geometric fields and isolated farmsteads are the product of the nineteenth-century enclosure of open downland. The thick curving hedge running from top left to bottom centre is the Fleam Dyke. The curving line from bottom left to top right is the long-abandoned Newmarket Railway. The main road is the London–Norwich

Plate 23 Barrington. The huge village green is clearly visible. The encroachment on it in the centre probably dates from the seventeenth century. The lack of houses along the right-hand edge of the green is due to their removal as a result of emparking, perhaps in the eighteenth century.

Plate 24 Conington Hall. Built in the early eighteenth century, the house is surrounded by a small and unpretentious park. This example of the work of the local squirearchy is more typical of the county than is the massive emparking of Wimpole.

Plate 25 Egerton House, near Newmarket. The basic field pattern here is the result of nineteenth-century parliamentary enclosure, but it has been modified later for the breeding of racehorses. Hence the small paddocks and thick shelter belts.

parish of Swaffham Prior, finally enclosed around 1814, three farmsteads were soon erected, but a fourth, Cadenham Farm, dates from around 1840.

Although parliamentary enclosure was mainly concerned with the making of new fields, it often also rapidly changed the form of some villages and prepared the way for modern building expansion of the late nineteenth and twentieth centuries. Villages which originally had greens sometimes lost them on enclosure, when they were divided up and the land allotted to adjacent landowners. Encroachments on village greens had, of course, gone on centuries before enclosure. At Barrington, the huge village green has a large circular area within it near its north side occupied by houses and their gardens (Plate 23). Judging by the existing buildings there this encroachment had taken place by 1657 which is the earliest dated house.

But it was parliamentary enclosure which saw the end of many village greens. At Kingston in west Cambridgeshire, up to 1815 the village lay around a large square green where four roads met. This green was then divided up and during the later nineteenth century was completely built over. The village thus changed its layout and character completely, though the original edges of the green can still be seen as old fence lines behind the modern houses. The hamlet of Willingham in the parish of Carlton-cum-Willingham in the south-east of the county also had a similar square green. By the time of enclosure in 1800 this hamlet was largely deserted. The green was then enclosed and the resulting allotments built over to provide homes for the increasing number of people in the parish. The result was that the hamlet grew up again in an entirely different form.

At Great Shelford the picture is slightly different. There, between the two original Saxon villages, was an open triangular area of meadowland. As both villages grew during the medieval period, houses were built all along the edges of this meadow and gradually the two villages became one. This produced a central open space, called High Green, which functioned as a village green even though it did not originate as one. On enclosure in 1834 this 'green' was divided up into long plots fronting the old houses, and turned into gardens. As the century advanced, houses were built on these plots, the earliest in about 1845, and by 1900 half of the old green was built over. In the last thirty years, as Shelford has been drawn into the suburban sprawl of Cambridge, more and more new houses have been erected on these plots and the green has disappeared for ever. Once again though, in spite of modern development, one can still see the boundaries of the original Saxon meadow. Customers of the butcher still have to walk up a long drive to buy their meat, for this shop, a seventeenth-century house, is on the edge of the meadow eighty yards back from the present road.

By the 1880s the rural landscape of upland Cambridgeshire had taken on its modern appearance. Apart from the massive modern expansion of the villages, little has happened since to change it. This does not mean that the more recent alterations are of no interest. They sometimes are. For example, in the east of the county on the higher parts of the parishes of Cheveley, Woodditton, Stetchworth and Swaffham Prior and extending across the county boundary into West Suffolk, the modern fields have a pattern virtually unique in this country (Plate 25). Though the basic shapes of geometrical form are the result of late-eighteenth- and early-nineteenth-century downland enclosure the actual fields are bounded by wide shelter belts of trees and sub-divided into smaller tree-lined paddocks set with tree clumps. This is the result of the late-nineteenth- and early-twentieth-century growth of the racehorse training and breeding industry, centred on Newmarket, whose racecourses lie mainly within Cambridgeshire. These characteristic fields, often centred on large Victorian and Edwardian houses and stable ranges, are a unique and well-marked feature of this corner of the English landscape.

SELECT BIBLIOGRAPHY

Darby, H. C. *The Cambridge Region* (1938).
R.C.H.M. *Cambridgeshire*, Vols I and II (1968 and 1972).
Tate, W. E. 'Cambridgeshire Field Systems', *Procs. C.A.S.* (1944).
V.C.H. *Cambridgeshire*, Vol. II (1948).

6. The drainage of the fens

The general background. The drainage of Swaffham and Burwell Fens.

The general background

IN SOME RESPECTS the history of the fenland landscape from 1600 is very similar to that of the uplands. The same types of houses are found there, there is the same population explosion during the nineteenth century and on the fen islands the medieval common fields were swept away by parliamentary enclosure between 1790 and 1857. But the dominating aspect of the fenland landscape today is the result of the work of fen drainage from the seventeenth century onwards. It is to this work and its remains in the modern landscape that we must now direct our attention (Fig. 13).

In late medieval times the northern silt fens were rich pasturelands supporting large flocks of sheep and bringing great prosperity to the farmers there. On the southern peat fens there were large areas of drained pasture, grazed by innumerable sheep and cattle, and even arable land along the fen edges, bounded and crossed by a multitude of ditches. Beyond these were thousands of acres of 'summer lands', that is ground dry enough to be grazed or cropped in the summer months, as well as smaller areas of 'winter lands' which could be grazed throughout the year. In the late-medieval period the fens were extensively rather than intensively used and such exploitation as there was took place on a local scale. As Professor Darby has written,

"The fourteenth and fifteenth centuries were marked not by visionary projects for a general drainage, but by the diligent and humdrum labours of successive generations . . . battling against the difficulties of drains." The economic and technological basis of society was not yet ready for any great drainage work.

From this statement one must make an exception, that of the work of Bishop Morton. He seems to have been the first person after the Romans to plan and carry out a large-scale drainage scheme. As early as 1490 he grasped the problem that will always be a major difficulty, that of carrying the waters of upland rivers across the fens and into the sea without flooding the adjacent fenland. In the late-medieval period these upland rivers, the Welland, Nene, Ouse, Cam, Lark and Wissey, all wound their way across the flat fens to the sea by devious routes. In winter or at other times of heavy rain the flood waters overtopped the banks and drowned the surrounding fens. Morton's solution, taken up by all the later drainage engineers, was to speed up the flow of the rivers by constructing long straight artificial cuts so that the water was sent quickly into the Wash. Morton organised the construction of a massive drain twelve miles long, forty feet wide and four feet deep which collected the water of the River Nene near Peterborough and carried it straight across the fens through Whittlesey and Elm parishes back into the old course of the river at Guyhirn, south-west of Wisbech (Fig. 13). The cut bearing his name, Morton's Leam, is still used to this day. It has, as with all fenland rivers and drains, been recut and modified many times since it was constructed.

This is a feature of the fens which is both the despair of the lover of beautiful countryside, and the fascination for the landscape historian. All fenland drains and cuts look alike and together with the endless flat land in which they lie give the impression of a dull, lifeless and uninteresting

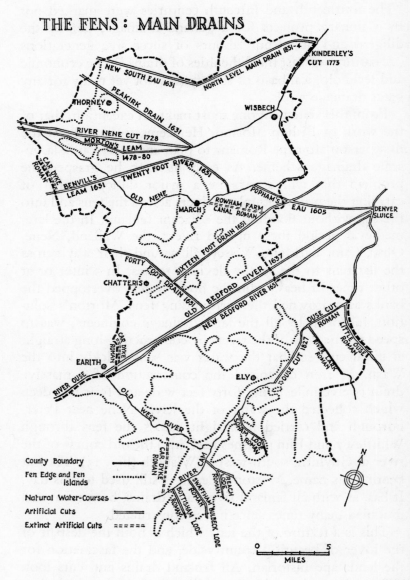

THE FENS: MAIN DRAINS

NEW SOUTH EAU 1631
NORTH LEVEL MAIN DRAIN 1831-4
KINDERLEY'S CUT 1773
THORNEY
PEAKIRK DRAIN 1631
WISBECH
RIVER NENE CUT 1728
MORTON'S LEAM 1478-80
CAR DYKE ROMAN
BENVILL'S LEAM 1631
TWENTY FOOT RIVER 1651
OLD NENE
MARCH
ROWHAM FARM CANAL ROMAN
POPHAM'S EAU 1605
DENVER SLUICE
FORTY FOOT DRAIN 1651
SIXTEEN FOOT DRAIN 1651
CHATTERIS
OLD BEDFORD RIVER 1637
NEW BEDFORD RIVER 1651
OUSE CUT ROMAN
LITTLE OUSE ROMAN
CAR DYKE ROMAN
OUSE CUT 1827
RIVER LARK ROMAN
EARITH
ELY
RIVER OUSE
OLD WEST RIVER
CAR DYKE ROMAN
SOHAM LODE ROMAN
RIVER CAM
SWAFFHAM ROMAN
REACH ROMAN
BOTTISHAM LODE
BULBECK LODE

County Boundary
Fen Edge and Fen Islands
Natural Water-Courses
Artificial Cuts
Extinct Artificial Cuts

N

0   5
MILES

Fig. 13

landscape. But for those prepared to carry out the necessary fieldwork and documentary work, the fenland landscape comes alive with history. Almost every drain and watercourse, whatever its size and form, can be dated, its original purpose ascertained, and its countless alterations understood. Soon the meaningless pattern takes on a new dimension and the jigsaw of drains falls into a complete and magnificent picture of man's conquest of nature.

The achievement of Morton stands alone in the late medieval period but it was the beginning of the great work which was to follow. First, however, there was a period of stagnation and even regression. The Dissolution of the great religious houses in the middle of the sixteenth century brought to an end the long period of monastic control of much of the fenland. In the resulting confused buying and selling of ecclesiastical land what overall organisation for drainage there was fell into abeyance. The result was a marked deterioration in the state of the fenlands. An Elizabethan survey of Thorney, quoted by Darby, shows this well. "It containeth 16,000 acres of fen grounds . . . which in memory have been dry and firm lye now surrounded (for the most part) by water, by reason of the drains ever sithence uncast and other the infinite watercourses suffered to grow up."

All was not lost, however, for the new generation of landowners, aware of new ideas and techniques in agriculture, and with the determination and financial resources to improve their lands, were arriving in increasing numbers. A new climate of opinion and hope was developing which was to spread rapidly. Not that the new ideas were quickly accepted or put into practice immediately. As well as being a supreme example of man's will to overcome his environment, the history of the drainage of the fens is a long story of his basic conservatism, greed and stubbornness. Nevertheless by the late sixteenth century a new spirit was abroad and men started to consider ways and means of improving the fens. Some small-scale drainage was undertaken in these years. For example in a document of 1591 there are references to new enclosures of fen near Ely, and a little later landowners in Elm parish in the northern fens carried out some minor drainage work. Between 1594 and 1600 there was reclamation of land round the edges of Soham Mere, a vast marshy lake on the fen edge between Soham and Wicken. These were all in the medieval tradition of piecemeal assarting and drainage but they indicate the efforts then being made to improve the fenland.

The beginning of the seventeenth century saw much more important ideas being developed. Many schemes, both on a large and a small scale, were mooted and though lack of capital prevented their being undertaken, the idea of carrying out large-scale drainage works was rapidly becoming an accepted aim. In 1605 a group of wealthy businessmen, led by Sir John Popham the Lord Chief Justice, agreed to drain an area of land around Upwell in Cambridgeshire and Norfolk. They undertook to construct and maintain various water-courses and in return they were to be allotted land from the fen. The scheme collapsed, though some land was reclaimed, but work recommenced in 1609 and the result was the construction of another new cut or channel to carry water from one of the choked distributaries of the River Nene, in Elm parish, seven miles across the fens to the River Ouse at Salters Lode in Norfolk. This cut, still known as Popham's Eau, remains to this day (Fig. 13). More important here was the concept of carrying out drainage by financing the actual engineering work in return for allotments in the newly drained land. This was to become characteristic of drainage work later in the century.

Some major new landlords could and did organise their own drainage scheme. At Littleport a great deal of land was purchased in 1602 by Sir John Peyton, Lieutenant of the Tower of London. A survey of the manor made a few years later states that 1490 acres of fenland had been embanked and divided into twelve plots of meadow, another 294½ acres enclosed but not embanked and a further 200 acres were in the process of being enclosed.

By the 1620s, probably as a result of silting at the mouths of the fenland rivers away in the Wash to the north, flooding and bad drainage were increasing. Something had to be done. In 1630 some of the larger landowners in the area approached Francis, fourth Earl of Bedford, owner of some 20,000 acres of land at Thorney. He agreed to drain the whole of the southern fenlands including parts of Lincolnshire, Huntingdonshire and Norfolk. In return the Earl was to have 95,000 acres of land from the fens to cover the cost. Of these, 40,000 acres were to be used to maintain the drainage and 12,000 acres were to go to the Crown. In 1631, thirteen other wealthy businessmen joined the Earl and calling themselves Adventurers, because they adventured their capital, formed themselves into the Bedford Level Corporation. This Corporation obtained the services of Cornelius Vermuyden, the great Dutch drainage engineer, who had already carried out a number of drainage schemes elsewhere in England. At last the major work of drainage commenced, a process which was to change the face of the Cambridgeshire fens for ever.

Vermuyden's plans for the fens were at first mainly concerned in preventing water from the great rivers from flooding the adjacent land. He reasoned that if the river waters could be passed into the sea quickly and safely there would be no problem in obtaining rich agricultural land all over the fens. His solution, the same as that of Bishop Morton and Sir John Popham, was to cut new straight embanked channels which would, he said, shorten the river courses and increase their gradient. Work started in 1631 and for six years the fenlands were filled with thousands of men cutting huge channels across the landscape. It is a great pity that no contemporary description of this work has come down to us for it must have been an enormous undertaking. The nearest parallel is the building of the railways in the nineteenth century, but it is not a close one, for here in the fens the work was on a larger scale considering the area of land involved and took place over a very short period of time. In 1631 two large cuts were completed to carry water from the River Nene near Peterborough across the northern edge of the county and back into the Nene lower downstream. One of these was the New South Eau in Thorney parish, which still exists as a major drain today. The other, The Peakirk Drain, seventeen feet wide and ten miles long, has since disappeared as a major channel but its line is still preserved by the straight run of the modern A47 road between East Wryde Farm, east of Thorney, and Guyhirn, in Elm parish. Further south Morton's Leam was recut and a new channel called Benvill's Leam, ten miles long, was made across Whittlesey parish to carry water from yet another branch of the Nene. Other cuts were made in Norfolk and a number of small cut-off channels and sluices were constructed.

Vermuyden's greatest work, however, was the Bedford River (now the Old Bedford River). This was a truly gigantic piece of work, a straight channel seventy feet wide and twenty-one miles long which carried the waters of the River Ouse from Earith, just inside Huntingdonshire, right across the Cambridgeshire fens to Denver in Norfolk. This completely by-passed the old course of the Ouse which flowed to the east of Ely. This fantastic piece of work still stands as one of the major engineering achievements of this country (Fig. 13 and Plate 26).

All this was not accomplished without opposition. Many people did not want the fens drained, others thought the methods used were wrong, and many smaller land-owners, tenants and labourers sincerely believed they would lose much of their livelihood as a result of drainage. Much of this opposition was confined to the publishing of pamphlets but some led to riots and the breaking down of drainage works. The work went on, however, and in 1637 the 'Bedford Level' was declared drained. At once there was an outcry that this was not so. Though the fenland as a whole was much improved many places were not and large areas were still being flooded. New works were started but before they were completed, political events overtook them and the county was plunged into civil war. All the drainage attempts stopped and the completed works were abandoned or neglected.

After the war Vermuyden returned and started again. The old cuts were repaired and a number of new ones were made to improve the internal drainage of parts of the fens and to continue to remove upland water. Of these the Forty Foot Drain running from near Ramsey in Huntingdonshire through Benwick, Doddington and Chatteris parishes to Welshes Dam on the Bedford River, ten and a half miles long, was a major one. The Sixteen Foot Drain from near Chatteris north-west through Wimblington to the Nene at Upwell, nine miles long, was another. The largest of these works was the New Bedford River which was cut almost parallel to the original (now Old) Bedford River. High barrier banks were constructed on each side of the two 'rivers' and the great strip of land between them, now called The Washes, was left to act as a reservoir for surplus water in time of flood (Plate 26).

By 1652 this was all completed and again the fens were declared to be drained. Then the 95,000 acres which had been allotted to the Adventurers in return for the capital spent on the works were finally laid out. These were blocks of land of various sizes distributed all over the fens. In many places these allotments were the first enclosures ever made there and most of them are still traceable today. Some are still shown on maps as Adventurers' Grounds or Lands or Fen and with a little practice one learns to recognise the boundaries and internal drains of these and other unnamed ones by their shape and layout where compared to the later enclosures around them. More rarely one finds similar fields called Undertakers' Lands. These are the lands allotted to the men who *undertook* to carry out the actual work of drainage as opposed to the Adventurers who put up the money.

With the achievement of reasonably drained fenland the area prospered. Most of the fens continued to be used for pasture, though this was much better than before. But in many places improving landlords and competent farmers soon enclosed large areas of land much of which was cropped. In an account dated 1683 of the activities of some French refugees who had settled in Thorney it is stated that cabbage and cereals were being grown on newly reclaimed fen. Though the actual fields these refugees made have not been identified exactly, they must have been in the area of the present French Drove and French Farm whose names still give us the clue to these pioneers.

Elsewhere other late-seventeenth-century enclosures still remain in the landscape, though they are not at first sight very different from later ones (Plate 28). It often requires detailed documentary research as well as fieldwork to identify them but if this is done the story of the slow reclamation of the fens is possible. In the fenlands of Sutton parish, west of Ely, is a whole series of variously orientated blocks of fields which, in the fens, usually indicates different periods of drainage and enclosure (Fig. 9B). Indeed one block is cut by the Old Bedford River, showing that its enclosure must date from before 1637. In the magnificent records of the Bedford Level Corporation, which are the basis for all work on the history of fenland drainage, there is a note referring to lands belonging to a Mr Hammond here in 1656. Mr Hammond's land is still recognisable on the ground, north-west of Sutton Gault, as a long strip of enclosed fen bounded by a continuous ditch, subdivided into long, narrow fields and bisected by its own main drain still called Hammond's Eau. This is obviously a single mid-seventeenth-century piece of fenland enclosure carried out by one enterprising farmer. Further south on the side of another rectangular block of fenland fields is the modern Tubb's Farm. In 1665, when describing the position of a break in the bank of the Old Bedford River, the Bedford Corporation Records note that it is "in Bedford North Bank neere Tubbes his house". This is exactly where Tubb's Farm stands and its land is still recognisable. So here we have evidence not only of enclosure and drainage but the establishment of outlying farmsteads as well. If we look carefully in this area of Sutton Fen we can see a whole set of variously orientated blocks of fenland fields, all presumably the work of individual farmers and most apparently dating from the seventeenth century.

Perhaps the best remains of late-seventeenth-century enclosure can be seen at Soham. Up to 1664, the fenland south of the village was largely occupied by Soham Mere, a roughly circular area of water covering some 1500 acres. Encroachment around the edges of this mere by the people of both Wicken and Soham had been going on for centuries. The small ditched fields lying round the continuous drain marking the boundary of the mere in the seventeenth century still survive today and some of these, called The Bracks, are recorded in a Soham Court Roll of 1393 as *Brakelake*, that is newly broken land near a stream. Other fields around the mere date from the late sixteenth century. But in 1664 a concerted plan resulted in the total drainage and enclosure of the mere as well as much of the other fenland in the parish and the details are recorded in a document belonging to Pembroke College. The fields that were formed in the bed of the mere at this time remain today, as does the central main drain, the twelve-foot-wide ring drain and the Counter Bank which protected it from flooding. Most of this newly drained land was used as pasture but elsewhere in the same parish "Divers parts of the fens have been converted to arable for corne and hemp. Several new houses have been erected by the new owners of the fen grounds."

The years following the mid-seventeenth-century drainage works then were prosperous ones. The improvement to the land was marked and everywhere farmers were enclosing land and building farmsteads in the fen. Sir William Dugdale who visited the fens in 1657 reported that onions, peas and hemp were being grown near Willingham, while north-east of Ely he saw flax, hemp, oats, wheat, cole-seed and rape. At Whittlesey he noted that there were rich meadows and cornland as well as plantations of fruit trees, willows and vegetables. The fenland even produced poets who wrote of the achievements.

> I sing Floods muzled and the Ocean tam'd
> Luxurious Rivers govern'd and reclaim'd,
> Water with Banks confin'd as in a Gaol
> Till kinder Sluces let them go on Bail.
> Streams curb'd with Dammes like Bridles, taught t'obey
> And run as strait, as if they saw their way.

But this prosperity was only temporary. Very soon new and unforeseen difficulties appeared that were to bring disaster to the county's fenland.

Of these, by far the most important was the lowering of the surface of the southern peat fens as a result of the drainage. Neither Vermuyden nor any of the other drainage engineers foresaw this. As the water was removed from the vast thickness of peat which covered the southern fens the surface dried out, the peat compacted and the land sank. In addition the dry surface was then either blown away by the wind or wasted away by bacteriological action. Further north on the silt fens there was some shrinkage, though it was very slight when compared with the peat fen. This produced the effect of making the southern peat fens lower than the silt fens nearer the sea and thus it became difficult to carry the upland water across the fens. The large channels and new cuts as well as all the old rivers had to be embanked as the surrounding land sank and in a very short time they were flowing at levels considerably higher than the adjacent fens. This meant that danger from flooding when the banks burst was increased and also that the cost of maintaining these banks was considerable. Even more important was the fact that the water within the fens themselves could no longer flow into the main channels. As Professor Darby has said, "it is difficult to exaggerate the importance of this factor . . . of shrinkage in the failure to drain the Fenland."

The present landscape shows this lowering of the peat surface very clearly (Plates 26 and 27). All the major channels and many of the smaller ones stand high above the surrounding land. Perhaps the most remarkable view in the fens is on the Littleport–March road (the B1411), where it runs parallel to the New Bedford River. To the south-east is flat fenland, but immediately north-west of the road is a massive embankment over twenty feet high which is the retaining bank of the Bedford River along which the waters of the River Ouse pass safely to the sea over fifteen feet above the fens. In the late seventeenth century these banks which had been only recently built were not safe. The early drainage workers made them by digging out the surrounding peat and piling it up alongside the rivers and channels.

However, being of peat these banks dried out and when under pressure in times of flood often burst, with disastrous results. The Bedford Level records of the late seventeenth century are full of complaints of flooding and orders to repair broken banks. Thus in 1696 under 'Works to be Done' we find "to amend the worst places of the banks of this level from Isleham Chair round by Ely, and so up to Soham on the North of Soham River – £110". When the weakness of these peat banks was understood the underlying clay was dug out and used for rebuilding them. However this cost a great deal of money and took generations to complete, and as the peat continued to shrink and the land sank these banks had to be continually heightened.

The results of both the breaking of the banks in times of flood and the constant battle to repair them and keep them safe are still visible in the fens. Many old breaks are marked by semi-circular bends in otherwise straight banks. These are often called Gulls or Gullets, and a particularly good one exists on the north-west side of the Old Bedford River in Sutton parish at a place called The Gullet (Fig. 9B). The remains of the repair and rebuilding work also take the form of now waterlogged pits where clay has been dug out and taken to adjacent banks. A very large pit lies south-west of Mepal village near the New Bedford River and is still called the Gault Hole after the clay which was dug there. A group of much smaller ones lies on the north-east side of Bottisham Lode, in Lode parish. The work of repairing banks, dredging channels and cutting new ones which was started in the mid-seventeenth century had to go on endlessly and still goes on today.

In the late seventeenth century much of this work was in vain. Celia Fiennes, who crossed the fens in 1695, said that the area around Sutton was 'mostly under water'. What had seemed to be the beginning of great prosperity in 1652 when the major drainage works were completed had become

Plate 26 The Old and New Bedford Rivers in winter. The great expanse of The Washes between the rivers holds the flood waters of the River Ouse behind the high barrier banks. These protect the adjacent fenland, here actually below sea level.

Plate 27 The Washes of the River Cam in flood time. The actual river is in the middle distance but here in the winter floods the land on either side of it is under water. The high wash bank on the left of the picture prevents the water drowning the fens, here nearly twelve feet below it.

Plate 28 The peat fens. Here on the fens, east of Doddington, the complicated pattern of pre-drainage water-courses can only be appreciated from the air, though they are all actually visible on the ground. The large water-course in the right-hand corner is the Sixteen Foot Drain, cut by Vermuyden in 1651. The rectangular fields to the left of it all date from the late seventeenth century, though the farmsteads are later.

Plate 29   Site of windpump, Bottisham Fen. The rectangular pond is all that is left of a windpumping mill, erected in 1821 to drain the surrounding land. The pond acted as a reservoir for the mill which stood on its left-hand side and lifted the water into the adjacent high-level drain.

Plate 30 Stretham Engine. Built 1831 to drain the Waterbeach Level, it still retains most of its original machinery. The left-hand block with the chimney is the Boiler House with the walled coalyard in front. The tall central block is the Engine House, while the small building on the right contains the huge scoop wheel. The building on the extreme right houses a diesel engine, installed in 1924. In the foreground is the main Engine Drain.

Plate 31 Engine Drain, Swaffham Fen. This straight ditch, five miles long, is the Main or Engine Drain of this area. It was cut in 1821 to enable the fen to be drained by the first steam-pumping engine in the county.

a disaster by 1700. However, the fenland farmers found an answer even though it was a somewhat inefficient one. This was the windpump which enabled water in the low-lying fens to be lifted from ditch to drain and from drain to river and so keep large parts of the fens reasonably dry. These windpumps were very similar to the more normal windmill used for grinding corn, except that instead of driving grind-stones they turned large-diameter wooden wheels fitted with paddles or ladles which lifted or rather scooped water a few feet at a time out of the lower drains into higher ones. By the early eighteenth century there were a number of these windpumps in operation and as time went by more and more were erected so that gradually the whole fenland became dotted by countless mills whose slowly turning sails showed that they were engaged in the work of draining the fens.

All these windpumps have now gone. The sole remaining survivor, now re-erected in Wicken Fen, is of no great antiquity and hardly typical. But the sites of these wind-pumps may still be discovered once the peculiar form that their remains take is recognised. The actual structures themselves have usually left no trace at all, though occa-sionally a slight mound, with brick foundation rubble and other occupation debris, in the corner of a field near a main drain turns out to be the former site of a windpump. More often it is the associated waterworks that show where mills were. Some had small ponds or reservoirs next to them into which water flowed before it was lifted, and some of these still remain. There are two in the Swaffham Fen district along Bottisham Lode (Plate 29). These rectangular reser-voirs have to be distinguished from almost identical clay-pits in similar situations, but the existence of old approach drains and the definite rectangular outline usually makes it clear when one is dealing with an old mill site. More often there is no reservoir, but the drains which led the water to these mills often still remain and can be recognised on large-scale maps as well as on the ground even though they have long been abandoned for drainage purposes. There are often places on the edges of rivers or main drains where three or four minor drains all meet in a series of sharp bends or in a semi-circular ditch which indicates the site of an old windpump. The sites of all the eighteenth-century windpumps in Waterbeach Fen have been identified by looking for these characteristics in conjunction with old maps and drainage records.

The first of these windpumps were erected in the late seventeenth and early eighteenth centuries by individual farmers whose land was being flooded and for whom the erection of the windpump was the only possible solution to their problems. As the eighteenth century advanced, however, it became obvious that in many areas a much-improved drainage could be obtained by co-operation between landowners. Gradually groups of landowners and farmers set up Drainage Commissions to enable the internal drainage of blocks of fenland to be organised on a proper basis. All the land in these areas was taxed and the money spent on erecting and maintaining windpumps and the cutting and cleaning-out of drains. The organisation of the work was directed by a committee of landowners, called Drainage Commissioners, who employed men to look after the main drains and the windpumps and who also saw that all minor drains were kept clear and in good order by their respective owners. The first such Drainage Commission was set up by Act of Parliament in 1727 to organise the drainage of the fenlands of Haddenham, Wilburton and parts of Sutton and Stretham, known as the Haddenham Level.

In the following sixty years a whole host of private acts were passed to set up Drainage Commissions and with the help of the ubiquitous windpump the disasters of the late seventeenth century were overcome and the fenlands entered a new period of prosperity. With this improvement went a new phase of enclosure. As more and more land became reasonably dry for the first time, enterprising farmers were quick to enclose it by dividing it up into new fields, each bounded by long straight ditches linked to the main drains. The process can, by detailed research into parish records and Drainage Commissions' minute books, be worked out for many places in the fens. More important, it can still be recognised on the ground today, though it is usually necessary to have a large-scale Ordnance Survey map to see the details. Very often each block of these eighteenth-century new fields, though in itself geometrically laid out and divided into rectangular fields, was for reasons of convenience of drainage set at slightly different angles to older blocks of fields. Therefore as time went on the whole pattern of modern fields slowly emerged, not as huge areas of similar fields as they appear at first sight, but as many different blocks all orientated in slightly different directions. The result is that today we can see, even in the most uncompromising piece of fenland, which fields originated in the medieval period, which are the mid-seventeenth-century Adventurers' allotments, which are later seventeenth-century enclosures and which are eighteenth- and nineteenth-century fields.

The parliamentary enclosure movement was almost the last stage in this development. For as well as ending the existence of the wastes and common fields of the uplands and most of the common fields around the villages on the fen islands, parliamentary enclosure also enabled large tracts of still-open fen to be divided into the fields we can see there today. From 1791, when much of the fenland of Wimblington was enclosed, until 1857 when Grunty Fen, now in Wilburton parish, was enclosed, thousands of acres of fenland were divided up and drained. The amount of fen, as opposed to fen-island common field, that was enclosed during the years varied from parish to parish depending on how much enclosure had been carried out privately at an earlier date.

With these private and parliamentary enclosures of the eighteenth and nineteenth centuries went new farmsteads. They were set up all over the newly drained fens, often in remote places. But they were not placed as haphazardly as they appear today. By the eighteenth century the problem of peat shrinkage was known, if not understood. Any building placed on the peat soon fell down as its foundations tipped and walls cracked. Farmers did their best to place their new buildings where shrinkage was least likely to affect them and they usually chose the silt and gravel beds of the old pre-drainage streams and rivers which, as the surrounding peat shrank, gradually emerged as relatively stable, long, low ridges known as roddons. Therefore the vast majority of fenland farmsteads of the eighteenth and nineteenth centuries were built either on these roddons, or along the banks of main drains or rivers where there was also stable ground. These roddons can be seen winding their way across the fens as light-coloured low banks contrasting with the surrounding black peat, often with farmsteads safely perched upon them. Of course not all the chosen places were permanently safe and many farmhouses and other buildings collapsed. Even those that remain are sometimes characterised by cracked and tilted walls and by iron tie-rods holding them together.

The names of some of these late fenland farmsteads are just as interesting as the earlier medieval ones and often give us clues as to their builders and history. Of particular interest is Colony Farm in a remote part of Manea parish on the side of the Old Bedford River. The site was selected in the 1840s for an Owenite co-operative experiment whereby between 100 and 200 colonists came to work 150 acres of land in common. They even published a periodical called the *Working Bee*. But after a year the scheme collapsed and Gardener's *Directory of Cambridgeshire* for 1851 said "But alas! for the mutability of human institutions! the socialists have fled." Only the name survives to record this minor nineteenth-century social experiment.

The tiny hamlet of Welshes Dam, also on the north side of the Old Bedford River, takes its name from Edmund Welsh, one of the contractors for the drainage works in 1651. He was in charge of the building of a sluice gate here where the Forty Foot Drain emptied into the Bedford River and the houses which later grew up here took their name from Welsh and his dam.

Few of these fenland farmsteads and cottages are of any architectural or aesthetic merit. Many have been rebuilt again and again. But, dull though they are to look at, they all reflect the slow improvement of drainage and agricultural prosperity of the fenlands over the last 300 years.

Though the eighteenth century saw the recovery of the fens, there were still problems, and by the early nineteenth century the worst of these was the continual shrinkage of the peat. The advent of the windpump had solved this problem during the eighteenth century but as the level of the fenland continued to drop even windpumps with their limited lifting power could not cope. This was partly overcome by constructing double or even triple windpumps, by which water was gradually lifted by one pump at a time. By 1821 there were two windpumps working together at Littleport Bridge, draining Burnt Fen, while at Soham Mere by the same date there were three windpumps lying close together in a line and lifting the water from the land of the old mere.[1] At Soham Mere the site of all three windpumps can still be seen on the ground. Even so, this method of draining was not satisfactory and once again the

[1] Baker's Map of Cambridgeshire (1821) shows well over 200 windpumps in the county's fens.

fenlands were threatened with disaster. As before, however, it was saved by the introduction of a new technique, this time the steam engine.

An inscription on the existing engine house built for the Littleport and Downham Drainage Commissioners in 1830 on the side of the New Bedford River records this in verse:

> These Fens have oft times been by Water drown'd.
> Science a remedy in Water found.
> The powers of Steam she said shall be employ'd
> And the Destroyer by Itself destroy'd.

The first steam engine to be erected in Cambridgeshire was in 1821 at Upware for the Swaffham and Bottisham Drainage Commissioners, and by 1850 there were at least fourteen others at work in the county. These were huge rotative beam engines, housed in tall brick sheds with a long, low building on one side which held the boilers and a smaller building on the other in which was the scoop wheel. The latter was similar to the wheels on the windpumps but much larger and capable of lifting as much as fifty tons of water a minute. As one of these engines was capable of draining as much land as ten or more windpumps had done, and much more efficiently too, the old windpumps were gradually abandoned and the drainage channels altered so that the water in a single drainage district was directed to the one steam engine. Today most of these great monuments to nineteenth-century industrial power have gone. The characteristic tripartite building comprising boiler, engine and scoop-wheel houses, erected in 1830, still remains on the New Bedford River in Downham parish, while a similar but much smaller one built in 1841 for the Burwell Drainage Commission at Upware has also managed to survive. The pride of the fens however is the Stretham Engine, built in 1831 for the Waterbeach Level Drainage Commission

(Plate 30). Here we can see the only remaining steam pumping engine with all its machinery and buildings still intact. It is a remarkable structure and it should be visited by anyone interested in the history of the fens.

Though most of these 'Saviours of the Fens' have now gone they have all left traces in the landscape. Sometimes these are hard to find. The site of the first steam engine to be erected in the county is now a patch of uneven ground, with bricks and slate scattered around, buried in a small thicket at Upware close to the bank of the River Cam. And its main drain, now long filled in, can still be seen as a shallow depression running across the adjacent fen, while its outfall channel where the water was thrown into the river is still clearly marked below the flood protection banks.

All over the fens the main 'Engine Drains' which were cut across the fens to link these engines with the minor drains still survive, even when the engines themselves have gone. There are now other means of lifting the water from the fens, but the great drains dug for the steam engines still exist and are still used. They are often marked on maps as 'Main Drain' or 'Engine Drain' or 'Commissioners' Drain', but even where they are not named, it soon becomes easy to pick them out from the multitude of other channels. Like the major high-level drainage cuts they sometimes cut obliquely across the older pre-nineteenth-century field drains, making use of some almost imperceptible low-lying level. Elsewhere they twist and turn through many angles to pick up water from the many and various blocks of fields which pre-date them. An example of the former type may be seen in Swaffham Fen in the south-east of the fens where the main engine drain runs absolutely straight for over three miles along the course of an extinct river (Plate 31). At Mepal south-east of the Old Bedford River is an example of an engine drain which turns constantly to take the water from individual blocks of fields dating from the seventeenth to the nineteenth century. Another characteristic of these main internal fen drains is that they often pass through tunnels or culverts below the high-level channels. Thus the water in Padney Fen, in Soham parish, though it lies adjacent to the River Cam, is drawn along the main internal drain of Soham Fen for three and a half miles passing under the higher level Soham Lode before it is pumped into the River Ouse near Ely.

By the end of the nineteenth century yet another pumping technique came to the fens, that of the diesel engine. These, driving centrifugal pumps instead of the old-fashioned scoop wheel, brought a new level of ease and efficiency to fenland drainage. Soon the fenland was, and still is, dotted by small brick or wooden sheds which house the engines and pumps. These, while hardly as picturesque as the wind-pumps or as impressive as the steam engines, continue to drain the fens more efficiently than ever. A particularly good place to see this method of drainage in operation is along the B1098 road between How Fen in Chatteris and Boat Bridge near Wimblington. The road runs parallel to the Sixteen Foot Main Drain cut by Vermuyden in 1651. To the west of the drain is a whole series of small blocks of enclosed fenland, Normoor, Benson's Fen, Block Fen, etc., each of which is drained by a small diesel pump. The result is that one passes the most motley and decrepit collection of brick and wooden shacks that it is possible to see anywhere. Yet each houses an engine and pump on whose efficiency depends the very existence of each piece of fenland. In recent years there has been a tendency to replace or supplant even the diesel engine by the more convenient electric pumps and these too, in even smaller buildings, are becoming a characteristic feature of the fenland landscape.

The eighteenth and nineteenth centuries also saw the

continuation of Vermuyden's main work in cutting large, straight channels to carry upland water across the fens as well as to remove water lifted by the various types of pumping machinery (Fig. 13). These have all remained in the present landscape as massive embanked channels, gashing their way across the fens and overriding all earlier drains in their path. The main channel of the River Nene from Peterborough to Guyhirn, a truly gigantic cut, was made in 1728, while the massive diversion of the River Ouse between Ely and Littleport was constructed in 1827. The latter left the old sinuous course of the river away to the east, and this still exists as a high-level minor channel. In 1834 the North Level Main Drain was cut across the northern fenland of the county.

The bare recital of names and dates of such channels perhaps means little on the printed page, but when one sees them on the ground the staggering achievements of the history of fen drainage in Cambridgeshire become clear. When we cross a large water-course at Tydd Gate in the extreme north of the county it may seem of little consequence. But that water-course is the North Level Main Drain which runs into the River Nene a mile to the east. And to the south-west it runs exactly straight for over seven miles through the parishes of Tydd St Giles, Newton and Parson Drove to Clough's Cross where it turns and runs west for a further six and a half miles through Thorney parish to its beginning in the north-west corner of Cambridgeshire. It is this drain which carries the water from most of the fens in the north of the county, as well as those in parts of south Lincolnshire, safely to the sea.

So the county's fens are now drained. But the process has not ended, nor will it ever end. The work of drainage started by the Romans nearly 2000 years ago has gone on and will go on as long as men need to gain a living from what is now the richest agricultural land in England.

o

The Drainage of Swaffham and Burwell Fens

The best way of understanding the real complexities of the history of fen drainage is to examine in detail the history of one small area. This has been carried out in the Swaffham and Burwell Fens in the south-east of the county.[2] It is not certain if this area is typical of the rest of the county, for little work has been done elsewhere. Nevertheless it is perhaps worth looking at this area to see how a small piece of flat fenland has developed from a marshy wilderness to rich agricultural land and how the landscape historian can trace this growth (Figs. 14–17).

The Swaffham and Burwell Fens are a roughly rectangular area bounded on the north-west by the River Cam, and on the other sides by the uplands of Wicken, Burwell, Swaffham Prior, Swaffham Bulbeck, Bottisham, Quy, Horningsea and Fen Ditton parishes, all of whose land extends into the fen. The first problem in understanding the history of the landscape here is to reconstruct the natural drainage of the area before man started to alter it. To do this one has to discover the old extinct river and stream beds, which now often stand up as low silt or gravel ridges above the surrounding fens. This can be done by laborious fieldwork, though air-photographs, soil surveys and geological surveys help here. The result is that it is possible to identify a major stream crossing the fen from south-west to north-east and then turning north to meet the present River Cam at Upware. This stream picked up the waters of various tributary streams flowing off the uplands to the south-east and north-east.

The earliest alteration of this natural drainage took place in the Roman period, when in order to connect the rich

---

[2] R.C.H.M. *Cambridgeshire North East* (1972), pp. liv-lxv.

agricultural uplands to the River Cam a series of canals were cut straight across the fens from the uplands to the river (Fig. 14). These are the present Bottisham, Swaffham Bulbeck and Reach Lodes (Plate 32). These Lodes completely altered the natural drainage pattern by cutting it at right-angles in three places and diverting the water from the old stream into the Lodes.

What happened in the centuries following the end of Roman rule is not known. All that one can say is that of the villages along the fen edge, only the inhabitants of one, Burwell, appear to have carried out reclamation and drainage during the medieval period. There a whole series of small fields was laid out along the fen edge below the village and in a larger area to the north in a wide inlet of fenland called The Broads. By the standards of other villages further north in the fenlands this was on a fairly small scale, but the fact that it occurred here and not in the neighbouring villages illustrates a feature of all fenland drainage at all dates. That is, even in identical areas and backgrounds, individual parishes have very different drainage histories depending on the initiative and requirements of the local lords and peasants.

The first major drainage attempts which affected the whole of this fenland took place in the mid-seventeenth century following Vermuyden's work elsewhere. As a result of this the Adventurers who had provided the capital for the drainage were allotted 2600 acres of land here. These areas, still called Adventurers' Fen in Burwell and Adventurers' Ground in Swaffham Bulbeck, consisted of four large, roughly rectangular blocks whose original boundaries and some internal divisions are still traceable today (Fig. 15). They were first laid out in 1655–6 when Vermuyden's general drainage work was finally completed. The actual positions of these allotments are not fortuitous, though they may appear so. Care was taken to use land

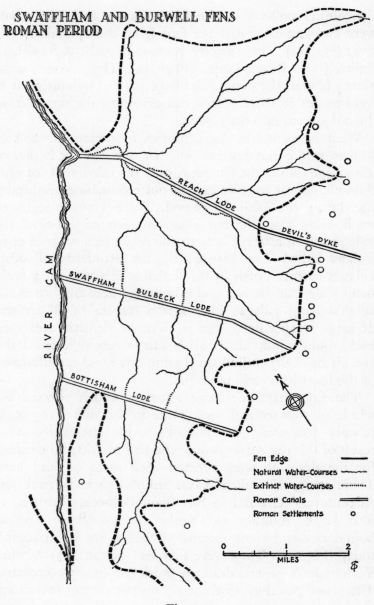

SWAFFHAM AND BURWELL FENS
ROMAN PERIOD

REACH LODE

DEVIL'S DYKE

RIVER CAM

SWAFFHAM BULBECK LODE

BOTTISHAM LODE

N

Fen Edge
Natural Water-Courses
Extinct Water-Courses
Roman Canals
Roman Settlements   o

0   1   2
MILES

Fig. 14

which could be easily drained. The blocks of land were sited not on the fen edge but along the centre of the fen so that the original natural drainage could be used. This was achieved by reconstituting part of this natural drainage. A main drain was cut from one block of Adventurers' land to another down the centre of the fen roughly on the line of the old natural streams. This passed under Bottisham and Swaffham Bulbeck Lodes in culverts and then ran into Reach Lode and so out into the River Cam. Parts of this main drain exist on the ground today and can easily be recognised once the history of the area is understood, though it no longer functions as a main drain nor is it now even a continuous water-course.

By the early eighteenth century peat shrinkage had started to affect the area, and the water in these fens would no longer run out into Reach Lode. So just before 1719 a windpump was erected near the mouth of the Lode and a new main drain cut to it from the old one. The site of this windpump is known, though nothing remains, for, as we shall see, it lay on the one place where all later drainage machinery was erected. This single windpump managed, fitfully, to keep these fens reasonably dry for the next fifty years.

Even before this pump had been built, work had started on enclosing and draining other areas of the fen. The amount of land drained and the date of the work vary considerably from parish to parish. In Swaffham Prior all the fenland of the parish was enclosed and a number of outlying farmsteads erected before 1700. To judge from the complicated pattern of the blocks of fields which remain, this was done by a number of different owners with little regard to the needs of their neighbours, and the resulting drains connecting these lands to the main drain ran through many odd angles in order to serve them all. In Burwell parish to the north-east the majority of the fenland there was also

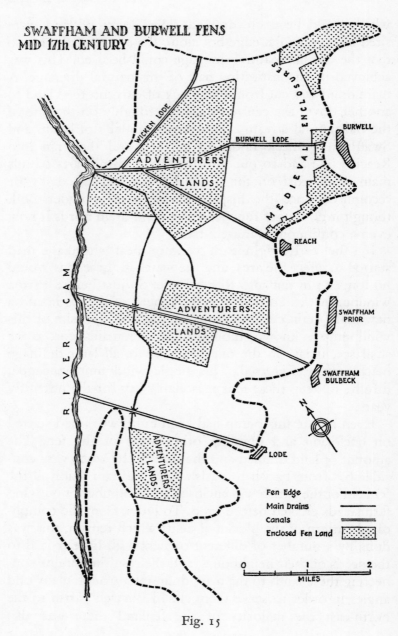

SWAFFHAM AND BURWELL FENS
MID 17th CENTURY

WICKEN LODE

BURWELL LODE

BURWELL

ADVENTURERS'
LANDS

MEDIEVAL ENCLOSURES

REACH

RIVER CAM

ADVENTURERS'
LANDS

SWAFFHAM
PRIOR

SWAFFHAM
BULBECK

N

ADVENTURERS'
LANDS

LODE

Fen Edge ----
Main Drains ——
Canals ====
Enclosed Fen Land [dotted]

0   1   2
MILES

Fig. 15

enclosed by the early eighteenth century. Here, however, it seems that it was all carried out at one moment in time, and with some degree of co-operation. All the fields in the present Hallards Fen and the surrounding area are laid out in one large block with straight drains and droveways all aligned on Burwell Lode, an artificial water-course cut in the late seventeenth century to enable barges to reach Burwell village. In the fenlands of Quy, Fen Ditton and Horningsea, all but a tiny area was enclosed piecemeal during the eighteenth century, again apparently by individual farmers. In contrast, in the fens of Swaffham Bulbeck and Bottisham, only a few small fields along the fen edge were made during the eighteenth century and most of the land there remained open.

Shrinkage of the peat and the consequent lowering of the land surface continued through the eighteenth century and it became more and more difficult to remove the water from the area. As a result, in 1766 a committee of landowners was set up with the intention of establishing a Drainage Commission to undertake full-scale drainage work. However, there was immediate dissention in the ranks of the landowners. Those in Burwell refused to allow their land to be drained, largely due to the fact that in Burwell there were particularly deep peat deposits which were dug for fuel on an enormous scale to the great financial benefit of the owners. Drainage would have ended this and therefore they looked on any scheme to remove water from the fens as a financial disaster. The landowners in the Swaffham and Bottisham fens ignored the Burwell people and went ahead to obtain an Act of Parliament for their land alone. As a result the Swaffham and Bottisham Drainage Commission was set up in 1767 (Fig. 16).

Because it was impossible any longer to drain the fen by the single windpump at Upware the Commissioners built a new one in Bottisham parish on the side of the River Cam

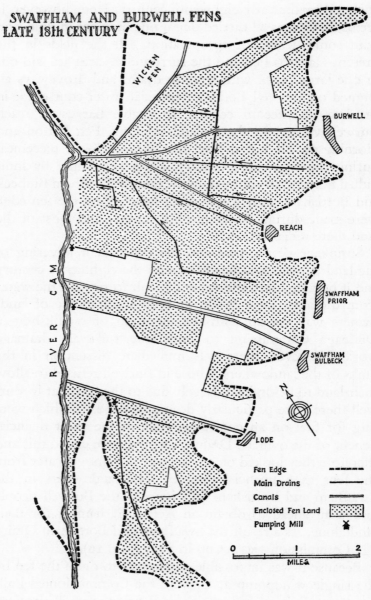

SWAFFHAM AND BURWELL FENS
LATE 18th CENTURY

WICKEN FEN

BURWELL

REACH

RIVER CAM

SWAFFHAM PRIOR

SWAFFHAM BULBECK

LODE

N

Fen Edge
Main Drains
Canals
Enclosed Fen Land
Pumping Mill

0   1   2
MILES

Fig. 16

216

to drain the south-west part of the fen, leaving the one at Upware to drain the north-east. Again new drains were cut and the one to Bottisham Mill is still traceable and indeed is called the Mill Drain even today. The site of the mill itself is visible tucked under the river bank, surrounded by its old inlet drains. Soon after 1800 all the remaining open fenland in Bottisham and Swaffham Bulbeck parishes was enclosed by Acts of Parliament along with the common fields and pastures of the uplands. The resulting rigidly geometric fields were fitted around the older Adventurers' lands and can be clearly distinguished from them. To cope with the new land which needed drainage, and to keep pace with the continued lowering of the land surface, the Drainage Commissioners had to build yet another mill, in Swaffham Prior parish, on the riverside to lift water out of the Swaffham Bulbeck fens, and in 1820 some private landowners erected a further mill to drain land in Horningsea parish. Once again the actual sites of these mills and their associated drains can be recognised today (Plate 29).

This work altered the direction of drainage in these fens. The natural south-west to north-east drainage had been turned through right-angles by the Romans. It was reconstituted by the Adventurers in the seventeenth century and then turned at right-angles yet again by the building of the four windpumps along the river bank during the eighteenth and early nineteenth centuries. Finally it was to be reversed again.

By 1820 it was clear that these fens were still not being drained successfully. With a boldness, not usual in fenland drainage history, the Swaffham Drainage Commissioners brought in the engineer John Rennie the elder, to review the situation. He not only realised that the natural drainage line ought to be reconstituted down the centre of the fens, but he also advocated the installation of a steam engine to pump the water out. Both recommendations were accepted and work commenced in 1821. A Main Drain or Engine Drain five and a half miles long was driven right across the centre of the district on the line of the old natural stream cutting indiscriminately seventeenth-, eighteenth- and nineteenth-century drains and fields and passing under Bottisham and Swaffham Bulbeck Lodes in culverts (Fig. 17 and Plate 31). At the end of the drain a thirty-horse-power steam engine was built to lift the water into the river. The scheme was not entirely successful. Being the first steam pump in the county it was too small and failed to keep up with the peat shrinkage. All the windpumps had to be retained and even another one built in 1830 to drain the far south-west of the area. In 1850 this steam engine was scrapped and a much larger one built. This proved effective and continued to drain the whole area until it was replaced by diesel pumps in the 1920s and '30s. This final achieve- ment of drainage enabled all the old windpumps to be aban- doned and led to the setting up of new farmsteads all over the fenland.

In the far north-east of the area, Burwell Fen, left outside the Swaffham district in 1767, had its own history. No attempt was made to carry out any effective drainage until well into the nineteenth century, by which time much of the fenland was so waterlogged that, peat-digging or not, something had to be done. Therefore in 1841 the Burwell landowners set up their own Drainage Commission and attempted to carry out an effective method of draining their land. Due to their late start and the existence of the well- organised Swaffham Fen drainage works they were unable to take advantage of either the Swaffham district scheme or the natural drainage of the area. The Commissioners were forced to cut a new Engine Drain across the line of the natural drainage to their own steam engine built at Upware near the Swaffham engine. This proved to be a serious mistake, for they were in effect trying to make water run

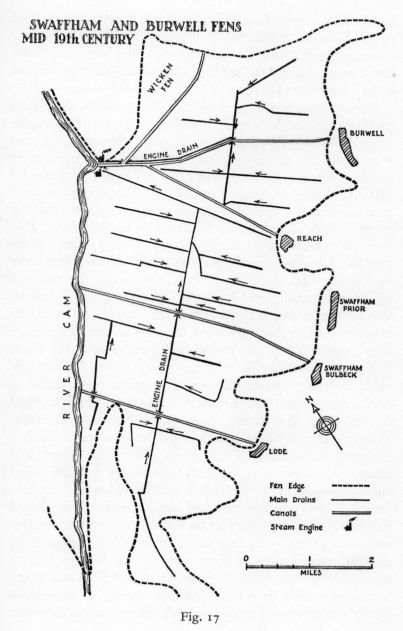

SWAFFHAM AND BURWELL FENS
MID 19th CENTURY

WICKEN FEN

BURWELL

ENGINE DRAIN

REACH

RIVER CAM

SWAFFHAM
PRIOR

ENGINE DRAIN

SWAFFHAM
BULBECK

N

LODE

Fen Edge — — — —
Main Drains ————
Canals ══════
Steam Engine

0   1   2
MILES

Fig. 17

uphill. This, combined with continued peat-digging and severe financial difficulties, partly brought about by having to reconstruct all the flood banks after they had been badly and cheaply built, resulted in the complete waterlogging of most of the area by 1900.

Various new power sources including paraffin, diesel and producer gas engines were installed to try to improve the drainage but all failed and by the 1930s almost all the area was derelict land. Some farmers tried to keep the water at bay in the late nineteenth and early twentieth centuries by erecting small windpumps in the fen. The sites of at least nine of these are traceable and the remaining one, built in 1908, is now re-erected in Wicken Fen to the north. This latter is misleadingly said to be typical of fenland wind-pumps. All these pumps proved costly failures and were eventually abandoned. Finally in 1940, under the pressure of the wartime demand for agricultural land, a new culvert was cut under Reach Lode and all the water in Burwell Fen was reversed to flow along the line of the natural drainage into Swaffham Fen and thence by its pumps into the river.

This complex history of a tiny patch of the Cambridge-shire fenlands, and much else of importance in terms of social, agricultural and engineering history has been worked out by using the minute books of the Drainage Commissioners, the records of the Bedford Level Commissioners, manorial documents, Tithe Maps, Enclosure Maps, old newspapers, air-photographs as well as soil and geological survey maps. It has meant delving into problems of mechanical and civil engineering, and endless talks with retired fen-drainage men as well as with the present Fen Superintendent and his staff. But most of all it has required the detailed examination of every part of the area on foot to appreciate the position of every drain and field and every bank and culvert. It is long and slow work, but the results justify the effort, for in the end one learns exactly how one seemingly flat and very dull part of the English landscape has evolved through nearly 2000 years of man's work upon it.

If now I stand at Upware, I see a very different landscape from the one I looked at four years ago. From the high river flood bank I can see across the fens lying twelve feet below the river. In front of me is Reach Lode, the Roman canal, used and re-used, cut and re-cut through the ages and now raised on a huge embankment above the fens. On my right, standing around the battered brick foundations of the steam-engine house of 1850, are the two dirty sheds housing the diesel pumps and a smart modern brick one with an electric pump which all now drain the whole fen. Below them, stretching back across the fens, is the Engine Drain, and the sharp double bend in its otherwise straight alignment marks the point where the drain once turned to meet the first steam engine here, built in 1821, whose site is hidden in a clump of bushes further to my right. Beyond this the flat fenland on the far right was enclosed in the late seventeenth century, though that immediately in front of me was part of the original Adventurers' lands of the 1650s. On my extreme left are the remains of the 1841 steam-engine house of the Burwell Drainage Commissioners with its now abandoned Engine Drain a boggy morass leading to it. Beyond that a white scar across a newly ploughed field is the now raised bed of an old fenland river, while further away still a belt of trees indicates the edge of Wicken Fen, the only piece of natural fenland left in the county. Even this is not all. Almost behind me, yet another brick shed houses a diesel pump, which belongs to the Great Ouse River Authority, whose purpose is to lift water out of the lode in times of flood to prevent it from drowning the fens. To see and understand all this is the beginning of a true appreciation of the history of the landscape of the Cambridgeshire fens.

The Cambridgeshire Landscape

SELECT BIBLIOGRAPHY

Astbury, A. K. *The Black Fens* (1958).

Bloom, A. *The Farm in the Fen* (1944).

Darby, H. C. *The Draining of the Fens* (1940).

Fowler, G. 'Shrinkage of the Peat Covered Fenlands', *Geog. Journal* (1933).

Hills, R. L. 'Drainage by Windmills in Waterbeach Level', *Procs. C.A.S.* (1964).

Hills, R. L. *Machines, Mills and Uncountable Costly Necessities* (1967).

R.C.H.M. *Cambridgeshire*, Vol. II (1972).

V.C.H. *Cambridgeshire*, Vol. II (1948).

7. Communications and industry

Roads and tracks. Railways. Water traffic. Industry and the landscape.

Roads and tracks

CAMBRIDGESHIRE HAS A number of examples of the old so-called prehistoric trackways. The most famous of all is the Icknield Way which extends across the chalklands of the county on its way from Norfolk to Wessex. Today it exists either as a grassy lane, such as the section known as Ashwell Street through Guilden Morden, Steeple Morden, Litlington and Bassingbourn parishes, or as the main A505–A11 road from Royston to Newmarket. The attractions of the former, rather than the latter, are obvious, but neither has any real connection with the prehistoric Icknield Way except in the remotest sense. For both lanes and modern roads are only 150 to 200 years old. Their straight alignments and wide verges are not the work of prehistoric ingenuity or Roman engineering but the result of eighteenth- and nineteenth-century turnpike road construction and the work of Enclosure Commissioners who were concerned to confine the older pattern of dozens of parallel tracks across open downland into clearly defined roads.

A splendid example of this can be seen in the old Street Way, a delightful length of empty lanes from Great Wilbraham to Newmarket. It is always said to be the prehistoric Icknield Way, but if we walk along it, it has features that belie this idea. The first section in Great Wilbraham is

exactly straight. Then it suddenly turns into a new alignment as it crosses the boundary into Little Wilbraham
parish. This change is due to the two separate Enclosure
Commissions for the parishes laying out slightly different
roads in 1797. Then where the Street Way crosses the
boundary between Little Wilbraham and Bottisham it turns
through a double right-angle. Here the Bottisham Enclosure Commissioners who were laying out their roads and
fields later on found it convenient to have their parish lane
in a slightly different place. The Street Way bends again on
the Bottisham–Swaffham Bulbeck boundary, and once more
on the Swaffham Bulbeck-Swaffham Prior boundary, again
for the same reason. Therefore, though these lanes are a
pleasant aspect of the county's landscape they are not prehistoric trackways. They are all that remains of a broad zone
of communication up to five and a half miles wide which
crossed the county from south-west to north-east along
which prehistoric, Romano-British, medieval and later
peoples journeyed.

Though, therefore, the Icknield Way hardly exists any
longer, its effects on the present landscape are marked and
can be clearly seen. The very existence of the great linear
defence works such as the Devil's Dyke, Fleam Dyke and
the Heydon Ditch, discussed in Chapter 2, indicates the
width of this broad zone of communication and the need
to block it at some time in the early post-Roman period.
Far more interesting is to see how the existence of the
Icknield Way has controlled the appearance and layout of
Saxon and medieval villages that lay in its path. This broad
way across the chalklands crosses two major river valleys,
the Saffron Walden branch of the River Cam, south of
Cambridge, and the Linton branch of the Cam further east.
Medieval traffic moving along this zone was funnelled
through a limited number of fords when it reached these
rivers before spreading out again on the other side. As a

result the villages at these river crossings tended to develop long streets at right-angles to the river.

Thus in the Saffron Walden Cam valley, Whittlesford, Duxford and Ickleton all have long east-to-west High Streets because they lay close to fords, while their near neighbours of Hinxton, Pampisford[1] and Sawston, which were not sited at major crossing places, developed very different plans. On the Linton Cam Babraham, Great and Little Abington and Hildersham also developed as long street villages at right-angles to the river. The result of this development has produced both visually pleasing and extremely inconvenient results in more recent times as the main east–west routes have declined in importance or disappeared altogether and have been replaced by north-to-south traffic running along the river edges. At Duxford and Ickleton (Fig. 18) it has produced long dog-legs in the modern road pattern as north-to-south traffic has to turn sharply along the old east–west street and then back again. This produces visually attractive places and at Ickleton helps to make it one of the prettiest villages in the area. On the other hand, at Great and Little Abington this same kind of double bend became the main A604 road between Cambridge and Colchester and modern traffic threatened to wreck the villages completely. A long and expensive bypass has had to be constructed to remove the congestion and save the villages. So in a curious way the line of a prehistoric routeway has caused a major twentieth-century traffic problem.

The impact of the Romans on the county's landscape is also reflected in modern roads and lanes. The existence of a Roman town at Cambridge meant that four major roads were driven straight across the county towards it, while the main road from London to the North passed through

---

[1] Despite its name, Pampisford is not near a ford. It was originally known as Pampesworth—the enclosure of Pampa.

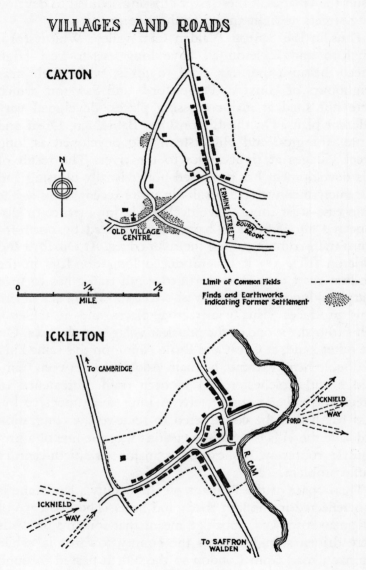

VILLAGES AND ROADS

CAXTON

N

ERMINE STREET

BOURN BROOK

OLD VILLAGE CENTRE

0   ¼   ½
MILE

Limit of Common Fields - - - - - - - -

Finds and Earthworks
indicating Former Settlement

ICKLETON

To CAMBRIDGE

ICKNIELD
WAY

FORD

R. CAM

ICKNIELD
WAY

To SAFFRON
WALDEN

Fig. 18

the western corner of the county. Today these roads differ widely in their appearance. The one approaching Cambridge from the south-east is now an almost continuous line of green lanes through the fields of that part of the county. It has long been replaced by a more indirect route through the villages along the valley of the Linton Cam. On the other hand its continuation north-west of Cambridge towards Godmanchester in Huntingdonshire is a modern and dangerous three-lane highway, hopelessly overloaded and soon to be made a dual carriageway. Again, however, there is perhaps more interest in how these roads have affected the landscape around them, though it was not until the medieval period that this happened.

The best example of this is the Ermine Street or Old North Road which crosses the western corner of the county from south to north. Though there are now four villages, Kneesworth, Arrington, Caxton and Papworth Everard, lying on it, these have all gradually moved to the road as it developed into the main route to the north during the medieval period. Of these villages, Caxton is the best one in which to see the process at work (Fig. 18). The original Saxon village of Caxton lay some distance from its present site, around the now almost isolated church south-west of the Roman road. Traces of this village can still be detected on the ground in the form of deeply cut narrow lanes, now disused, and early medieval and even Roman pottery from the adjoining fields. Then gradually as the Roman Ermine Street was transformed into the Old North Road, the village moved towards the road and houses grew up along both sides of it. We can even see that these houses were built on existing strips of the common fields of Caxton, for the gardens of the houses there are long, narrow, curved strips running back to meet the traces of ridge-and-furrow which lie beyond them. As time went on almost all the village moved to the main road, and only the church and the abandoned streets are left today to show where it once was. The importance of the Old North Road until recent times can also be seen in the present architecture of the village. There are still three huge houses which were once inns, two of them seventeenth century in date and the other converted to an inn in the eighteenth century. One retains its original entrance for carriages and though one of the others, now Caxton Manor, appears at first sight to be just a large house, a closer examination reveals that the present front door and hall is a later insertion in the wide carriage entrance through to the stables beyond.

By the seventeenth century many of the major roads of the county were becoming of considerable importance and yet their upkeep was usually organised on a parish basis which failed dismally to provide good and reliable highways. The hopeless inadequacy of this method of coping with road repairs led to the setting up of the first Turnpike Trust in the county on the Old North Road (now the A14) including the section through Cambridgeshire. This, by collecting tolls from travellers, was able to greatly improve the state of this major routeway, though the actual line of the road was not altered. During the eighteenth century other Turnpike Trusts were set up in the county. One for the Chesterford–Newmarket road (A11) was set up in 1724 and another from Fowlmere to Cambridge came into being in the same year. Again, both these trusts only improved the existing roads. However, the Godmanchester-Newmarket Turnpike Trust set up in 1745 did carry out large-scale alterations to part of the road for which it was responsible. The section between Quy Bridge and Bottisham to the east of Cambridge (now the A45) was built as a new three-mile road to cut out an older more devious route through Bottisham village.

Easily the best example of how these turnpike roads affected the landscape can be seen on the great Dark Age

Devil's Dyke which spans the Icknield Way. This, as we have seen, was originally built as a continuous defence line with no entrances or gaps in it at all. When it was abandoned and traffic started to move again, various gaps were cut through it. By the eighteenth century there were at least twelve of these in various places. When the Newmarket Heath Turnpike Trust was established a new straight road was made through the largest of the gaps. However, it was soon found that travellers, to avoid paying tolls at the turnpike house situated in the gap, merely swung off the road and after passing through one of the other gaps rejoined it. For obvious reasons this did not suit the Trust and they attempted to stop this by blocking the gaps in the Dyke. However, the Jockey Club at Newmarket then protested strongly that people were unable to move from one racecourse to another on race days. As a compromise the gaps were blocked, but gates were put in which "in future be shut up except at times of the Newmarket Meeting".[2] The results of this compromise still exist. At the so-called Well Gap and the Cambridge Gap, the massive bank of the Dyke is replaced by a lower and narrower bank with a small opening in its centre. These low banks are the eighteenth-century blocking of the old medieval trackways and the small openings the sites of the gates.

During the late eighteenth and nineteenth centuries the minor roads of the county underwent a revolution as a result of the enclosure movement and a very large proportion of the lanes of the county date from this period. Their characteristic straight alignments and wide verges show this well. On the fenlands, too, wide droveways were a result of drainage and enclosure, all laid out with an eye to providing easy access for herds of cattle or flocks of sheep. However, it has to be remembered that even as late as the

[2] Cambridgeshire County Record Office, Minutes of the Newmarket Heath Turnpike Trust.

1930s many of the fen roads were rutted, boggy tracks, often impassable, which had to be regularly ploughed and harrowed to remove the deeper holes. As we speed along the minor fen roads today it is easy to forget that the present hard surface is often covering a strip of concrete hurriedly laid down after 1940 by the War Agricultural Committees when the fens were being developed under the pressure of the war economy. For fenland people these wartime roads were just as great a revolution in their way of life as anything before or since.

Railways

To an older generation of railway enthusiasts, Cambridgeshire and Cambridge in particular had a special fascination. Because of the history of railway development in the county the variety of locomotives and rolling stock from a host of railway companies which ran through the county in the pre-1922 era has become famous.[3] All this has gone. Today the ubiquitous green or blue diesels of British Railways run on the few remaining lines and everywhere overgrown tracks and abandoned stations can be seen. For the landscape historian, however, there is still much of this age of steam to be seen. The complex railway history of the county is still vividly preserved in almost every corner, particularly in terms of railway architecture.

The earliest railway in the county was constructed in 1845 by the Eastern Counties Railway Company who laid their main line from London to Norwich through Cambridgeshire. They built two magnificent stations, one at Cambridge in an Italianate style fitted grandly to the new functional requirements, which remains largely intact, and another at Ely, now sadly mutilated. All along the line the village stations were built to a standard form, including a

[3] e.g. R. Lloyd, *The Fascination of Railways* (1951), pp. 105–12.

neat square office block with a low-pitched slate roof and stationmaster's house at the rear. Those at Great Shelford and Waterbeach are good examples. At every level-crossing were small square or cruciform bungalows, also with low-pitched slate roofs, for the keepers, and a number of these also remain.

Within a few years more lines were constructed. In 1846 the line from Ely to Peterborough via March was opened and in 1847 the March to Wisbech, Cambridge to Huntingdon and Ely to King's Lynn routes were completed. All these, and later lines built by other railway companies, had dissimilar stations whose remains reflect the individual history of each company. The line from Royston to Cambridge, built by the Great Northern Railway in 1851, has completely different stations from those built a few years earlier by the Eastern Counties Railway (later the Great Eastern). Here the offices and stationmaster's house are in one long block with a two-storey bay projecting on to the platform. The ground floor of this bay was the station office and the upper floor the stationmaster's bedroom. From both a good view along the line was possible. The stations at Melbourn and Shepreth show this well. In 1862 the LNWR constructed the line from Potton in Bedfordshire to Cambridge, and though now abandoned the stations that remain are built to a standard form with a curious trick of setting the entrance in the internal angle of the L-shaped buildings. Lord's Bridge Station, Old North Road Station, Longstowe and Gamlingay Stations are all of this form. Likewise the Cambridge to Mildenhall line via Fordham, constructed by the Great Eastern Railway in 1884–5, is characterised by stations in a typical late-Victorian style with half-hipped roofs and heavy barge boards on the gables. These remain at Swaffham Prior, Lode and Barnwell Junction.

Perhaps the most interesting of all the county's railways

both in its history and architecture is the short-lived Chesterford–Newmarket railway. It was built in 1846–7 from Chesterford in Essex on the main London–Cambridge line, across south-east Cambridgeshire to Newmarket, with a branch back to Cambridge. The company was an independent one and was supported by the Jockey Club who felt "that a railway to Newmarket will not only be a great convenience to parties anxious to participate in the truly British sport of racing, but will enable Members of Parliament to superintend a race and run back to London in time for the same night's debate". The line was opened in 1848 but almost immediately became unwillingly involved in one of the early railway company wars. It was finally taken over by the Eastern Counties Railway and by 1851 its main line was closed. This line can still be traced across the chalklands of south-east Cambridgeshire for all its cuttings, embankments and bridges remain, as do many of its original buildings, though these are now used for very different purposes. The architect had a habit of putting crude brick pediments over all the doors and these still give a clue to the origins of a number of buildings along the old line. A tiny brick cottage near the junction of the A505 and A11 at Bourn Bridge, near Pampisford, has a pediment of this kind above its door. It is the original crossing-keeper's house on this section of the line and there are two others further east. Even on the still-used branch line, two houses on the side of the railway, one at Fulbourn and the other at Cherry Hinton, have this same distinctive pediment and can be recognised as the original stations now abandoned or moved.

Once more, however, it is the impact of this form of transport in a wider landscape that has left the major marks. Though, as we shall see in the next chapter, the apparently classic picture of a railway affecting the growth of Cambridge itself is not exactly true, both March and Chatteris

Plate 32 Reach Lode. This massive canal was cut across the fens during the Roman period. From then until the early twentieth century it was used for commercial and agricultural water traffic. The cruisers now moored along it reflect its new function as part of the recreational facilities of the fenland waterways.

Plate 33   The Hythe, Reach. This flat promontory of land on the fen edge and at the end of Reach Lode is an artificial wharf. Here, throughout the medieval period and later, countless barges were loaded and unloaded.

Plate 34 Railway yards, March. In a curiously rural landscape are the important freight sidings sited here as a result of the accidental development of a major railway junction. The old town of March lies well to the south.

Plate 35 Ely. The cathedral dominates the town. In front of it is Palace Green, the last remnant of the large triangular green of the earliest settlement. To the left of the cathedral the outline of the now largely filled-in Market Place is visible, as is the long run of Fore Hill leading down to the fen edge and the medieval wharves.

have been altered by the coming of the railways (Plate 34). Even small villages were rapidly affected by them, especially those close to Cambridge where railway commuter traffic developed early. At Great Shelford, the remarkable late-nineteenth-century growth of the village as a smart middle-class dormitory suburb was entirely due to the fact that its station was the first on the line south of Cambridge. The whole shape of the village was altered as houses grew up in the area of the station which lay some distance east of the original settlement.[4] The same is true north of Cambridge where the original Histon Station lay well south of the two villages of Histon and Impington. Both villages spread rapidly south to the station and beyond and soon formed an amorphous sprawl from which the old centres around the medieval parish churches still stand aloof. In this century, villages, at least in the pre-planning era, have been pulled in other directions as the motor car and omnibus took over from the railway. Thus at Great Shelford, in the 1920s and '30s, the village suddenly spread north along the road to Cambridge while the earlier expansion around the station came to a halt.

Water traffic

Not surprisingly, the fenland with its large rivers and many artificial channels, combined with near impassable roads, has always been an important area for water-borne trade. Even during the Roman period there was considerable traffic across the fens, and stone from Northamptonshire and Rutland was certainly brought into the county as was pottery from west of Peterborough. It is also probable that much agricultural produce was shipped north along the Car Dyke and other canals and rivers to the military areas in northern England.

[4] C. C. Taylor (ed.), *Domesday to Dormitory* (1971).

This large-scale trade lapsed during the Saxon period, but certainly from the twelfth century onwards it became very important. The Northamptonshire stone in the majority of the medieval churches in the county must have come across the fens in barges, and there was major traffic in agricultural products. Local stone, called *clunch*, a particularly hard form of chalk which occurs in certain areas in the south of the county, was also sent by barge to a multitude of places. For example, clunch from Reach, east of Cambridge, was used in the rebuilding of Ely Cathedral as well as in a number of Cambridge colleges, as the Sacrist Rolls of the cathedral and medieval college accounts specify. Many other types of goods were also shipped across the fens during the medieval period, and again from the Ely Cathedral records it is known that timber and nails were brought in by water for work on the abbey church. By the eighteenth century, when more complete documentation is available, it is clear that all these materials and many other local products such as bricks and peat were being transported by water, and in addition coal, wines and spirits and Scandinavian timber, imported via Wisbech and King's Lynn, were being sent on by barge for distribution over a wide area.

This trade led to the development of ports both large and small all over the county. It is often forgotten that until the last century Cambridge itself was a major inland port. A large part of its medieval prosperity was based on waterborne trade. The famous Stourbridge Fair, one of the great fairs of medieval England, was dependent to a large degree on water traffic along the River Cam. Ely too, certainly from the thirteenth century onwards, was an important port for traffic originating within and far beyond the fenlands of the county. Elsewhere many small villages and even hamlets, which were on or close to major rivers or navigable canals, often became ports, while other villages actually had specifically constructed canals connecting them to major water-courses. The coming of the railways in the nineteenth century dealt a death blow to this trade and though it lingered on into the early years of this century it has now disappeared and the waterways have taken on a new role as an important source of recreation for town and country dwellers alike.

Although this trade has gone, its mark is firmly stamped on the landscape for all to see. At Swavesey the old dock, now overgrown and abandoned, can still be seen at the north end of the village near the church. At Littleport, the hythe remains at the end of the canal which links it to the River Ouse. Out on the New Bedford River at Mepal are the crumbling remains of a small wharf, which perhaps dates from the mid-seventeenth century when the river was cut.

By far the best examples of two, very different, inland ports may be seen at Reach and Swaffham Bulbeck, east of Cambridge. Both are situated at the landward ends of two Roman canals, re-used in later times. Each has an entirely different history of water-borne trade which is reflected in what we see there today. At Reach, by the early fourteenth century, there was a small but flourishing port. An annual fair was held there and the documented exports through this port include local stone (clunch), timber, iron and agricultural products, while stone from Northamptonshire is known to have been imported. Later sixteenth-century records list stone, cloth, shoes, horses and barley being traded here and by the seventeenth century coal was being imported from north-east England. In the eighteenth century trade declined, though we have details of coal, Scandinavian timber, wine, spirits, salt and bricks all being brought in. Some trade continued during the nineteenth century but today it has all gone and the village remains a quiet backwater with a largely undistinguished appearance.

At least so it appears at first sight. In fact the history of the port is better recorded on the ground than in documents (Fig. 19).

The village lies on either side of a broad rectangular space, Fair Green, which stretches down to the fen edge and the landward end of Reach Lode, the Roman canal, which links it with the River Cam and which was the basis of all its trade (Plate 32). However, the village did not always look like this. Though there was certainly a port here in the Roman period, as archaeological discoveries have proved, when the great Devil's Dyke was erected it was driven right through this port to link with the canal and so form a continuous defence line. Thus the later Saxon settlement there took the form of two separate villages, East and West Reach lying on either side of the Dyke.

When trade developed in the medieval period two large-scale engineering works were carried out. First some 300 yards of the Dyke, where it met the canal, were completely destroyed, so producing the large green which could then be used as a fairground and space for general trading activities. That this is so can be proved by the jagged form of the present end of the Dyke where it was left in its dismantled state, as well as by the old parish boundary between the two original villages which passed across the centre of the green on the line of the Dyke. This remained as an administrative boundary until 1954. The second piece of work was the construction of a large landing place or hythe, as it is still known, to which barges could tie up, at the fenland end of the green (Plate 33). This is a large promontory projecting into the fen with water channels round two sides. That it is completely artificial was proved by watching the foundation trenches being dug for a sewage plant which now disfigures it. This showed that it was made of chalk rubble dumped on the old fen surface. Other visible

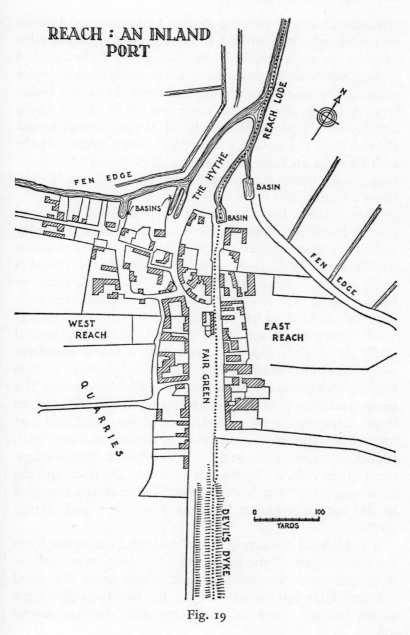

Fig. 19

237

remains of this port take the form of a whole series of basins or private wharves cut into the rising ground on the edge of the main water-course. These, though now silted up and overgrown, can be recognised fairly easily and in some cases can be related to existing buildings. Thus two basins lying side by side on the south-west side of the hythe belonged to a pretty late-medieval timber-framed house. Behind it, in the garden and parallel to the basins, are the wall footings and one remaining wall of the various warehouses and barns which were once part of a small merchant's commercial organisation.

Very different from Reach are the remains of the inland port at Swaffham Bulbeck. Here the old village centre lay well away from the end of the Roman canal known as Swaffham Bulbeck Lode. During the medieval period a small hamlet, known significantly as Newnham, grew up there, but there is no evidence whatsoever for large-scale trade of any kind. It was not until the seventeenth century, when nearby Reach was in decline, that any real commercial traffic developed, and even then only a single merchant was involved in the trade. This firm passed through various owners and gradually became a successful enterprise. The early-nineteenth-century concern acquired the status of an important organisation and account books which still survive show that trade included agricultural products, coal, timber, salt, iron, wines and spirits and bricks. The development of the railways finally put an end to the trade and the final sales of all the buildings and contents are recorded in the local newspaper between June 1877 and March 1878.

The physical remains of this commercial enterprise form the greater part of the hamlet of Newnham, now and for long known as Commercial End. There are a few rural cottages there but the majority of the buildings along the single curving street are connected with the commercial firm which was based there. The best is the house which was the centre of the whole enterprise, still called the Merchant's House. It is a fine brick building of around 1700 with Dutch gables and an eighteenth-century office or 'counting house' added on one side. This counting house once looked across an open yard which was surrounded by various buildings whose purpose and position are known from various sale plans. These included stables, barns, coal sheds, wine stores, etc., though now only the Granary converted to a modern house, the Salt House, now a garage, and one warehouse, all dating from the nineteenth century, remain. In the centre of this complex lay the wharf, which still exists as a wide, boggy, rectangular basin with a brick and stone revetment. To the north, part of the long, narrow 'canal', now almost totally overgrown, which connected the wharf to the main Lode, can be seen.

Outside the old merchant's yard there are other parts of the trading centre. Opposite the Merchant's House, in the main street, is a large eighteenth-century malt-house, though now misleadingly dated 1697 over the door. On one side of these maltings is the eighteenth-century maltster's house, which was enlarged in the early nineteenth century while on the other, a former inn, now a private house, was also part of the trading firm. There is also a row of sturdy brick cottages erected about 1820 for clerks working for the firm, as well as groups of cruder timber-framed and plastered cottages built for labourers at the same time. The latter are now greatly sought after as 'period' dwellings. The whole constitutes a nice example of commercial architecture resulting from fenland trade.

Industry and the landscape

Cambridgeshire, until relatively recently, has managed to escape the worst horrors of industrial development and even now this does not intrude overmuch in the modern landscape except at a few places. What does remain, in many forms, is often of interest when it is recognised.

Outside the urban areas medieval industry was mainly confined to a few places where suitable materials for building were extracted. There are many small pits dotted about the uplands from which chalk rubble for houses has been removed for many generations. More important are the larger chalkpits situated on the outcrop of Totternhoe Stone, a relatively hard band of chalk stretching across the county. This stone, known as clunch, was certainly worked in Roman times. During the medieval period, and indeed up to the nineteenth century, it was dug on a massive scale and used widely all over the county. The suitability of this stone for delicate carving meant that it was greatly prized for church work and the finest results may be seen in the magnificent fan vaulting in the Lady Chapel of Ely Cathedral. Almost every church in the county has clunch somewhere in its fabric and it can be identified in many of the Cambridge colleges. It was also used either as masonry or rubble in many country houses, farmsteads and cottages up to the beginning of this century, though the need to protect it from damp by rendering it with plaster or cement makes it difficult to see easily just how common it still is.

The pits, now usually overgrown, from which this clunch was taken can be seen right across the southern part of the county from Isleham in the east to Barrington in the west. One of the largest is at Cherry Hinton, clunch from which was certainly used in Corpus Christi, Trinity and Peterhouse Colleges in the late medieval period. Even larger are those at Reach, where some fifty acres of abandoned quarries exist. From here clunch was transported by water all over the county and beyond. It was certainly used in repairs to Cambridge Castle in 1295 and the records of

Caius, King's, Queen's and Trinity Colleges tell of its use on major buildings and repair work all through the medieval period and beyond. Clunch continued to be dug for the construction of minor domestic buildings, in the south of the county, until the beginning of this century and many hundreds of tons were also used on the fens for the repairing and reconstruction of the banks of water-courses.

By the fourteenth century a new building material, brick, was introduced into the county. At first it was used only in major buildings, especially in some of the Cambridge colleges. The earliest bricks were apparently made outside the county and some were certainly imported, once again emphasising the importance of the fenland rivers as trade routes. By the fifteenth century, however, local bricks were certainly being made and used. As time went on brick became more and more important and its use gradually spread to all types of building. In the sixteenth and seventeenth centuries it was mainly confined to larger town and country houses, but by the eighteenth century its use had spread to farmhouses and cottages. Since then it has been widely used in all types of buildings.

The remains of the industry which coped with the steadily increasing demand for brick over the last few centuries are dotted along the outcrops of suitable clays especially on the gault clay zone in the south of the county and the Jurassic clays in the north-west. There are two very different types of site. Some are still working and completely disfigure the landscape. This is especially true around Whittlesey, where the industry is an offshoot of the even more ugly industrial landscape around Peterborough to the west. There the countryside is dotted with tall chimneys belching smoke, while the acrid fumes constantly assail the visitor. Huge brickpits, noisy with excavators and other machinery, lie all around, separated by lines of depressing terraced houses for the workers.

Far less disfiguring are the remains of much older and smaller brickworks which have long since been abandoned. Many were in use for only a short while during the eighteenth and nineteenth centuries, often for specific building projects. Some of them remain as small pits along the fen edges and within the river valleys but more often the original workings have disappeared and only uneven ground and the scatter of broken bricks and 'wasters' are left to be seen. Yet careful work on maps and documents can date the period when these brickworks were in use and sometimes even the actual buildings constructed from the bricks can be identified. Thus we know that a small and now overgrown brickpit at Horningsea was being worked in 1824 when a sale particular of the adjacent public house mentions it. In addition we know from Drainage Board records that some of the bricks used in the erection of the pumping engine house at Upware in 1850 were made here. This kind of detailed local study, while not in itself of great importance, can add greatly to the detailed knowledge of an area so that the stage is reached when almost every hollow and bump in the ground is finally explained.

Stone-quarrying and brick-making are extractive industries which have left their mark all over this country but Cambridgeshire does have the scars of an industry virtually unique in England. This was the digging of coprolites which developed in the second half of the nineteenth century and for thirty years or so played an important part in the economy of south Cambridgeshire.

The term 'coprolites' was given to phosphatised nodules of clay, shells, sponges or other fossils which are found on top of the gault clay. The idea of using these as fertiliser was suggested around 1850 when the county's farming was prosperous and farmers could afford a relatively expensive artificial manure. From around 1860 vast areas along the fen edge east of Cambridge and also in west Cambridgeshire from Grantchester through to Abington Pigotts, as well as on some of the fen islands, were worked for these coprolites. Owners of land leased blocks to prospectors who then dug the coprolites which usually lay up to twenty feet below the surface. Digging was done manually, usually by the open-cast method. A long trench was dug across the field, the top soil piled up along it and the coprolites removed. Then another adjacent strip was dug, the top soil being thrown back into the first trench. In this way the field was gradually dug over and at the end there remained a long mound of spoil at one side of the field and an open trench at the other. Normally the spoil was used to fill the trench but very often, especially towards the end of the century when the digging of coprolites was becoming uneconomic, this was not done. The result is that in many places today the water-filled trenches and mounds still exist to show where the coprolite diggers worked. In Stow-cum-Quy Fen, east of Cambridge, the land is dotted with this type of remains. More obvious is an enormous bank, resembling a disused railway embankment, which lies on the west side of the main London road into Cambridge just south of Trumpington. How many of the thousands of people who pass it every day realise that it is a relic of this curious industry?

The work of digging coprolites provided employment for hundreds of labourers and landowners. Merchants as well as the people who processed the raw coprolites into fertiliser prospered. Soon after 1880 a decline set in, due partly to exhaustion of the most easily worked seams, but also to the general economic depression of the times and the importation of cheap American fertilisers. The industry had a short-lived revival during the First World War when coprolites were dug for munition-making but it was totally uneconomic. Now the industry is largely forgotten and only in the landscape can we see its mark.

SELECT BIBLIOGRAPHY

Allen, C. J. *The Great Eastern Railway* (1968).
Brown, K. 'A Derelict Railway', *Procs. C.A.S.* (1931).
Fox, C. *The Archaeology of the Cambridge Region* (1923).
Spufford, M. 'The Street and Ditch Ways in S.E. Cambridge-
   shire', *Procs. C.A.S.* (1966).
V.C.H. *Cambridgeshire*, Vol. II (1948).

8. The landscape of towns

Ely. Wisbech. Cambridge.

CAMBRIDGESHIRE IS SINGULARLY lacking in urban areas. Cambridge itself dominates most of the southern half of the county, physically, economically and socially, while Ely does the same for the southern fens and Wisbech for the north. Apart from these there is little. Chatteris and March in the western fens are both relatively new as towns and their growth as urban centres has been late. Linton in the south of the county was technically a borough in the medieval period but it was always small and there is little today in the present village to indicate any real urban status.

Ely

The great cathedral at Ely, dominating both the surrounding town and fens from the summit of its island, is one of the glories of England (Plate 35). To see it, tens of thousands of people make the journey across the allegedly uninteresting fenland every year and spend an hour or so wandering around the towering medieval structure. Far fewer bother to look at the town of Ely, always a busy congested place, as it plays out its centuries-old role of major commercial centre of the southern fenland. One suspects that hardly any visitors bother to look carefully at either the buildings of the town or the layout of its streets. This is a pity for the origins and development of Ely can be seen in these physical remains just as clearly as the history of the cathedral can be seen in its stones.

The development of the present city starts with the foundation of a religious settlement on the site of the cathedral around A.D. 673 by Etheldreda (Fig. 20). There may have been an existing Saxon settlement close by already, for an early Saxon burial ground was discovered just north of the town in 1959. If our idea, that a dispersed pattern of settlement existed on the fen islands even in the Saxon period, is a correct one, the suggestion that there was a pre-cathedral settlement at Ely is reasonable. In any case the existence of the religious foundation would soon have attracted a community of people around it. The obvious place for such a community to grow up would have been immediately to the west of the present cathedral along and around St Mary's Street. If we look carefully at this area we can see clearly that St Mary's Street, together with Palace Green, was once a very large triangular open space which has been reduced and almost obliterated by a large 'island' of buildings in its centre as well as by some encroachment on its north-eastern edge. The present St Mary's church, which stands on the south side of this 'green', is in a position which suggests that it could be on the site of an original church of this first settlement.

The second stage in the development of the city must have been its extension eastwards on to what is now Market Street, High Street and the Market Place. Again if we look closely at the pattern of streets here we see a feature common to many medieval towns. The area is generally rectangular and mostly occupied by lanes, alleys and buildings, but the very existence of these alleys such as Chequers Lane and Butchers Row suggests that the whole rectangle originated as a large open market place. This has been gradually encroached upon as what were once temporary market stalls became over the centuries permanent shops. The encroachment was certainly taking place in the middle of the thirteenth century, for in a survey

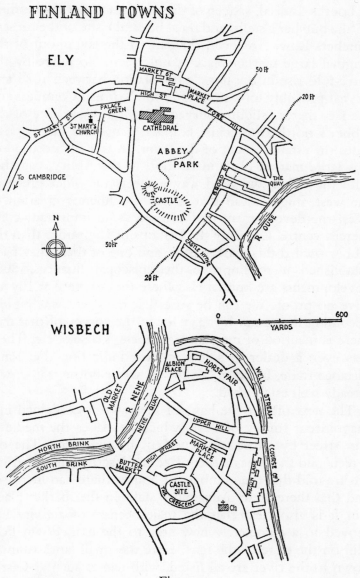

FENLAND TOWNS

ELY

WISBECH

Fig. 20

247

of 1251 there were twenty freeholders in the town with stalls or booths. Indeed, sixteen of these appear under the heading of 'the butcher's stalls' and must be on the site of the present Butchers Row. However, the date of the laying-out of the original large market place is unknown. To judge by the three-fold rise in the town's population between 1086 and 1251 it probably took place after the Norman Conquest and the fact that its slightly curved sides follow the line of the Abbey's northern precinct boundary suggests that it post-dates the establishment of the latter. In fact the position of this large market place in relation to the Abbey, together with the rather awkward way it meets the older green to the west, might mean that it was a deliberate creation to assist the development of the town as an important commercial centre. Certainly the Bishops of Ely rather than the Abbey owned this market place and one of them may have established it to improve the episcopal finances. Such developments are known elsewhere though here at Ely we have no proof. We can be sure that the town was rapidly becoming important by 1251 for in the survey of that date there is mention of merchants, tanners, glaziers, etc. There was even a dealer in spices, a clear indication that long-distance trade, based no doubt on water-borne traffic, was already well established.

The next picture we have of the town is contained in a magnificent survey of 1416, which describes the medieval city street by street and tenement by tenement. The old 'green' and the later market place are described in detail and we are told that the numbers of houses there had increased and that there were many more stalls in the market place. But it is also clear that the major centre of activity had moved to a completely new area to the east, down Fore Hill on the edge of the fens. Here the small lanes running down to the river are all listed, with names such as Castle, Monk's Broad and Stock Hythes, indicating that they were all the sites of wharves. This relatively late extension of the town reflects the growing importance of water-borne trade which was to continue for many centuries. This development was considerably aided by a massive alteration of the course of the River Ouse. Today the river swings west to pass along the fen edge and so serve all these wharves, but in earlier times it lay further south-east where its old line can still be traced as a drainage ditch. This alteration probably took place around 1300 and again may have been carried out by one of the Bishops of Ely though there is no proof of this. Today this part of the town still has remains of the inland port which flourished here. Not only do the individual lanes running down to the river preserve the form of the original wharves, but to the north, Fore Hill continues on to become the present Waterside. This is a long open space or market place with a quay at its east end. The remains of seventeenth- and eighteenth-century warehouses and barns still line it and indicate its long period of importance as a place where barges were unloaded and goods traded and stored.

The variety of goods which passed through these wharves and quays in the later medieval period is well documented. Cloth came from Bury St Edmunds and Newmarket in Suffolk, clunch and timber came from Reach, lead and wax from Boston in Lincolnshire, glass from Yarmouth, canvas from St Ives in Huntingdonshire, tin from King's Lynn, bricks from Wisbech and limestone from Peterborough. An enormous number of imports are recorded as coming from the great Stourbridge Fair at Cambridge, including spices, iron, lead and timber.

The end of the monastery at Ely in the sixteenth century had little effect on the town itself. It continued to be an important market town and its water-borne trade went on. However, we must be careful not to see the town at this time, or later, as an island paradise. The surrounding fens, then still mainly undrained, made it a very different place from that which we see today. Camden in 1580 wrote that it was not "to be boasted for beauty". A hundred years later Celia Fiennes had a very low opinion of it, though a day begun by floundering through the waterlogged main streets and ending in a slug-infested bed-chamber probably made her a biased visitor. The drainage of the surrounding fens and the growth of a local market-gardening industry whose products were shipped out to many parts of eastern England during the eighteenth century improved the appearance and prosperity of the town. From then on the town grew rapidly in size and like most other places acquired the usual suburbs of little historical interest or aesthetic merit. The coming of the railway in the mid-nineteenth century and the development of road transport in this century have ended its prosperity as a port but Ely still remains as a local market centre, a position it has held for many centuries.

Wisbech

As at Ely much of the history of Wisbech is still preserved in the present plan of the town, despite the efforts of the twentieth century to obliterate it. Though Wisbech is still a most attractive place, by virtue of its eighteenth-century buildings, a much older story is recorded in the pattern of its streets (Fig. 20).

The town grew up at the junction of two rivers, the 'Wysbech', now the River Nene, and the Well Stream, then the main outfall of the River Ouse and now a modern road carving its way round the east side of the old town. It is probable that the original settlement lay not in the angle between the two rivers where the town centre now is, but on the west side of the Wysbech or Nene around the present Old Market. Not far away is the site of the medieval manor house which was probably the administrative centre of the area before the late eleventh century. The Old Market was so called as early as 1221 and this suggests that some form of trading centre existed here in early times.

The main growth of the town, however, seems to have followed the erection of a castle here in the late eleventh or early twelfth century. This was, by tradition, built by William I after he had finally conquered the fenlands but there is no absolute proof of this and it may well have been erected by one of the early Bishops of Ely, to whom the manor of Wisbech passed in 1109, to protect a growing or intended town near it. Certainly the town with the castle, lying across the neck of the peninsula between the two rivers and dominating the market place, is, as the Victoria County History has said, "a good example of a manorial borough".

The castle itself has long since disappeared. It was a motte-and-bailey castle of the normal eleventh- and twelfth-century type, the motte standing within the circular street now called The Crescent with its bailey to the north. The line of the bailey ditch is still reflected by the curving line of High Street and the south side of the Market Place. The castle either encouraged the main commercial centre of the old settlement to move east across the river, to come under its protection, or the castle and a new town were part of a coherent plan. Whatever the reason was, the town grew up here north of the castle between the rivers with a large market place, called the New Market, immediately outside the bailey. As at Ely, it is quite clear that the market place was much larger than it is now and probably extended as far north as Upper Hill Street so forming a neat near-square area. It has since been encroached upon from the north and east.

Presumably about the same time the parish church, tucked under the castle walls to the east, was built to provide the townsfolk with a place to worship. The earliest surviving part of this church is the north arcade of the nave which dates from a little after 1150 and this may well be part of the first building on the site.

In spite of the apparently good site and auspicious beginnings, Wisbech as a trading centre was severely handicapped during the later medieval period by various difficulties. The basic problem was the continuous silting up of the lower reaches of the River Nene, below the town, where the river spread out before entering The Wash. This prevented all but the smallest ships from reaching the town. In addition, around 1300 the River Ouse was diverted from Wisbech to its present course via King's Lynn and the Well Stream was reduced to a minor water-course. This cut off the town from a great part of its hinterland and also prevented growth. This latter event, however, did play a part in the physical appearance of the town. The reduction of the old broad River Ouse to a much narrower stream left a wide area of marsh on either side of it. On the town side, at least, this seems to have been encroached upon and used for trading and market activities. The original edge of the River Ouse is still visible as a continuous curving building line on the north side of the town-centre from New Quay, along the south side of the Horse Fair through Falcon Lane to the parish church. The space left between this line and the reduced Well Stream after 1300 was used as two other market places or quays. The largest is the present Horse Fair and Albion Place on the north while the other is a much smaller wedge-shaped area now Canal Row and Falcon Lane to the east. Both these have been partly built over and much reduced in size since but their original outlines may still be traced. The town in the medieval period had yet another open space, known as the Butter Market, now an open square in Bridge Street. Though its name gives us a clue to its medieval usage, its position close to the River Nene implies that it started life as a quay or hythe.

Despite the physical advantages of new quays the problems of Wisbech remained, and little was done to alter the situation until the late fifteenth century. Then the cutting of Morton's Leam from Peterborough to Guyhirn around 1480 improved the flow of the River Nene and this seems to have led to an increase in trade. The town was made a corporate borough in 1549 and by 1566 there were a number of small ships trading into the port, mainly engaged in carrying coal and cereals.

A disastrous flood occurred in 1613 and an investigation afterwards found that silting in the Nene was so bad that little or no water could pass along it. During the seventeenth century after much argument and discussion work was again carried out to improve access to the port. Vermuyden, as part of his general drainage work in the fenlands, constructed a sluice on the Nene just north of the town in 1631 to prevent sea floods, and in 1638 a two and a half mile straight cut was made lower downstream to improve navigation and to stop the silting. This resulted in a renewed growth of trade and the town became prosperous. By the early eighteenth century the town was rapidly becoming a major port. In 1718–19, 241 ships entered the town and £4000 were collected in customs dues. In the same year the export of oats alone amounted to 40,000 quarters. This period of prosperity is still reflected in the architecture of the town. There are a number of extremely fine early-eighteenth-century houses built by rich merchants or bankers amongst which Peckover House, on the North Brink, is by far the best.

The middle of the eighteenth century brought yet more problems. Silting of the Nene continued and resulted in a whole series of disastrous floods between 1763 and 1770. At the same time in dry years there was almost no water in the river at Wisbech and boats had to unload six or eight miles away downstream. This problem was finally solved by the construction of 'Kimberley's Cut', a new embanked channel for the Nene below Wisbech which was completed in 1772, though a number of other improvements were carried out on the Nene outfall channel right through the nineteenth century. In 1794, to help improve trade, the old course of the River Ouse, the Well Stream, was canalised, giving the port easy access to a large and rich agricultural area in north-east Cambridgeshire and west Norfolk. These works brought a new era of prosperity to the town. A custom house was built in 1801 and in 1825–6, 1209 ships entered the port and customs dues brought in almost £30,000. At this time the exports were mainly cereals and rape seed while timber and coal were the principal imports. In this period of prosperous farming, Wisbech was the largest cereal-shipping port in the United Kingdom.

Again this period has left its mark on Wisbech today and some of the best late-Georgian and Regency architecture in the county is here. Though much of it has been and still is being demolished or mutilated in an attempt to make Wisbech look like every other mid-twentieth-century town, enough remains not only to show the history of this period but to make Wisbech still one of the most attractive towns in East Anglia. The houses along North Brink "form one of the finest pieces of Georgian street architecture in the country"[1] and the streets laid out between 1793 and 1816 on the site of the castle, The Crescent, Castle and Museum Squares and Market Street, are not only a superb example of early town planning but a particularly attractive piece of provincial architecture of the time. Elsewhere in the town are numerous examples of fine late-eighteenth-century and early-nineteenth-century houses.

The arrival of the railway in 1847 caused a decline in the

[1] V.C.H. *Cambridgeshire*, Vol. IV, p. 242.

ship-borne trade of Wisbech, and though it still continues it is now on a relatively small scale. The town, however, has remained the marketing centre for an increasingly prosperous agricultural area, and has continued to expand rapidly.

Outside Ely, Wisbech and Cambridge, only Chatteris and March function as urban centres and then on a relatively small scale. Both are late developers in the urban stakes.

Chatteris is visually a rather dull and uninteresting small town, though it has a few nice houses of the eighteenth century for those with the time to discover them. It consists largely of a long main street which grew up on the main road from Ely to Peterborough where it crosses an elongated fen island.

Of much more interest is *March*, seven miles to the north. Like many fenland towns and villages it appears rather dull with an over-abundance of nineteenth-century buildings in the characteristic fenland white (now dirty grey) brick. In spite of this there is much of the history of the town in its present appearance. March is situated on the northern edge of a fen island where the Wisbech–Chatteris road crosses what was once a distributary of the River Nene. This is now, as a result of drainage, reduced to a rather unattractive water-course.

March in the medieval period was a relatively small place. Until the mid-nineteenth century it was always a chapelry of Doddington, a village well to the south, and in 1086 Domesday Book records a population of only twelve indicating perhaps no more than fifty or sixty people in all. In the following 200 years it gradually became a small trading port based both on road and river traffic. Certainly by 1221 records indicate that March had become a considerable village. It is during this period that the present town-centre probably took on its modern form. On either side of the river there developed open spaces, ringed by houses, which acted as market places and quays. The one on the north of the river, the present rectangular area called Broad Street, still remains almost completely intact. On the south side a much larger and more irregular open area, formerly extending along the river edge, has been largely encroached upon by houses and shops in the usual manner but part of it still remains in the form of the present Market Place.

In the sixteenth century the town remained a port, albeit only a small one, and boats trading in coal and grain are recorded at that period. This commercial activity continued into the eighteenth century and the town grew slowly. A 'town hall' existed in 1669 and in 1670 a market with two annual fairs was granted. Trade seems to have declined in the late eighteenth century and though it revived in the nineteenth century, the subsequent expansion of the town was caused by the arrival of a very different form of transport, the railway. The first line from Ely to Peterborough was opened in 1846 and lines to Wisbech, St Ives and Spalding were laid between then and 1867. The latter line was particularly important as it connected some of the industrial and mining areas of north-east England and the north Midlands with London and East Anglia. March Station and the main railway junction lay on poor-quality cheap land to the north of the old town and as a result the town spread out in that direction in an untidy sprawl. In the 1930s a major marshalling yard was laid out here which for a long time was the largest in the country (Plate 34). Thus March became a railway town in the tradition of Crewe, Swindon and Wolverton.

Cambridge
There can be few towns in England which have had so much written on their history and architecture as Cambridge, much of it by eminent historians. These scholars

have dealt with the growth and development of the town and the visual appearance has also been magnificently covered by other workers and organisations. Yet the majority of the books and articles on Cambridge have concentrated on the growth of the medieval city and more particularly on the growth and architecture of the University. This is not to decry these works nor to dismiss the great beauty of the University and colleges. Cambridge remains a major living monument to Western civilisation both in its visual appearance and in its educational impact. Yet in the past, and still today, Cambridge has been and is much more than just a university town. Though the many thousands of visitors who flock to Cambridge from all over the world see and rightly admire the old town centre and the University buildings, these cover only a tiny part of what is now an important industrial and commercial centre with a population of over 100,000. Even in the medieval period the city was a major inland port and market town with connections stretching far beyond East Anglia or even this country. Here, therefore, we will largely ignore the University and its buildings and look at less impressive aspects of the history of Cambridge which are nevertheless still preserved in the landscape of the city.

Today we see Cambridge as the apparent result of an excellent choice of site (Plate 36). It stands at the point on a slow-moving river where the flood plain is narrow and it passes hard, well-drained land on either side, so providing an easy river crossing and suitable areas for settlement. However, these advantages were not apparent to prehistoric peoples. These certainly lived around what is now Cambridge, but they also occupied similar as well as less suitable places both up and down stream from the city. This is an important point to realise, for the present site of Cambridge was not necessarily the only place where a town could have been developed. In strict geographical terms

R

there are other situations just as convenient both above and below the city. Its actual siting was the result of purely human factors, which even if we cannot understand we must at least recognise and so avoid falling into the trap of geographical determinism.

The actual choice of the present position of Cambridge rather than any other must be the result of some unknown Roman military engineer of the first century A.D. The need for a military road linking Colchester with the main route to the north at Godmanchester in Huntingdonshire, led to the construction of the so-called Via Devana which passed through the centre of modern Cambridge and crossed the River Cam at Magdalene Bridge. The reason why this crossing was chosen rather than another is not known and certainly a number of alternatives might just as easily have been chosen. The decision made, however, the whole history of Cambridge's development inevitably followed. The new road crossing had presumably to be protected and an early military post, perhaps a fort, was erected on the gravel-capped chalk ridge of Castle Hill, north-west of the river, now occupied by the Shire Hall. As was usual in Roman times a civil settlement grew up around it and developed into a small urban centre which was eventually walled for its protection. The line of the walls around this Roman town is known and indeed part of it can still be seen. The present Pound Hill, Mount Pleasant and Pleasant Row on the south-west side of Castle Hill are on the line of the Roman town ditch and the still huge earthen scarp in Mount Pleasant is the edge of the rampart. Though never a major town, Cambridge in the Roman period already exhibited some of the functions of the medieval city. Its position on a river connected to the Roman fenland canal system meant that it became a port and archaeologically trade is attested by the use of Northamptonshire stone there and the existence of pottery imported from the Peterborough area.

The Roman town continued to be occupied well into the fifth century at a time when there was considerable Anglo-Saxon settlement in the area. As was noted earlier the existence of Anglo-Saxon burials within Roman cemeteries and associated with late Roman objects and hybrid Roman/Saxon pottery shows that Saxons and Romano-Britons were living together. As the details of Cambridge history slide into the 'Dark Ages' it is possible to see that while Romano-British survivors, already intermarried with Saxons, still remained within the old town on Castle Hill, other Saxon newcomers were settling down south-east of the river crossing around the present town-centre.

The details of the development of the town during the succeeding 300 years are hazy and little remains in the present landscape to illuminate it. Tradition has it that Cambridge was laid waste and abandoned by the seventh century, for when the monks of Ely came to find a coffin for the body of St Etheldreda in 695, they found Cambridge a *"civitatula quondam desolata"*. Whether this was strictly true is doubtful. The old Roman town where they discovered a Roman coffin may have been partly derelict but it is unlikely that the settlement was completely abandoned. In any case the picture of destruction that the monks recorded may well have been only a temporary phase resulting from the savage wars between Mercia and East Anglia earlier in the seventh century.

Certainly by the eighth century Cambridge was reviving and it has been suggested that King Offa (757–96) built the bridge over the River Cam that gives the city its name. Towards the end of the ninth century Cambridge was occupied by the Danes and in 878 it actually became part of the Danelaw. Though it was severely damaged during the wars of the early eleventh century, it is clear that during the 200 years following the Danish occupation Cambridge was developing as a port and commercial town, largely centred to the south-east of the river crossing. The distribution of late-Saxon pottery and other finds shows this well, and the now long-vanished King's Ditch,[2] which in later medieval times encircled this part of the town, was probably cut as a defensive work during this period. We also have a record of 'Irish Merchants', perhaps Danes from Dublin, occupying wharves near the river crossing which shows the growing status of the town as an inland port.

There is still in the modern landscape evidence of this period of prosperity. St Clement's church, near Magdalene Bridge, though rebuilt many times, preserves in its dedication Danish influence, and its position close to the wharves of the Irish Merchants probably means that there was a Danish trading quarter there. Likewise the churches of St Botolph and St Edward by their dedications indicate that they are both pre-Norman Conquest foundations, and a Saxon grave slab found in the latter supports this. At St Benet's church the existence of a chancel, nave and fine west tower, all dating from the early eleventh century, is a visual reminder of the prosperity of the town at this time. In addition there is documentary evidence that the church of St Mary the Less is a pre-Conquest foundation and again there are Saxon grave slabs there. While the total evidence is smaller, there is no doubt that there was also a flourishing community north-west of the river on the site of the Roman town. Archaeological and documentary research have pointed to extensive occupation within the old Roman walls as well as the existence of at least one pre-Conquest church there. Thus there can be little doubt that by the late tenth century Cambridge was a prosperous and flourishing town.

It was to this commercial centre that William the Conqueror came in 1068 and erected on the top of Castle Hill the large motte-and-bailey castle, part of which still

[2] The last trace of this Saxon defensive ditch can still be seen as a slightly sunken area in the Fellows' Garden at Sydney Sussex College.

survives, to control the river crossing, protect the bridge and dominate the town. To make way for it twenty-seven houses were demolished, additional proof that the old Roman town was well populated at this time.

From the twelfth century the development of the town is well documented and the stages of its growth can be seen on the ground. The main commercial part of Cambridge south of the river soon started to expand beyond the line of the encircling King's Ditch and in particular development took place along three of the main routes out of the town to the south-east and south, i.e. along Trumpington Street, St Andrew's Street and Jesus Lane. Beyond the latter, on a large piece of common land close to the river, there soon started an annual fair, known as Stourbridge Fair, which became one of the most important in the country. This attracted merchants from all over England and beyond and, combined with the continued growth of Cambridge as an inland port, gave the town great prosperity during the medieval period.

The main town-centre was then very different from that which we see today. The present market place certainly existed, but to the west, in what is now King's Parade and Trinity Street, there were no fine college buildings but a mass of houses, barns and warehouses extending down to quays along the river, occupied by merchants and others engaged in local and long-distance trade. Indeed at this time King's Parade and Trinity Street were known as High Street, a clear indication of the commercial importance of this part of the town. Around this commercial centre there were still many open spaces within the city limits and beyond and completely surrounding all lay the common fields stretching in every direction.

Up to the thirteenth century then, Cambridge was an important and increasingly prosperous trading centre, perhaps not very different from many others in England. In the early years of the century King John established the town as a corporate body and everything seemed set fair for the continued development of a normal market town. However, in 1209 an event occurred which was to radically alter all its subsequent history and growth. In that year a group of scholars migrated from Oxford to Cambridge and from then on the University gradually came into being. In the same century Hugh of Balsham, Bishop of Ely, established a community of scholars which was to become Peterhouse. These events did not at first greatly alter the physical appearance of the town but in the early fourteenth century a number of other colleges were founded and their locations resulted in considerable changes in the layout of Cambridge. Michael House, now absorbed into Trinity College, was established in 1324, Clare College in 1326 (Plate 37) and Trinity Hall and Gonville Hall were founded soon after. All these foundations grew and expanded their original sites and in doing so they gradually took over a large part of the area occupied by warehouses and quays along the river. The University itself also gradually acquired land and developed it in the same area, and in the middle of the fourteenth century Pembroke and Corpus Christi Colleges were established further to the south. In the fifteenth century King's and Queen's Colleges were founded and the result of all this was that a large section of the town was gradually taken over by University establishments. In effect the western part of the commercial centre of the town was displaced by the University and pushed sideways thus completely altering the normal development of Cambridge (Plate 39). The growth of all the colleges and the University into the architectural splendours that we see today must not allow us to forget that it was a relatively late and disruptive influence in the long history of the town's landscape.

The great series of later college foundations which began

with Jesus College in 1496 and ended with Sydney Sussex in 1594 changed the topography of the town to a much lesser degree, for they were all on the sites of earlier religious foundations and did not entail the acquisition of houses and other property on the scale of the earlier colleges. Nevertheless, both town and University were expanding fast and by the sixteenth century land in the town was in short supply, a problem that was to beset the city for 300 years. The riverside colleges particularly started to reclaim land along the Cam, and in so doing took over pieces of common land. This caused an outcry in the town and though the results of their efforts produced the justly famous Backs the early stages in this work were somewhat different from the present delightful setting. Trinity College especially aroused the fury of the townsfolk who claimed that "the said college doth commonly use to lay their muck and their manure on their backside upon the aforesaid common green, where they will suffer no man else to do the like and have builded a common jakes upon part of the same."

Throughout the seventeenth and eighteenth centuries Cambridge appears to have changed very little in layout though architecturally both the town and the University were altered considerably. The confining effect of the surrounding common fields prevents any major expansion and such growth as there was took place within the old town. There is evidence here of severe overcrowding and subdivision of existing buildings into tenements. Then in the first few years of the nineteenth century events took place that were to alter the city more than any others in its history. These were the enclosures of the common fields and the results were of such magnitude and are so little appreciated by either visitors or inhabitants that it is worth looking at them in some detail.[3]

[3] This section is based on work carried out by Mr A. P. Baggs. I am grateful to him for permission to use some of his material.

The nineteenth-century expansion of Cambridge and indeed most of the more recent developments occurred on the east and south-east of the old town, so that even today the city has a markedly lopsided layout with the country-side still close at hand just to the north-west but with almost three miles of built-up area to the south-east. This expansion was in the direction of, and later beyond, the great arc of the railway which came to the city in 1845. It is easy, therefore, to fall into the trap of assuming that the town developed in this direction because of the railway and its associated industries in a way that is typical of so much nineteenth-century urban growth and also that this development took the form of steady outward expansion. Neither of these assumptions is correct as can be easily seen by a detailed study of the existing architecture of the nine-teenth-century parts of Cambridge.

Unfortunately, neither the casual visitor nor even the devoted landscape historian ever journeys into these parts of the town to see for themselves just how a large nine-teenth-century urban area actually developed. If we do this, we find many curious anomalies in the apparently straight-forward growth of the suburbs of Cambridge. As one walks south-east from the old town-centre the periods of building are curiously muddled. A group of fine neat houses of around 1820 is succeeded by huge ugly terraces of the 1880s and beyond less pretentious buildings of about 1840 followed by more from the 1830s (Plate 38). By examining every building, noting every street name and every bend or turn in the roads one finally concludes that there is a great deal more to nineteenth-century Cambridge than first seems possible.

The population of Cambridge in 1801 was around 10,000. By 1901 this had risen to over 40,000, but at this time there were still only 12,000 people living in the area occupied by the medieval city. The greater part of the

Plate 36 Cambridge today. The colleges and their grounds line the Cam while the commercial centre of the town lies huddled behind them, having been pushed back from the river. The long almost straight street is on the line of the road leading into the Roman town of Cambridge which lay in the bottom left-hand corner of the picture.

Plate 37   Clare College Court and King's College Chapel. This is the part of Cambridge that the visitor knows well. Even so, the magnificent architectural heritage that the University has given the world never fails to impress.

Plate 38   Benet Place, Lensfield Road, Cambridge. These semi-detached town houses were built around 1820 on land then only recently enclosed from the former common fields.

Plate 39   Cambridge Market Place in 1842 before the planners and developers of the twentieth century imposed their ideas upon it. Medieval houses and the Old Guildhall lie around the square in which is Hobson's Fountain, the town's water supply. Beyond, the pinnacles of King's College Chapel stand aloof from the busy commercial activity close by.

Plate 40 The modern rural landscape. The old village street of Burwell lies in the foreground. Under the pressure of continuously rising population new housing estates are spreading outwards in an ever-increasing sprawl.

increase had been housed east and south-east of the town on what had been the old East or Barnwell Field. This great area was enclosed by Act of Parliament in 1807 and the land divided up into allotments or fields as was usual on enclosure. Many of the colleges received allotments of land in return for various strips that they had held in the common fields as did a considerable number of private landowners. But the largest area of allotments was made to one Thomas Panton who at that time was Lord of the Manor of Barnwell, then a village east of Cambridge whose inhabitants also cultivated this East Field. It was this initial allotment of land on enclosure which largely controlled all the later growth of the town in this direction and made certain that it did not expand gradually outwards.

What happened, in simple terms, was that except near the town-centre the land allotted to the colleges tended to be developed later than privately owned land. When this college land was built up it was usually occupied by good-quality houses and sold leasehold which was of more value to these perpetual institutions. Land which belonged to private individuals tended to be sold off quickly in freehold blocks and to be developed by speculative builders to a much lower standard. This basic difference was accentuated by the fact that Thomas Panton, the major landowner, actually died before the allotment under the Enclosure Act was made, and his executors sold off his land fairly quickly. This was resold in smaller and smaller plots for development by builders. It is this basic difference between the attitudes of private and institutional landowners and the arbitrary imposition of their allotments following enclosure that accounts for the appearance of much of nineteenth-century Cambridge today.

For example Station Road, which was laid out in 1845 when the station was built, is not lined with contemporary houses but by much later buildings of the 1870s and '80s.

This was because the land there was owned by Jesus College, who first held up development and then finally erected large detached houses and semi-detached villas for the wealthy. This is in sharp contrast to the more typical lower class dwellings that we usually find on the approaches to stations. In Cambridge the railway workers were housed not near the station, but away to the north in Romsey Town on land which was originally allotted to Panton and then sold up and developed later by individual builders. Here we can see the more usual narrow streets and long, cramped terraces of the railway age.

The history of individual parts of nineteenth-century Cambridge is often more complex and depends on a multitude of factors, though the results are usually still clear in the present landscape. A superb example is the block of land known as Newtown, which lies on the south side of the old city, bounded by Hills Road, Lensfield Road, Trumpington Road and Brooklands Avenue. The original common field land here was divided up and allotted to a number of very different owners in 1807. These included the University, Trinity Hall, Addenbrooke's Hospital and various private landlords. The allotment in the north-east corner went to Thomas Musgrave, who in 1819 erected a very pretty range of thirteen houses, called Downing Terrace, facing Lensfield Road. These still exist, and though mutilated at one end, retain their character as one of the most interesting early-nineteenth-century architectural compositions in the town. Behind these superior dwellings Musgrave went on to develop a series of ill-designed and -built, squalid, back-to-back houses whose condition, as early as 1850, brought unfavourable comment from the Board of Improvement Commissioners. The area in fact soon became a slum and has now, mercifully, been cleared. To the east of this area, also facing Lensfield Road, a larger block was acquired by the architect William Wilkins who erected a large and splendid private house for himself. This too has now gone and its replacement, the University Chemical Laboratories, is not an improvement.

South of Wilkins's land were a number of allotments belonging to various small owners and one to Addenbrooke's Hospital. All these rapidly developed their property between 1820 and 1835, and this area is still characterised by narrow streets and long rows of seemingly standard brick terraces now being demolished for redevelopment. However, the terraces are not all the same. Even individual houses vary considerably in minor architectural details. Some have doorways with flat arches while other doors have round, elliptical or segmental-headed arches. The windows too vary, some having flat heads and some segmental heads. Even the glazing bars are of different patterns. Occasionally there are isolated better-class houses with double fronts or even a coach house in the garden. These minor details may not be very obvious, and perhaps seem of little importance, but they in fact reflect the whims of individual builders, developers and clients.

The fact that an institution, Addenbrooke's Hospital, was engaged in fast speculative building may seem to contradict the earlier statement that on the whole institutions were slower to develop their land. However, when we look at the governors of the hospital at this time, and see they were largely local landowners and builders, the hospital's attitude is not very surprising.

The area of Newtown west of the last and south of Musgrave's land was granted to the Pembertons, a wealthy local landowning family. Here again the treatment was different. The site was potentially a very favourable one looking out as it did on to Brookside, a pleasant open space. The Pembertons therefore held on to their land and developed it slowly with high-quality houses for middle-class buyers. But the overall value of the land was depressed by Musgrave's slums to the north and so the Pembertons started building at the south end and gradually moved north.

To the south and east again the land was held by Trinity Hall and the University respectively. The two institutions exchanged their plots so that the University could develop the Botanic Gardens which now occupy the south-west part of Newtown. Trinity Hall then attempted to develop what is known as Bateman Street and Norfolk Street in the form of high-class individual houses. Unfortunately, perhaps as a result of the proximity of the existing lower-class houses to the north, the scheme failed and the college was ultimately forced to build the depressing, tall, continuous terraces there in the late nineteenth century. This kind of complex development is repeated all over the outer suburbs of nineteenth-century Cambridge with only minor differences.

The early expansion of Cambridge to the south-east from the 1820s onwards was not matched by similar development in other directions. To the north-east across the river and outside the bounds of the old Roman town, building was restricted until almost the middle of the century. This was because the land here was occupied by the common fields of the village of Chesterton which were not enclosed until 1840. Then there was a sudden burst of activity and within forty years most of the land close to the old town was almost completely built over. One reason for the rapid expansion here was that though colleges held land in Chesterton, when it was reallotted on enclosure it was in areas furthest from the town and most of the land close to Cambridge fell into the hands of private owners who developed their property or sold it quickly to builders. The result is that New Chesterton, as it is known, is largely composed of houses of a later date than much of south-east Cambridge, though the minor variations of architectural

detail still reflect its piecemeal expansion and the individual
fields laid out by the Enclosure Commissioners are still
traceable in house type and street plan.

To the west of the city on the old West Field, development was even later, though enclosure had taken place in
1802. There was some early-nineteenth-century building
around Newnham and along the Barton Road, but as the
greater part of the land here was held by the colleges almost
all the existing houses are post-1880. Most were built
especially for dons and wealthy townsfolk and much of the
area is characterised by large late-Victorian and Edwardian
mansions standing in their own often considerable grounds.
There are some extremely fine examples of Neo-Classical,
-Jacobean and -Georgian architecture nearly all very much
in the 'heavyweight' class.

In this century Cambridge has continued to expand outwards, though still mainly to the north, south and east
because of the hold on land by the University and the
colleges. The present borough has now gobbled up the
older villages of Chesterton, Cherry Hinton and Trumpington and physically if not administratively extended to Shelford in the south, Histon and Impington to the north and
Girton to the north-west.

SELECT BIBLIOGRAPHY

Gray, A. 'The Dual Origin of the Town of Cambridge', *Procs.
C.A.S.* (1908).
Gray, A. *The Town of Cambridge* (1925).
R.C.H.M. *City of Cambridge* (1959).
V.C.H. *Cambridgeshire*, Vols. III and IV (1959 and 1953).
Watson, W. *An Historical Account of . . . Wisbech* (1827).

9. The landscape today

THIS THEN IS the story of the making of the Cambridge-shire landscape. If at times it has seemed to be a complicated one this is not because Cambridgeshire is special but because the making of any part of the English landscape is always complex. It is for us to try to see the details of this history which still remain about us. Every generation which has gone before us has left something for us to appreciate, enjoy and pass on to our descendants. Whether our generation will be able to do the same hangs in the balance. The pressures of modern society, its technology and, perhaps most important, the sheer numbers of people are rapidly threatening to overwhelm our entire environment. Cambridgeshire is, like everywhere else, suffering from these pressures. Almost every village is being rapidly expanded, historic buildings are being demolished and the hedges and coppices of the countryside removed. New trunk roads, by-passes and motorways are being planned and constructed and the towns, Cambridge most of all, are being slowly choked by traffic. Our generation will be the last to see much that now remains of our ancestors' hopes, achievements and failures. Our children will have to rely on what we remember.

Though the scars of the recent past and the blatant horrors of the present become more and more evident there is much to be thankful for. Many people in the county have for long striven to retain much of that which is best in its landscape. Amongst the most important of these people are the planners. These much-maligned men continue to struggle to control the flood of modern developments which threaten to overwhelm both them and us.

They, like all of us, have made mistakes, and for these they collect the brickbats of the conservationists and the developers. But their achievements rarely receive approval for by their very success they are not noticed. It is a salutary experience to see maps of Cambridgeshire villages showing the applications for proposed developments which have been turned down by the planners in the last twenty years. What we have been spared should make us grateful to these planners.

In many places the careful way that modern expansion has been grafted on to old villages is remarkable. The existence in the still delightful village of Swaffham Bulbeck of a large estate of council houses and a slightly smaller one of private houses is hardly noticed by even the observant visitor. On a smaller scale the design of a group of modern houses in the main street of Ickleton has been carried out with such care that, though thoroughly modern in appearance, they fit in well with the rest of the older buildings around them. One must never forget the problems that the planners have. Even in the simplest terms, that of numbers of people, the pressures are enormous. The population of the county has risen from just over 250,000 in 1951 to over 300,000 in 1971 and it is still growing. All these new people have had to be housed to a higher standard than ever before and provided with the modern amenities that we all demand. Inevitably something of the past has had to be destroyed to make way for them (Plate 40).

Not all modern destruction means the obliteration of the past. The outcry against the removal of hedges in the southern part of the county, to facilitate modern agricultural methods, may be justifiable in biological terms. But we must remember that many of the hedges are relatively new features of the landscape dating from the parliamentary enclosures of the late eighteenth and early nineteenth centuries. In many places the landscape of the county is beginning to look exactly as it did for a thousand years before 1800.

Even in the worst excesses of twentieth-century man one can still see something of interest. Cambridgeshire, like most of the eastern counties, has acquired more than its fair share of wartime airfields. The majority are now derelict and remain as ugly scars on the landscape, but at least one is worth noting. This is the disused airfield at Duxford, south of Cambridge, which is very different from all the rest. It has only a single runway and its remaining hangars have a curious old-fashioned look to students of twentieth-century military architecture. Its ancillary buildings too are surprisingly archaic and these include massive neo-Georgian barrack blocks dated 1933 and a group of houses which might easily be taken to be of the 1880s except for the date 1935 on them. In fact Duxford is a pre-war RAF station whose existence and position led to its establishment as a Sector Control Airfield during the Battle of Britain. It was here, in those desperate days, that the immortal Duxford Wing was born and so gave the place an honoured position in national as well as local history.

Even on the most mundane journey the past is all around us. A drive to work by the hasty early morning traveller from country village to city is seen in very different terms by the landscape historian. When I set off for Cambridge I have a much more interesting journey than others taking the same route. It starts with my passing down the village High Street, whose line follows one of the ancient routes of the prehistoric Icknield Way as it approached a ford across the River Cam. Then turning north along the river-edge road I pass through a small hamlet, now almost part of the modern village, which already existed when the Normans came here and on whose site Romano-British people had lived centuries before. Hidden deep in a wood on the left I can just make out the still water-filled ditches of the moat which surrounded the medieval manor house there. Then along a minor road, marked by sweeping curves and wide verges, whose present appearance is the result of it being turnpiked as a main road from Cambridge in 1729. The parish boundary between my village and the next is clearly marked as a thick hedge half-way along. The various farms I pass were all erected after the enclosure of the common fields of both parishes in 1814 and 1817 and the surrounding square fields with their straight hedges date from the same period.

Entering the next village I cross the river and immediately meet two sharp bends. These I know are not just an accident of history but the result partly of the realigning of the original road when the prehistoric ford was replaced by a bridge further upstream long before the late fourteenth century when the bridge is first mentioned in documents, and partly due to further realignment in the eighteenth century when a local landowner extended his park. A short length of straight road follows which was once the main street of the original Saxon village. On the left stands the church, a fine example of early-fifteenth-century architecture erected largely at the expense of one man, the then rector. Almost opposite is the original manor house, largely rebuilt in 1890 by a man who made his wealth developing much of late-nineteenth-century Cambridge, but with fragments of a late-sixteenth-century wing. It stands on the site of a much earlier building where lived generations of bailiffs who ran the estate for the Abbey of Ely from long before the Norman Conquest. Another sharp bend follows marking the point where the Saxon village ended and a great piece of meadowland began. This has now been entirely built over, for it was obliterated on enclosure in 1835. But the original Saxon boundary can still be traced in the building line of the existing houses which gradually swing back from the present street.

s

I turn left on to the busy main road to Cambridge and immediately cross a railway on a hump-backed and curving bridge. Again its position is not accidental. It was dictated by the need to build it slightly to one side of the existing road in order to keep traffic moving during its erection in the late nineteenth century. The old road is still there below the approach embankments to the bridge. From here on I am in modern suburbia, but the houses are not all of the same date. They represent the piecemeal speculative development by a host of people for over 100 years. There are one or two large late Victorian mansions, a number of short terraces of early Edwardian houses, characterised by bay windows with castellated parapets, and a group of 1920s municipal 'semis'. These are intermixed with timber-framed bungalows with asbestos tiled roofs and mock-tudor dwellings of the 1930s as well as one rather nice example of the late 'Hollywood' style of the same period. More recently the remaining gaps have been filled with rather stark red-bricked houses of the late 1940s and early '50s and by even more recent trendy designs. So at last after a journey of some fifteen minutes I arrive at work having in the space of about six miles passed through and seen nearly 7000 years of man's accomplishments in the making of the Cambridgeshire landscape.

Index